# Bridge Squeezes for Everyone*

## *Yes, Even You!

# Bridge Squeezes for Everyone*

## *Yes, Even You!

### David Bird

MASTER POINT PRESS • TORONTO

**Master Point Press**
331 Douglas Ave.
Toronto, Ontario Canada
M5M 1H2
(416) 781-0351
Internet www.masterpointpress.com

**Distributed by General Distribution Services Ltd.**
35 Humber College Blvd.
Toronto, ON M9W 7C3
United States 1-800-805-1083
Quebec/Ontario 1-800-387-0141
Northwestern Ontario/rest of Canada 1-800-387-0172

**Canadian Cataloguing in Publication Data**
Bird, David, 1946-
Squeezes for everyone

ISBN 1-894154-42-8

1. Contract bridge — Squeeze I. Title
GV1282.435.B57314 2002      C2001-904146-2

| | |
|---|---|
| *Editor* | Ray Lee |
| *Cover and Interior design* | Olena S. Sullivan |
| *Interior format and copyediting* | Deanna Bourassa |

Printed and bound in Canada by Webcom Ltd.

1 2 3 4 5 6 7    06 05 04 03 02

# Contents

# Bridge Squeezes

## FOR
# Everyone*

*Yes, Even You!

# Introduction

There is nothing at all complicated about most squeeze deals. A defender holds the sole guard in two suits and is forced to discard one of his guards when you play your winners in the other suits. Here is an example of the technique at its most basic:

```
                    ♠ K 10 4 2
                    ♡ J 8
                    ◇ A K 7 2
                    ♣ A J 6
    ♠ 7 3                              ♠ 9 6
    ♡ K Q 10 7 5        N             ♡ 9 6 4 3
    ◇ J 9 8 6      W         E        ◇ 10 4
    ♣ 9 4              S             ♣ 10 8 7 5 3
                    ♠ A Q J 8 5
                    ♡ A 2
                    ◇ Q 5 3
                    ♣ K Q 2
```

You reach a grand slam in spades and West leads the ♡K. How would you play the contract?

There are twelve tricks on top and all will be well if the diamond suit divides 3-3. Another chance is that West holds four or more diamonds along with his queen of hearts. In this case he will be unable to retain both red-suit guards when you cash your winners in the black suits. Can you visualize the end position?

This will be the layout as West starts to feel uncomfortable:

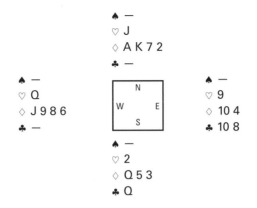

```
              ♠ —
              ♡ J
              ◇ A K 7 2
              ♣ —
♠ —                          ♠ —
♡ Q          ┌─────────┐     ♡ 9
◇ J 9 8 6    │    N    │     ◇ 10 4
♣ —          │ W     E │     ♣ 10 8
             │    S    │
             └─────────┘
              ♠ —
              ♡ 2
              ◇ Q 5 3
              ♣ Q
```

All of West's cards are 'busy'. They are guarding the threats that lie over him, in the dummy. The ♡J is threatening to score a trick and West's ♡Q guards against this. Similarly all of West's diamonds are needed to guard against the threat posed by dummy's fourth diamond. When you play the ♣Q West is in big trouble. He has to release one of his guards and you will score your thirteenth trick in whichever suit he decides to throw.

Did you need to make a note of every card that was thrown? Not at all! You needed to watch out only for one card — the queen of hearts. If that had not appeared by the time you had played your last club, you would throw the ♡J from dummy and hope that the diamonds were good.

Now try a squeeze for yourself. You must identify two suits that are guarded by only one defender, then work out how you can squeeze him.

```
                    ♠ A Q 9 3
                    ♡ A 8
                    ◇ A K 2
                    ♣ K 7 6 3
♠ 10 7 4 2       ┌─────────┐      ♠ 8 6
♡ J 10 9 3       │    N    │      ♡ K 7 5 4
◇ 9 8 7 4        │ W     E │      ◇ 10 6
♣ 9 5            │    S    │      ♣ J 10 8 4
                 └─────────┘
                    ♠ K J 5
                    ♡ Q 6 2
                    ◇ Q J 5 3
                    ♣ A Q 2
```

This time you are in 7NT and West leads the ♡J. Since only a madman would lead from K-J-10 against a grand slam, you place the ♡K with East and rise with dummy's ace. You have twelve tricks on top and a 3-3 club break will give you an easy thirteenth trick. If the clubs don't break 3-3, can you foresee a squeeze that might rescue you?

There is no potential for extra tricks in spades or diamonds. A squeeze will be possible only if the same defender holds the ♡K and four or more clubs. Since you place the ♡K with East, he will be your intended victim. You cash four rounds of spades, throwing the ♡6 from your hand, then start on the diamond suit. This position will arise:

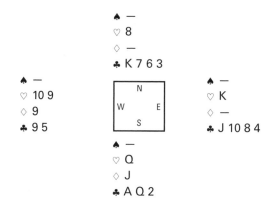

```
              ♠ —
              ♡ 8
              ◇ —
              ♣ K 7 6 3
♠ —                          ♠ —
♡ 10 9      ┌─────────┐      ♡ K
◇ 9         │    N    │      ◇ —
♣ 9 5       │ W     E │      ♣ J 10 8 4
            │    S    │
            └─────────┘
              ♠ —
              ♡ Q
              ◇ J
              ♣ A Q 2
```

You lead the ◇J, throwing dummy's ♡8. East has to throw one of his guards (he is 'squeezed in hearts and clubs') and you make the grand slam. Once again you needed to watch for only one card — this time the ♡K. If the defenders kept that card you would play for four club tricks at the end. There was no need at all to keep track of any club discards.

The two deals we have just seen are examples of the **simple squeeze**. This term refers to an ending where one defender holds the sole guard in two suits and is forced to discard one of them. It is by far the most common type of squeeze and — as we have just seen — not at all difficult to play.

In the next few chapters we will look closely at the elements of a squeeze and at some preparatory moves that may be necessary before a squeeze can operate. If you're already familiar with this basic stuff, you have license to skip over this part. But please rejoin us later as we explore in turn the many weird and wonderful forms of the squeeze. It will be an exciting journey, like walking round a zoo! By the time you have passed through the exit gate you will have an excellent chance of recognizing these magnificent creatures, next time you sit down to play.

# CHAPTER 2

# The Elements of a Squeeze

Think of a squeeze as a duel fought by declarer against one or both defenders. Declarer's main weapons are his **threat cards** — cards that are not yet winners, but threaten to become so. The defenders rely on their **guards**, cards that prevent a threat from scoring a trick. By playing the **squeeze card** (usually his last winner in another suit), declarer hopes to force a defender to part with a critical guard.

Let's look at the end position in a typical simple squeeze:

```
                    ♠ A J
                    ♡ —
                    ◇ —
                    ♣ J
        ♠ K Q                       ♠ 10 2
        ♡ —         ┌─────────┐     ♡ —
        ◇ —         │    N    │     ◇ —
        ♣ Q         │ W     E │     ♣ 10
                    │    S    │
                    └─────────┘
                    ♠ 8 7
                    ♡ 5
                    ◇ —
                    ♣ —
```

South is the declarer and these are his weapons:

    a one-card threat (the ♣J)

    a two-card threat (the ♠AJ)

    the squeeze card (the ♡5).

West, the only defender who can influence the outcome, has two items in his armory:

    a guard against the one-card threat (the ♣Q)

    a guard against the two-card threat (the ♠KQ).

When the squeeze card is led, West has to discard one of his guards. If he throws the ♣Q, declarer will throw the ♠J from dummy and score the last two tricks with the ♠A and the established ♣J. If instead West throws one of his spade honors, declarer will throw the ♣J from dummy and make two spade tricks.

Nearly all squeezes require there to be a one-card threat and a two-card threat that includes an entry (here the ♠A). Why is this entry necessary? Because otherwise the defender could safely abandon one of his guards and you would not be able to reach the threat card that had become established.

Suppose that you had mistakenly cashed the ace of spades earlier in the play of our last deal. This would then be the end position:

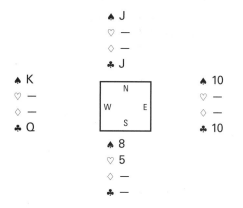

No good, is it? Dummy has two one-card threats and West guards both of them. However, when you play your last heart West can safely throw the ♣Q. Since there is no entry to dummy, you cannot reach the established ♣J. So, fix these basic requirements for a squeeze in your mind: *you need a squeeze card, a one-card threat and a two-card threat that includes an entry*.

# The positional squeeze

Let's take one more look at the successful end position from the previous pages:

```
              ♠ A J
              ♡ —
              ◇ —
              ♣ J
  ♠ K Q     ┌───────┐     ♠ 10 2
  ♡ —       │   N   │     ♡ —
  ◇ —       │ W   E │     ◇ —
  ♣ Q       │   S   │     ♣ 10
            └───────┘
              ♠ 8 7
              ♡ 5
              ◇ —
              ♣ —
```

Why does West have to give way when you lead the ♡5? It's because he has to make his key discard before the dummy does. This is known as a **positional squeeze** and can succeed only against a specific defender, in this case West.

If instead East holds the two black-suit guards, he will not be squeezed. This will be the end position:

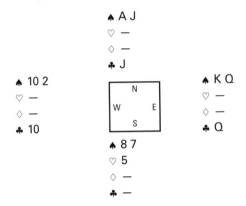

East will simply wait to see what you throw from the dummy. He will then throw the same suit himself and the squeeze will fail.

So, a positional squeeze is one that works because the key defender has to discard first, before the hand that contains the two threats. The most common setting for such a squeeze is where the one-card and two-card threats both lie in the hand opposite the squeeze card. Here declarer's ♡5 is the squeeze card and the two black-suit threats lie in the opposite hand.

# The automatic squeeze

Sometimes a simple squeeze will work against either defender. This happens most frequently when the one-card threat is in the same hand as the squeeze card. This creates an extra space in the hand opposite and you will not be forced to make a critical discard from that hand. Look at this end position:

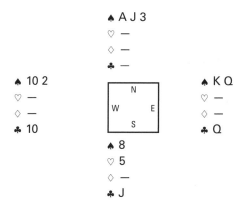

This time the one-card threat (♣J) lies in the same hand as the squeeze card (♡5). As a result, there is room for a spare card in the dummy, the ♠3. You throw this card on the last heart and, in our diagram, East is squeezed.

Why was East squeezed in this position? It was not because he had to discard before someone else. It was because he could not hold in just one hand sufficient cards to guard against the threats you could hold in two different hands. You held ♣J in one hand, ♠A J in the other. He would need to retain three cards to guard against these two threats and he was forced to reduce to two cards.

Such an ending is known as an **automatic squeeze**. It will operate successfully against either defender.

You would like to see complete deals to illustrate the positional and automatic squeezes? Your wish is my command! Look back to the deal on Page 9. This is an example of the positional squeeze. West had to discard before the dummy and the squeeze succeeded. Switch the East and West hands and it would have failed. Look next at the following deal, on Page 10. The single threat (♡Q) lies in the same hand as the squeeze card (♢J) and the squeeze will therefore operate against either defender.

# Extra winners with the two-card threat

Before we move to the next chapter, I would like to clarify my use of one piece of terminology. I will be using the phrase 'two-card threat' rather than the more verbose 'threat card accompanied by an entry'. Sometimes the presence of an extra winner will make this term inaccurate in a strict sense. Look at these holdings, each of which contains a threat card accompanied by an entry:

**1.**

♣ A J

```
    N
W       E
    S
```

♣ 2

**2.**

♢ A J 4

```
    N
W       E
    S
```

♢ K 3

The club holding in (1) is the most elementary form of the two-card threat. The ♣J is the actual threat card and it is accompanied by an entry (♣A). The diamond holding in (2) contains a spare winner in the South hand (♢K). If you play the king, the position is simplified to that in (1). Either holding would work fine as the 'two-card threat' in a slam. The same is true of these holdings:

**3.**

♡ A K 9

```
    N
W       E
    S
```

♡ 8 6

**4.**

♠ A 9 7 2

```
    N
W       E
    S
```

♠ K Q 5

In both cases the nine is the actual threat card. Cash the ace in (3) and you would revert to the basic form. Cash the king-queen in (4) to have the same effect.

So, when you look for a possible two-card threat on some deal, don't be put off by the presence of extra winners in a suit.

# CHAPTER 3

# Rectifying the Count

What preparation was required for the squeezes that we have seen so far? Absolutely none! Life is not meant to be easy, as you may have discovered, and in many cases a squeeze will not function unless some preparatory steps are taken. In this chapter we will look at the most important of these techniques — ensuring that the key defender has no spare discard at the moment of the squeeze.

In general, a defender cannot be squeezed unless all his cards are 'busy', guarding against some threat or other. If he has a spare card somewhere he will simply discard that instead, retaining all his guards. To make sure that the key defender's cards are all busy, you should aim to lose at an early stage all those tricks that you can afford to lose. In a small slam, for example, you should aim to lose one early trick. In a major-suit game you should aim to lose three tricks. Each time you lose such a trick you will remove one idle card from the defender's hand. This technique — deliberately losing one or more tricks to tighten the end position — is known as **rectifying the count**.

It's not an easy idea to grasp and we will need an example or two to make it clear. Look at this 6NT contract:

```
                   ♠ Q J 8
                   ♡ A 5 2
                   ♢ A 7 4
                   ♣ A Q 8 5
   ♠ 10 7 4 3          N          ♠ 6 2
   ♡ K Q J 7 3                     ♡ 10 9 6
   ♢ 9 6          W       E        ♢ J 10 5 3
   ♣ 10 4             S            ♣ J 9 6 3
                   ♠ A K 9 5
                   ♡ 8 4
                   ♢ K Q 8 2
                   ♣ K 7 2
```

West leads the ♡K and you see that there are eleven top tricks. All will be well if either minor suit breaks 3-3. There is also the chance of a squeeze if the same defender holds four or more cards in both diamonds and clubs.

Let's suppose you win the first trick with the ace of hearts and test the diamonds, finding that they break 4-2. Perhaps it is now that the thought of a squeeze comes to mind. You decide to cash four rounds of spades, hoping to apply some pressure. This position will arise:

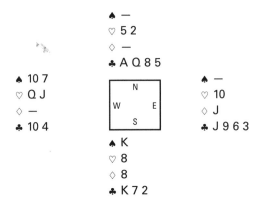

East is alone in guarding the diamonds and the clubs. Does your last spade make him wince? It does not! He has a spare card in his hand, the ♡10, and can afford to throw that. East's cards in the minors were busy but they were accompanied by one idle card, his remaining heart. The slam will fail.

To make the squeeze succeed, you must remove East's idle card. This can be done by ducking the very first trick, allowing West's ♡K to win. This essential move is an example of rectifying the count. You are deliberately losing, at a convenient moment, the one trick that you can afford to lose in a small slam. You win the heart continuation and proceed as before. The end position will be different in one vitally important way:

                ♠ —
                ♡ 5
                ◇ —
                ♣ A Q 8 5
    ♠ 10 7                      ♠ —
    ♡ J           N             ♡ —
    ◇ —       W       E         ◇ J
    ♣ 10 4        S             ♣ J 9 6 3
                ♠ K
                ♡ —
                ◇ 8
                ♣ K 7 2

Compare this with the first ending on this page. Now East's cards are all busy. He has no card to spare on your ♠K (you will throw the ♡5 from dummy) and the slam is made.

Does it seem a strange idea to you — ducking the first trick when you could have won it? If so, you will soon get used to it. Most squeezes simply will not work unless you have lost the requisite number of tricks beforehand. On this deal the only chance to lose a trick safely is to duck the very first trick. (Winning the first heart trick and ducking the second would not have impressed anyone!)

Let's look at some more deals where it is necessary to rectify the count. To extract the most benefit from them, you should make some attempt to plan the play yourself, before reading on. (Sorry if I sound like your least favorite school-teacher. When I read similar recommendations myself in some bridge book, I usually ignore them. I would doubtless be a better player if I didn't and I always feel a bit guilty about it.)

I leave it to your conscience, then. Here's the next deal:

```
North-South Vul.            ♠ A 8 4 3
Dealer South                ♡ Q 4 3
                            ◇ K 9
                            ♣ K Q 4 2
      ♠ 9 7                  ┌─────┐        ♠ J 10 6 5 2
      ♡ A J 10 8 5 2         │  N  │        ♡ 6
      ◇ 10 8 6 4           W │     │ E      ◇ 5 3 2
      ♣ 10                   │  S  │        ♣ J 9 8 3
                            └─────┘
                            ♠ K Q
                            ♡ K 9 7
                            ◇ A Q J 7
                            ♣ A 7 6 5
```

| West | North | East | South |
|------|-------|------|-------|
|      |       |      | 1◇    |
| 2♡   | dbl   | pass | 3NT   |
| pass | 4NT   | pass | 6NT   |
| all pass |   |      |       |

You win West's ♠9 with the king and can see ten tricks on top — with one more to come from the heart suit, when the ace is knocked out. A twelfth trick will be easy if clubs break 3-2. If East holds the guards in both black suits he can surely be squeezed. How would you plan the play?

It may seem a good idea to play a low heart towards the queen at Trick 2, setting up the eleventh trick. Let's see what happens if you do that. West will cover your card and dummy's queen will win. You play a spade to the queen and cross to king of diamonds. Then you play the ace of spades, followed by the remaining diamonds. This will be the position:

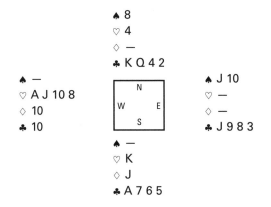

East has the sole guard on both black suits. You play your squeeze card, the ◊J, but East is not squeezed! He has a spare card in his hand, the second spade. He can throw that card away and the slam will fail.

The slam failed because you did not rectify the count. To do this, you needed to force West to take his ♡A on the first round. See what happens if you lead the ♡K at Trick 2. West then has to win, or you will score two heart tricks. You capture his return and subsequently play dummy's ♡Q, extracting East's spare card. The end position will then be:

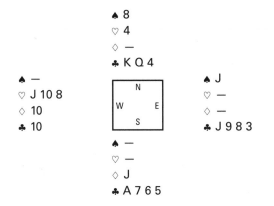

You play your last diamond, throwing the ♡4 from dummy, and East has no answer. Every card in his hand is busy and he must unguard one of the black suits.

Once again, you needed to think carefully about rectifying the count. If you played a heart to the queen before considering the matter, it would be too late. There would be no safe way to concede a trick. Ducking a spade or a club would be no good, of course, since this would destroy one of your precious threat cards.

We will end this section with a deal that presents two good examples of rectifying the count.

*Neither Vul.*
*Dealer East*

```
                    ♠ Q J 7 6 5
                    ♡ A Q 10 4 3
                    ◇ Q 8 4
                    ♣ —
   ♠ 10 8 3 2                        ♠ 9
   ♡ 9 6          ┌──────────┐       ♡ 7 5 2
   ◇ 7 5 2        │    N     │       ◇ K J 10 3
   ♣ 10 9 8 5     │  W   E   │       ♣ A K J 4 3
                  │    S     │
                  └──────────┘
                    ♠ A K 4
                    ♡ K J 8
                    ◇ A 9 6
                    ♣ Q 7 6 2
```

| West | North | East | South |
|------|-------|------|-------|
|      |       | 1♣ | 1NT |
| pass | 2♡ (transfer) | pass | 2♠ |
| pass | 3♡ | pass | 3♠ |
| pass | 4♣ | pass | 4◇ |
| pass | 4♡ | pass | 6♠ |
| all pass |   |   |   |

You reach six spades on a transfer sequence (3♡ was forcing to game, so South's 3♠ was a stronger bid than 4♠ would have been) and West leads the ♣10. How would you play the contract?

East's opening bid makes it a near certainty that he holds the three big cards in the minors. You can catch him in a simple squeeze, provided you find a safe way to rectify the count. If you ruff the opening lead, the 4-1 trump break will prevent you from ducking a trick later (even if you manage to duck the trick to East, who cannot play a diamond, a club return will force you to ruff again in the long hand and promote a trump trick for West.)

The only way to make the slam is to discard a diamond from dummy at Trick 1. East wins with the ♣K and exits safely in trumps. You then draw trumps and run the major suits. East will be squeezed in this three-card end position:

```
                    ♠ 7
                    ♡ —
                    ◇ Q 8
                    ♣ —
                                     ♠ —
                  ┌──────────┐       ♡ —
   immaterial     │    N     │       ◇ K J
                  │  W   E   │       ♣ A
                  │    S     │
                  └──────────┘
                    ♠ —
                    ♡ —
                    ◇ A 9
                    ♣ Q
```

You play the last trump from dummy. If East throws the ◇J you will discard the ♣Q from the South hand and then score the diamond ace and queen.

Suppose instead that West finds a diamond lead. Now you rectify the count by allowing East's ◇10 to win the first trick! Again the defenders will have no way to prevent a simple minor-suit squeeze on East. Strange, isn't it, that losing tricks can be just as important as winning them?

# The stars come out to play:
## rectifying the count

Each chapter from now on will include a section in which top-class players execute exactly the type of play that has been described. The first such deal comes from the 2001 European Pairs.

```
                    ♠ A 9 2
                    ♡ A 10 2
                    ◇ A 9 3
                    ♣ A K Q 2
    ♠ 7 4                            ♠ 10 8 3
    ♡ K Q J 8          N            ♡ 7 6 5 4 3
    ◇ 8 2         W         E       ◇ Q J 10 7 5
    ♣ J 10 9 7 5          S         ♣ —
                    ♠ K Q J 6 5
                    ♡ 9
                    ◇ K 6 4
                    ♣ 8 6 4 3
```

West holds the sole guard in both hearts and clubs and can be subjected to a simple squeeze. Some pairs bid to 6NT and made it easily by ducking a heart to rectify the count. One top club revealed the situation there and the declarers then ran their winners in spades and diamonds to squeeze West.

Suppose now that you are playing in 6♠ on the lead of the ♡K. How would you play that contract? Italian ace, Dano de Falco, tried the effect of ducking the ♡K at Trick 1, to rectify the count. Unlucky! West now switched to clubs, delivering a ruff.

At another table Bas Drijver, from Holland, faced the same situation and took a safer line. He won the opening lead and drew trumps. To rectify the count he then ducked a round of diamonds. The timing was now right for a simple squeeze on West.

Some unlucky declarers in 6♠ received a club lead, ruffed by East. They then had only ten top tricks and had to duck a diamond to rectify the count for one down. Do you see why? The extra trick they were seeking from the squeeze would bring them only a total of eleven tricks. This meant that two early tricks had to be surrendered.

Sometimes declarer does not have to face the task of rectifying the count — the defenders do the job for him! We will end this section with an instructive deal warning us of this defensive trap. Norwegian ace, Geir Helgemo, was the declarer, playing in the 1994 Cap Volmac tournament in The Hague.

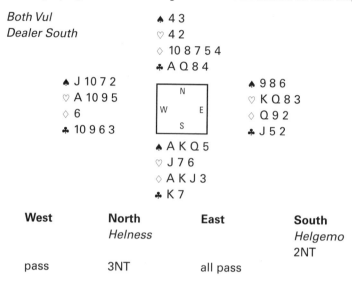

Both Vul
Dealer South

```
                      ♠ 4 3
                      ♡ 4 2
                      ◇ 10 8 7 5 4
                      ♣ A Q 8 4
  ♠ J 10 7 2                          ♠ 9 8 6
  ♡ A 10 9 5         N                ♡ K Q 8 3
  ◇ 6            W        E           ◇ Q 9 2
  ♣ 10 9 6 3         S                ♣ J 5 2
                      ♠ A K Q 5
                      ♡ J 7 6
                      ◇ A K J 3
                      ♣ K 7
```

| West | North | East | South |
|------|-------|------|-------|
|      | Helness |    | Helgemo |
|      |       |      | 2NT |
| pass | 3NT | all pass | |

West led the ♡10 to East's queen and the ♡3 was returned, the defenders swiftly claiming four tricks in the suit. Helgemo won the subsequent spade switch and seemingly had to guess diamonds correctly to make his contract. The diamond ace drew two small cards. Would you play for the drop on the next round or cross to dummy to take a finesse?

Since West has led from a four-card suit, there is no reason at all to play East for long diamonds. What is more, Helgemo could see that if West did show out on the king of diamonds he would almost certainly be squeezed in clubs and spades! His shape would have to be 4-4-1-4 unless he had — for no good reason — spurned the lead of a five-card suit. The second diamond did indeed squeeze West in the black suits and the game was made.

Do you see how the defenders could have made life more difficult for declarer? They should have refrained from cashing the fourth heart, the one that rectified the count. If West switched to a spade (or a club) at Trick 4, South would be forced to guess the lie of the diamond suit and would have no reason at all to get it right. Should declarer choose to play the diamonds from the top, West would not be squeezed. He would have his last heart available as a discard and South would be able to manage only eight tricks.

# Quiz 🖉

**A.**

      ♠ A J 7
      ♡ Q 10 4 3
      ◇ A 5 4
      ♣ 5 3 2

        N
♠K led    W  E
        S

      ♠ 4
      ♡ A K 9 8 6 5 2
      ◇ Q 2
      ♣ A K 6

| West | North | East | South |
|------|-------|------|-------|
| 1♠ | pass | pass | 4♡ |
| pass | 4♠ | pass | 5♣ |
| pass | 5◇ | pass | 6♡ |
| all pass | | | |

You bid to a small slam in hearts after West has opened the bidding. How will you play the hand when West leads the spade king?

**B.**

      ♠ Q 10 4 2
      ♡ K 6 5
      ◇ K 8 5 4
      ♣ Q 3

        N
♡8 led    W  E
        S

      ♠ A K J 8 7 3
      ♡ A 9 3
      ◇ A 2
      ♣ A 10

| West | North | East | South |
|------|-------|------|-------|
| | | | 1♠ |
| 2NT | 3♣ | pass | 6♠ |
| all pass | | | |

West's 2NT shows at least 5-5 in the minor suits, and North's 3♣ indicates a sound raise in spades. How will you play 6♠ when West leads the ♡8?

# Answers ✎

**A.** You have eleven tricks on top and the near certainty of a spade-diamond squeeze against West. The only safe way to rectify the count is to duck West's ♠K at Trick 1. If instead you win the first trick, draw trumps, and attempt to rectify the count by ducking a club, East can destroy the squeeze by switching to diamonds. Nor can you win the spade ace now and later duck the second round of spades, since West would win and play a third round, destroying your threat card in the suit.

   After ducking the first trick, you win West's switch to hearts or clubs and play all your winners in those suits. On the last of these, West will be unable to find a good discard from ♠Q ◇Kx.

**B.** West surely holds the ♣K, as well as five diamonds, and it should be possible to squeeze him. How can you rectify the count? It's not safe to duck the opening heart lead to East because you might then suffer a heart ruff. Win the opening lead, draw trumps, and duck a heart at that point. Win East's return (in the South hand, if he plays a diamond) and cash all the winners in your hand. The end position will be similar to this:

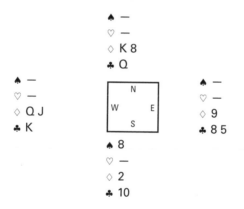

The last spade squeezes West in the minor suits.

# The Vienna Coup

In this chapter we will see another important preparatory move, one that bears an impressive name — the Vienna Coup. Suppose that one of your threats is contained in a suit like this:

◇ A 8

```
      N
  W       E
      S
```

◇ Q 7

Sometimes you will need the ace to be in place when the squeeze occurs. For example, dummy may contain a one-card threat in a different suit. If you are planning a positional squeeze against West, you may need the ◇A to reach the one-card threat, should it become established.

On other deals, as we will see in a moment, the ace of diamonds can prove a serious embarrassment. It can force you to guess the position of the enemy cards. Even worse, it can sometimes prevent a squeeze from functioning at all. You will fare much better in these situations if you cash the ◇A before playing for the squeeze.

To understand this, let's first see what can go wrong if the ace is left in position. Look at this deal:

```
              ♠ A J 9 6 4
              ♡ A K Q 2
              ◇ A 8
              ♣ 7 6
♠ 5                              ♠ 7
♡ 9 7          ┌───────────┐     ♡ J 10 6 5
◇ J 9 5 4 2    │     N     │     ◇ K 10 6 3
♣ K Q J 9 3    │ W       E │     ♣ 10 5 4 2
               │     S     │
               └───────────┘
              ♠ K Q 10 8 3 2
              ♡ 8 4 3
              ◇ Q 7
              ♣ A 8
```

You arrive in six spades and West leads the ♣K. You allow this card to hold, to rectify the count, and win the club continuation. All will be well if the hearts divide 3-3. There may also be a squeeze if the same defender holds the ◇K and four or more hearts. Let's see first what happens if you run the trump suit immediately. You will reach this position:

```
              ♠ —
              ♡ A K Q 2
              ◇ A 8
              ♣ —
♠ —                              ♠ —
♡ 9 7          ┌───────────┐     ♡ J 10 6 5
◇ J 9 5        │     N     │     ◇ K 10
♣ J            │ W       E │     ♣ —
               │     S     │
               └───────────┘
              ♠ 8
              ♡ 8 4 3
              ◇ Q 7
              ♣ —
```

The same defender holds both red-suit guards but... the squeeze does not work! When you lead the last trump you have to throw a card from dummy. If you throw the ♡2 you will destroy the threat in that suit, so you have to dispense with the ◇8. Now East can safely unguard the diamond king. The diamond suit is blocked and you will have no way to reach the established queen of diamonds. You will go one down.

The ace of diamonds is not needed as an entry to dummy and by cashing it earlier in the play you can avoid a blockage in the suit. In effect, you free the diamond queen to act as a threat against either defender. Suppose you cash the ◇A before running the trump suit. The end position will then be more favorable:

```
                        ♠ —
                        ♡ A K Q 2
                        ♢ 8
                        ♣ —
        ♠ —                             ♠ —
        ♡ 9 7          ┌──────────┐     ♡ J 10 6 5
        ♢ J 9          │    N     │     ♢ K
        ♣ J            │ W     E  │     ♣ —
                       │    S     │
                       └──────────┘
                        ♠ 8
                        ♡ 8 4 3
                        ♢ Q
                        ♣ —
```

Again you lead the last trump, throwing ♢8 from dummy. Now the squeeze succeeds. If East throws his diamond guard you will be able to cash the established ♢Q. The action of cashing the diamond ace is called a **Vienna Coup**.

We have seen the first purpose of the Vienna Coup — to prevent a threat card from becoming blocked. Suppose, on that same deal, that it was West who held both the red-suit guards. The Vienna Coup would then serve a different purpose. Let's rearrange the East-West cards:

```
                        ♠ A J 9 6 4
                        ♡ A K Q 2
                        ♢ A 8
                        ♣ 7 6
      ♠ 5                              ♠ 7
      ♡ J 9 7 6        ┌──────────┐    ♡ 10 5
      ♢ K 6 5 2        │    N     │    ♢ J 10 9 4 3
      ♣ K Q J 3        │ W     E  │    ♣ 10 9 5 4 2
                       │    S     │
                       └──────────┘
                        ♠ K Q 10 8 3 2
                        ♡ 8 4 3
                        ♢ Q 7
                        ♣ A 8
```

Again you win the second club and we will first imagine that you run the trumps without performing a Vienna Coup in diamonds. This will be the end position:

                    ♠ —
                    ♡ A K Q 2
                    ♢ A 8
                    ♣ —

    ♠ —                                    ♠ —
    ♡ J 9 7 6          N                   ♡ 10 5
    ♢ K 6         W         E              ♢ J 10 9 4
    ♣ —                S                   ♣ —

                    ♠ 8
                    ♡ 8 4 3
                    ♢ Q 7
                    ♣ —

You lead the last spade and West discards ♢6. Which card should you throw from the dummy? You have no idea! If the hearts are 3-3, you must throw the ♢8. If instead West started with both red-suit guards and has been squeezed down to a bare ♢K, you must throw the ♡2. In other words, you have been forced into a guess. It's true that you could have cashed two top hearts earlier, before running the spades. That would still leave you with the same guess to make on this lie of the cards,however.

Suppose now that you cash the diamond ace before running the trumps. There will be no guess in the end position:

                    ♠ —
                    ♡ A K Q 2
                    ♢ 8
                    ♣ —

    ♠ —                                    ♠ —
    ♡ J 9 7 6          N                   ♡ 10 5
    ♢ K           W         E              ♢ J 10 9
    ♣ —                S                   ♣ —

                    ♠ 8
                    ♡ 8 4 3
                    ♢ Q
                    ♣ —

When you play the last spade you can spare dummy's ♢8. You simply wait to see if either defender throws the diamond king. If they do, you cash the queen of diamonds. If they don't, you play for the hearts to be good. No guess-work is required and you make the slam whenever it can be made. That is the second purpose of the Vienna Coup, then. To avoid having to guess what to throw from dummy when the squeeze card is led.

Sometimes a Vienna Coup requires two cards to be cashed.

*East-West Vul.*
*Dealer North*

```
              ♠ A K Q 8
              ♡ K 10 7
              ◇ A 7
              ♣ A K 3 2
♠ 10 5 4              ♠ J 9 7 2
♡ 9 8 3 2      N      ♡ —
◇ K Q J 6 2  W   E    ◇ 10 9 8 5 3
♣ 6            S      ♣ Q J 9 5
              ♠ 6 3
              ♡ A Q J 6 5 4
              ◇ 4
              ♣ 10 8 7 4
```

| West | North | East | South |
|------|-------|------|-------|
|      | 2♣    | pass | 2♡    |
| pass | 2NT   | pass | 3♡    |
| pass | 3♠    | pass | 4◇    |
| pass | 5NT   | pass | 7♡    |
| all pass |    |      |       |

West leads the king of diamonds against your grand slam and you win with dummy's ace. What now?

Unless the queen and jack of clubs fall doubleton, you will need to find the same defender with both black-suit guards. It's no good running six rounds of hearts immediately. You will have to make two black-suit discards from dummy and East can simply match those discards. A better idea is to draw trumps and then cash the ace and king of clubs (a double Vienna Coup). Your ♣10 is then freed to act as a threat against either defender.

When the cards lie as in the diagram, West will show out on the second club. You can then cross to hand with a diamond ruff, leaving this position:

```
              ♠ A K Q 8
              ♡ —
              ◇ —
              ♣ 3
♠ 10 5 4              ♠ J 9 7 2
♡ —            N      ♡ —
◇ Q J        W   E    ◇ —
♣ —            S      ♣ Q
              ♠ 6 3
              ♡ 6
              ◇ —
              ♣ 10 8
```

On the last trump you throw the ♣3 from dummy and East is squeezed. It's time to apologize to the opponents for bidding such a miserable grand.

# The stars come out to play:
## the Vienna Coup

The declarer for our first real-life example of this play is Tim Seres, Australia's top card player for many decades. Here he is, competing in the 1979 New South Wales Open Pairs:

```
Both Vul.              ♠ 7 6 5
Dealer North           ♡ Q 2
                       ◊ A K Q 10
                       ♣ A 9 7 6

    ♠ K Q J 4        N         ♠ 8 3 2
    ♡ 9 6 4      W       E     ♡ J 5
    ◊ 9 8 3                    ◊ J 6 5 4
    ♣ J 10 3         S         ♣ K 5 4 2

                       ♠ A 10 9
                       ♡ A K 10 8 7 3
                       ◊ 7 2
                       ♣ Q 8
```

| West | North | East | South |
|------|-------|------|-------|
|      | 1NT   | pass | 3♡    |
| pass | 4♣    | pass | 4♠    |
| pass | 5◊    | pass | 6♡    |
| all pass |   |      |       |

Suppose you were the declarer. How would you play six hearts when West leads the ♠K?

Seres could count eleven top tricks, provided there was no loser in the trump suit. Paving the way for a possible squeeze later, he rectified the count by allowing West's ♠K to hold the first trick. He won the second round of spades, crossed to the queen of trumps and… yes, he cashed the ace of clubs! This was a Vienna Coup to free his ♣Q to act as a threat against either defender. When he ran the remaining trumps, East was squeezed in the minor suits. He had no good discard from ◊J654 ♣K. When he chose to throw a diamond Seres played for the drop in that suit, making the slam. (A diamond finesse could never gain. West had to keep the ♠Q to guard against South's ♠10, so he had no room for ◊J-x-x-x.)

Play the hand through again, this time without cashing the ♣A at an early stage. The squeeze will fail. Dummy will have no good discard on the last heart. If the ♣9 is thrown, the club suit will be blocked.

The second real-life deal was played in the 1998 Far East championship, with Australia's Jim Borin at the controls.

*North-South Vul.*
*Dealer North*

|  | ♠ A Q |
|---|---|
|  | ♡ K J 9 8 |
|  | ◇ A K Q |
|  | ♣ A 6 4 2 |

| ♠ J 8 6 4 | | ♠ K 10 7 3 2 |
|---|---|---|
| ♡ 10 6 3 2 | | ♡ 4 |
| ◇ J 9 | | ◇ 10 7 3 2 |
| ♣ J 10 5 | | ♣ Q 9 7 |

|  | ♠ 9 5 |
|---|---|
|  | ♡ A Q 7 5 |
|  | ◇ 8 6 5 4 |
|  | ♣ K 8 3 |

| West | North | East | South |
|---|---|---|---|
|  | *N. Borin* |  | *J. Borin* |
|  | 2♣ | pass | 2NT |
| pass | 6NT | all pass |  |

West led the ♣J against 6NT and on many similar deals it would have been a good idea to let this card hold, rectifying the count and possibly setting up a third club trick. Borin was not keen to do this since a spade switch would be unwelcome, putting him to a premature decision. He won the club lead with the king and led the ♣3. The ♣10 on the second round would have been awkward for declarer but West could hardly risk this play in case his partner had started with a doubleton queen. West in fact played low and Borin was able to duck the trick to East, the safe hand. East returned the ♣Q, the suit breaking 3-3, and then Borin threw a spade on the long club.

Declarer's next move was to play dummy's three top diamonds. The primary purpose of this was to unblock the suit, in case it should break 3-3. A secondary effect was to act as a Vienna Coup, freeing declarer's last diamond to act as a threat against either defender. West showed out on the third diamond, throwing a spade. Borin then played his heart winners, arriving at this end position:

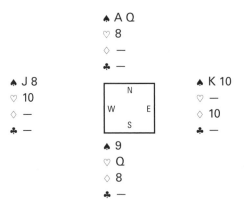

|  | ♠ A Q |
|---|---|
|  | ♡ 8 |
|  | ◇ — |
|  | ♣ — |

| ♠ J 8 | | ♠ K 10 |
|---|---|---|
| ♡ 10 | | ♡ — |
| ◇ — | | ◇ 10 |
| ♣ — | | ♣ — |

|  | ♠ 9 |
|---|---|
|  | ♡ Q |
|  | ◇ 8 |
|  | ♣ — |

On the last heart East threw the ♠10, baring the spade king. The average club player would probably have given the position away but East was a sturdy international player and bared the spade honor smoothly. When South led his spade at Trick 12 West produced an impassive jack. Suppose you had been South. Would you have finessed or played to drop the king offside?

When the defenders give nothing away with their mannerisms, you must refer back to the a priori odds. On this particular deal, you should play the holder of the majority of the spades to have started with the king. East had shown up with one heart, four diamonds and three clubs. He had therefore been dealt five spades to West's four and so was a '5-to-4 on' favorite to hold the missing king.

"Play the ace," said Borin. The king fell from East and the slam had been made.

# Quiz

**A.**

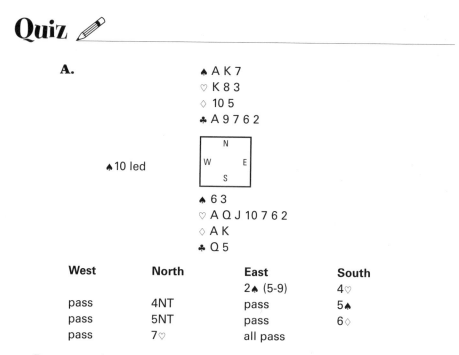

♠ A K 7
♡ K 8 3
◇ 10 5
♣ A 9 7 6 2

♠ 10 led

N
W    E
S

♠ 6 3
♡ A Q J 10 7 6 2
◇ A K
♣ Q 5

| West | North | East | South |
|------|-------|------|-------|
|      |       | 2♠ (5-9) | 4♡ |
| pass | 4NT   | pass | 5♠ |
| pass | 5NT   | pass | 6◇ |
| pass | 7♡    | all pass | |

Partner carries you to a grand slam via Roman Key Card Blackwood. How will you justify his faith? If you intend to cash the ♣A at some stage, what will be the purpose of this play?

**B.**

♠ 9 7 5
♡ 8 5 2
◇ J 9 5
♣ A 9 7 6

♡ Q led

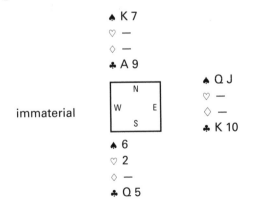

N
W    E
S

♠ A K Q J 6 3
♡ 10 9 4
◇ A K
♣ Q 5

| West | North | East | South |
|------|-------|------|-------|
|      |       | 2♡(5-9) | 4♠ |

all pass

West leads a singleton ♡ Q. East overtakes and cashes two more rounds of the suit, West throwing a diamond and a club. How will you play the hand when East continues with a fourth heart? If you intend to play the ♣A at any stage, what will be the purpose of the play?

# Answers 📝

**A.** You must hope to squeeze East in the black suits. This can be done if he holds the ♣K in addition to the six spades that his opening bid has suggested. Suppose you win the spade lead and cash all your red-suit winners. The position will be something like this:

♠ K 7
♡ —
◇ —
♣ A 9

                              ♠ Q J
                              ♡ —
immaterial           ◇ —
                              ♣ K 10

♠ 6
♡ 2
◇ —
♣ Q 5

Before East is put to a final discard you will have to throw a card from dummy. If you discard the ♣9 East can safely unguard his ♣K. The squeeze will not work. Instead, to free your ♣Q to act as a one-card threat against East, you should cash the ♣A (a Vienna Coup) after drawing trumps. When you subsequently run your winning cards in the red suits East will have no escape.

**B.** You should ruff the fourth round of hearts with a high trump in the South hand, preventing West from scoring his ♠10 (should he hold that card). Unless the ◇Q drops doubleton, you will need to find West with the ♣K and the ◇Q and to squeeze him in the minors. The ace of clubs is an essential entry to achieve this squeeze and there would be no point at all in cashing it early in the play. Indeed, it would kill the only entry to dummy. After ruffing the fourth round of hearts high, you should draw trumps and play the remaining winners in the South hand. If West does hold the two missing minor-suit honors, he will have to discard from ◇Q ♣Kx at Trick 11 and you will make the game.

Do you see how the defenders could have beaten you? Since West did not in fact have a promotable trump honor, East would have done better to switch to a club at Trick 4. This would remove the ace of clubs from dummy and prevent you from achieving a squeeze. West should have done his best to signal for a club switch. For example, if he held K-J-10-x in clubs, it would have been a good idea to throw the ♣J at his first opportunity.

# CHAPTER 5

# Isolating the Guard

A threat card generally wields more power when it is guarded by only one defender instead of both. Imagine you are playing in a diamond slam and are blessed with this club side suit:

```
              ♣ A J 5 4
                 ┌─────┐
                 │  N  │
  ♣ K 9 8 6 3    │W   E│    ♣ Q 10 7
                 │  S  │
                 └─────┘
              ♣ 2
```

Here both defenders guard the ♣J, so it may be of little use as a threat card. Now suppose you cash the ♣A and ruff two clubs in your hand. The remaining cards will lie like this:

```
              ♣ J
                 ┌─────┐
                 │  N  │
     ♣ K 9       │W   E│     ♣ —
                 │  S  │
                 └─────┘
              ♣ —
```

Now the ♣J acts as a threat against West alone. If he has the sole guard in some other suit too, a squeeze may be possible.

The technique of ruffing a round or two of a suit, to remove one defender's guard, is known as **isolating the guard**. Here you isolated the club guard in the West hand. Some writers describe the play, misleadingly, as 'isolating the menace' (where 'menace' is another word for 'threat card'). As you see, it is not the threat card that is isolated; it is the guard against it.

Let's look at a straightforward example of this technique, using the club holding above.

```
                    ♠ K 3
                    ♡ A Q 2
                    ◇ A 10 5 3
                    ♣ A J 5 4
  ♠ 9 6                              ♠ 7 5 2
  ♡ 10 9 7          ┌─────────┐      ♡ J 8 6 4 3
  ◇ J 9 6           │    N    │      ◇ Q 8
  ♣ K 9 8 6 3       │ W     E │      ♣ Q 10 7
                    │    S    │
                    └─────────┘
                    ♠ A Q J 10 8 4
                    ♡ K 5
                    ◇ K 7 4 2
                    ♣ 2
```

You stretch to a grand slam in spades and West leads the ♡10. Prospects are poor and, unless you find a miraculous lie in one of the minors, you will need a minor-suit squeeze. Only one of the defenders can guard the diamonds. For a squeeze to succeed, you will need to isolate the club guard in his hand alone.

You win the heart lead with the king and draw trumps in three rounds, throwing a diamond from dummy. You then set about isolating the club guard. Ace of clubs, club ruff, ace and queen of hearts (throwing a diamond from your hand), second club ruff.

After these preliminaries West is alone in guarding the clubs. By good fortune he holds the diamond guard too. These cards remain:

```
                    ♠ —
                    ♡ —
                    ◇ A 10 5
                    ♣ J
  ♠ —                                ♠ —
  ♡ —               ┌─────────┐      ♡ J 8
  ◇ J 9 6           │    N    │      ◇ Q 8
  ♣ K               │ W     E │      ♣ —
                    │    S    │
                    └─────────┘
                    ♠ 10
                    ♡ —
                    ◇ K 7 4
                    ♣ —
```

Your last trump catches West in a simple minor-suit squeeze and the grand slam is made. The squeeze would work equally well with the East and West cards swapped, since you can throw a diamond from dummy on the squeeze card.

Try the next deal yourself.

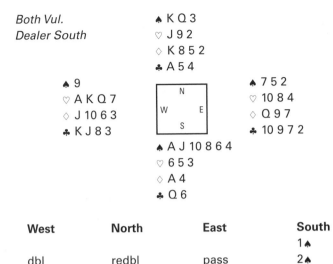

Both Vul.
Dealer South

♠ K Q 3
♡ J 9 2
◇ K 8 5 2
♣ A 5 4

♠ 9
♡ A K Q 7
◇ J 10 6 3
♣ K J 8 3

♠ 7 5 2
♡ 10 8 4
◇ Q 9 7
♣ 10 9 7 2

♠ A J 10 8 6 4
♡ 6 5 3
◇ A 4
♣ Q 6

| West | North | East | South |
|------|-------|------|-------|
|      |       |      | 1♠    |
| dbl  | redbl | pass | 2♠    |
| pass | 4♠    | all pass |   |

West scores three tricks in hearts and exits with a trump. How do you plan to make the spade game?

If West holds four or more diamonds and the king of clubs, a simple squeeze will produce your tenth trick. At the moment, however, both defenders guard the diamonds. You should aim to isolate the diamond guard in the West hand by taking one diamond ruff in your hand.

You win the trump switch and draw trumps in two more rounds. You then cash the ace and king of diamonds and ruff a diamond. East has no diamonds left and West's ◇J is the sole guard against dummy's ◇8. When you play your last two trumps West will have to discard one or other minor-suit guard.

Note that it would not be right on this deal to cash the ace of clubs early in the play, a Vienna Coup. You would free the queen of clubs to act as a threat against either defender, yes, but you would then need that defender to hold five or more diamonds. Here the bidding has provided strong evidence that West is likely to hold the club king. To make the contract you need him to hold (at least) four diamonds too.

# The stars come out to play:
## isolating the guard ☆

Our real-life example of this maneuver comes from the women's championship at the 2000 Olympiad in Maastricht. Wales faces Egypt and Jill Casey is sitting South.

```
Both Vul.              ♠ Q J 2
Dealer East            ♡ A Q 10 8 7 2
                       ◇ A 10 5
                       ♣ 4
        ♠ 84                          ♠ 10 9 7 6 5
        ♡ 93           ┌──── N ────┐   ♡ K 5 4
        ◇ Q 7 3 2      W          E    ◇ J 8
        ♣ Q 10 7 5 2   └──── S ────┘    ♣ K 6 3
                       ♠ A K 3
                       ♡ J 6
                       ◇ K 9 6 4
                       ♣ A J 9 8
```

| West | North | East | South |
|------|-------|------|-------|
| Agha | Kurbalija | Dossa | Casey |
|      |       | pass | 1NT (15-17) |
| pass | 2◇ (transfer) | pass | 2♡ |
| pass | 4♣ | pass | 4◇ |
| pass | 4♡ | pass | 4♠ |
| pass | 4NT | pass | 5♡ |
| pass | 6♡ | all pass | |

West led a trump and Casey rose with the ace. (It is a viable alternative to finesse, if you judge that West is more likely to have led from K-x-x than from 9-x-x-x.) The trump king did not fall and Casey continued with a second round of trumps. The Egyptian East won with the trump king and switched to a club. Declarer won with the ace and paused to assess her prospects. How would you have played the slam?

Unless there is a very friendly position in diamonds, the contract will depend on a minor-suit squeeze. For this to succeed one defender will have to hold at least four diamonds (or the queen and jack). You will also need her to hold the sole guard in clubs. It is quite likely that both defenders guard the club suit initially. By ruffing two clubs in the dummy, however, it may be possible to isolate the club guard in one defender's hand.

Casey ruffed a club at Trick 4 and drew the outstanding trump, throwing a diamond from her hand. She then crossed to the spade ace and ruffed another club, which in fact isolated the club guard in the West hand. Two more rounds of spades left this position, with the lead in dummy:

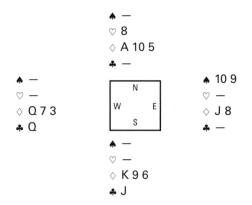

When Casey led dummy's last heart, throwing a diamond from her hand, West was squeezed in the minor suits and the slam was made.

# Quiz

**A.**

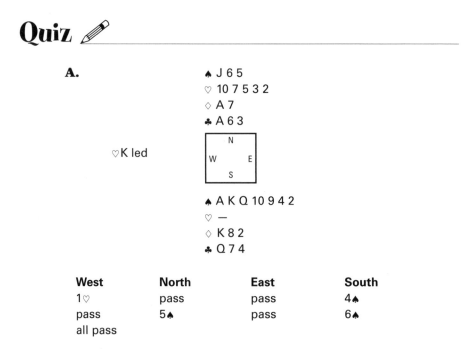

♠ J 6 5
♡ 10 7 5 3 2
♢ A 7
♣ A 6 3

♡K led

♠ A K Q 10 9 4 2
♡ —
♢ K 8 2
♣ Q 7 4

| West | North | East | South |
|------|-------|------|-------|
| 1♡ | pass | pass | 4♠ |
| pass | 5♠ | pass | 6♠ |
| all pass | | | |

West, whose opening bid guaranteed at least five hearts, leads the heart king against your small slam in spades. How will you plan the play?

**B.**

$\spadesuit$ K 8 6 2
$\heartsuit$ Q 6 4
$\diamond$ A 8 7 2
$\clubsuit$ A 8

```
        N
    W       E
        S
```

$\clubsuit$J led

$\spadesuit$ 3
$\heartsuit$ A K J 10 8 3 2
$\diamond$ Q 5 4
$\clubsuit$ K 5

| West | North | East | South |
|------|-------|------|-------|
|      |       |      | 1$\heartsuit$ |
| 1$\spadesuit$ | dbl | pass | 4$\heartsuit$ |
| pass | 4NT | pass | 5$\heartsuit$ |
| pass | 6$\heartsuit$ | all pass | |

West, who has overcalled 1$\spadesuit$, leads the $\clubsuit$J against your heart slam. How will you plan the play? (Trumps are 1-2 and West will rise with the spade ace when you lead a spade.)

# Answers 🖉

**A.** A diamond ruff will bring your total to eleven tricks and a twelfth trick is surely available via a heart-club squeeze against West. If hearts are 5-3 you will need to ruff three hearts in your hand, to isolate the heart guard with West. One big problem remains to be solved. How can you rectify the count? If you have not yet addressed this point, turn back to the problem and see if you can spot the answer.

To guard against a holding such as $\heartsuit$J-x-x with East, you must discard a club at Trick 1! If West shifts to a trump or a diamond, you use the $\diamond$A and a diamond ruff with the jack as entries to ruff two hearts. This will isolate the heart guard in the West hand. Finally you run the trumps. West's last three cards will be $\heartsuit$A $\clubsuit$Kx and he will be caught in a simple squeeze.

If instead you attempt to rectify the count by ducking the second or third round of hearts, East may win and break the squeeze with a club switch. (Duck a fourth round of hearts to West, of course, and he will kill your heart threat by playing a fifth round!)

**B.** You should win the club lead in your hand, draw trumps (in two rounds) and lead a spade towards dummy. West goes in with the ace and exits with another club. What now? If West holds the ◊ K, which is likely after his overcall, you can squeeze him in spades and diamonds. However, if spades were originally split 5-3 East currently guards the third round of spades. You should therefore cash the ♠ K, throwing a diamond, and then ruff a spade in your hand. This will remove East's last spade and leave West in sole command of the spade suit. You run your remaining trumps and arrive at this ending:

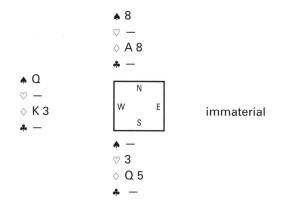

The last trump leaves West with no good discard.

You may wonder what would happen if West did not go up with the ace of spades. Would you then be left with two diamond losers? You could still make the slam, in fact, by using a type of squeeze that we will see in Chapter 11. By ruffing a spade, returning to dummy with a third trump and ruffing another spade, you would remove East's holding in the suit. You would then play your remaining trumps and cross to dummy with the ♣ A, reducing West to ♠ A ◊ Kx. Finally, you would throw him in with the spade ace to force a lead from the ◊ K.

# Transferring the Guard

The three preparatory moves we have already seen — rectifying the count, the Vienna Coup, and isolating the guard — are commonplace. In this chapter we will look briefly at a maneuver that is less frequently required, one that allows you to switch the guard in a suit from one defender to the other.

Let's see the play in the context of a full deal.

```
                        ♠ A J 8 7
                        ♡ Q 9 5
                        ◇ A 6 4
                        ♣ A K 5
        ♠ 6                             ♠ 9 3
        ♡ J 10 8 4 3         N          ♡ K 7 6 2
        ◇ K 10 8 3      W         E     ◇ J 9 7 2
        ♣ 9 4 3             S          ♣ 10 7 6
                        ♠ K Q 10 5 4 2
                        ♡ A
                        ◇ Q 5
                        ♣ Q J 8 2
```

You arrive in a spade grand slam and West leads the ♡J. How would you play the hand?

The only real chance of a thirteenth trick is a red-suit squeeze. East cannot be subjected to a squeeze because he sits over the threats in the dummy. If that is not apparent to you, imagine East holding both the red kings. Dummy's last three cards would be ♡Q ◇A6 and you would have to throw the ◇6 before East had to discard from ♡K ◇K9. No good!

You must therefore attempt to squeeze West. If you simply run your ten winners in the black suits you will need West to hold the ♡K, as well as the ◇K. Unfortunately there is not one chance in a hundred that West has the ♡K. Against a grand slam you should look for a safe lead. It would be out of the question to lead from a K-J-10 combination.

East is marked with the ♡K and therefore currently guards the heart suit. What you need to do is to switch the heart guard to the West hand. This can be done by leading the ♡Q from dummy, forcing East to cover.

You win the heart lead with the ace, draw trumps in two rounds and then lead the ♡Q. When East covers you ruff in the South hand. West now holds the guard on the heart suit (the ♡10 against dummy's ♡9). When you play your remaining black-suit winners, this end position will arise:

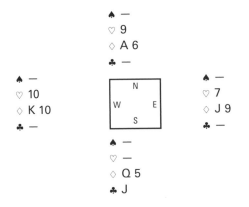

```
              ♠ —
              ♡ 9
              ◇ A 6
              ♣ —
  ♠ —                        ♠ —
  ♡ 10      ┌─────────┐      ♡ 7
  ◇ K 10    │    N    │      ◇ J 9
  ♣ —       │ W     E │      ♣ —
            │    S    │
            └─────────┘
              ♠ —
              ♡ —
              ◇ Q 5
              ♣ J
```

You play your last club and West has to surrender.

On that deal you could place the heart honors because of the opening lead. Sometimes it will be the bidding that helps you. 'East cannot hold the ♡K because that would give him enough to respond to his partner's one-bid. I will have to transfer the guard and play him for the ♡J instead.' That's the sort of reasoning you may be able to use.

# The stars come out to play:
## transferring the guard

Our real-life example of this type of play comes from the high-stake table at New York's Town Club. The declarer is Jimmy Rosenblum and the deal was related to me by his partner, Martin Hoffman.

```
Both Vul.              ♠ 2
Dealer North           ♡ A K 10 8
                       ◇ A Q 6 4
                       ♣ A Q 9 5
        ♠ J 9 8 6 4                      ♠ Q 7 5 3
        ♡ 5 4             N              ♡ 3 2
        ◇ K 5 3      W         E         ◇ 10 8 7
        ♣ 8 7 6           S              ♣ K J 10 3
                       ♠ A K 10
                       ♡ Q J 9 7 6
                       ◇ J 9 2
                       ♣ 4 2
```

| West | North | East | South |
|------|-------|------|-------|
|      | *Hoffman* |   | *Rosenblum* |
|      | 1♣ | pass | 1♡ |
| pass | 3♠ | pass | 3NT |
| pass | 4♡ | pass | 4♠ |
| pass | 6♡ | all pass | |

Hoffman's 3♠ was a splinter bid, agreeing hearts and showing a singleton or void spade. West appeared to have found the killing lead when he placed the ♣8 on the table. Suppose you had been the declarer. Would you have found a counter to this?

With a club loser exposed, declarer saw that he would need to find the diamond king onside. If he relied on the diamond suit to provide three tricks, he would have to find West with a doubleton king or East with a doubleton ten. What's more, declarer would have to choose between these two possibilities.

Rosenblum could see a better line — one that would succeed whenever East held the ten of diamonds (and West held the king, of course). He called for the nine of clubs on the first trick. East won with the 10 but could not continue the suit safely. Declarer won the spade switch, ruffed a spade high, and drew trumps. He then led the jack of diamonds, covered by the king and ace. Do you see the effect of this play? The diamond guard was transferred from West to East. The same defender was now guarding both minor suits! Declarer cashed the queen of diamonds (a Vienna Coup) and ran the remaining winners in the South hand. This was the eventual end position:

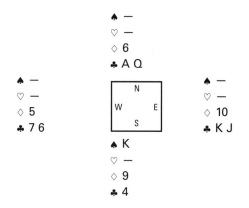

When declarer led the spade king, throwing a diamond from dummy, East had no card to spare. He was caught in an automatic simple squeeze. This is a painful fate at the best of times, but even more so at rubber bridge when the stakes are sky-high.

# Quiz

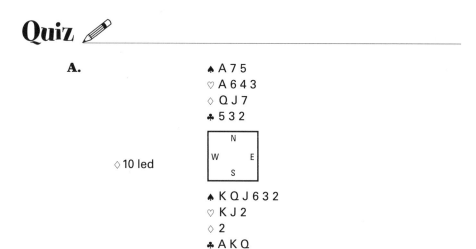

A.

♠ A 7 5
♡ A 6 4 3
♢ Q J 7
♣ 5 3 2

◊ 10 led

♠ K Q J 6 3 2
♡ K J 2
♢ 2
♣ A K Q

With no opposition bidding you arrive in six spades. West leads the ♢10, covered by the queen, and East wins with the king. How will you play the slam when East switches to the ♡9?

**B.**

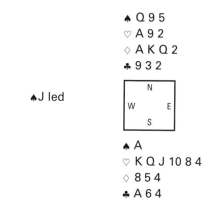

♠ Q 9 5
♡ A 9 2
◇ A K Q 2
♣ 9 3 2

♠ J led

N
W E
S

♠ A
♡ K Q J 10 8 4
◇ 8 5 4
♣ A 6 4

North opens a strong 1NT and you arrive in six hearts. How will you tackle this contract when West leads the ♠J?

# Answers 🖎

**A.** How do you think the diamond suit lies? East has made life easy for you by winning with the king instead of the ace. He must hold the ace too, and West may well have some holding headed by the 10-9-8. What about the heart suit? East's switch to the nine of hearts suggests that he does not hold the queen. Indeed, if he held that card he would surely have played a safe club at Trick 2. If your assumptions are right about the lie of the red suits, a simple squeeze against West comes into focus. By leading the jack of diamonds from dummy, forcing East to cover, you can transfer the diamond guard to West. He will then be left guarding both red suits.

The first step is to win the ♡9 switch with the king, retaining dummy's ace as an entry for the squeeze. Then you play three rounds of trumps, ending in the dummy. The diamond jack is covered and ruffed (and you can then draw the last trump if they broke 4-0). When you cash your remaining black-suit winners, West will be squeezed in the red suits. If you find this hard to follow, play it through with real cards, giving West a hand such as ♠ 9 8   ♡ Q 10 5   ◇ 10 9 8 5 4   ♣ 9 6 4.

**B.** There are eleven tricks on top. If diamonds don't break 3-3 you will probably need a spade-diamond squeeze against West. How do you think the spade suit lies? The odds are high that West has led from a holding headed by the J-10 and that East holds the spade king. After winning the spade lead and drawing trumps you should duck a club, to rectify the count. Win the return and lead the queen of spades from dummy. When East covers, you ruff in the South hand and run the winners there. If West started with four or more diamonds in addition to the J-10 of spades, he will be squeezed in spades and diamonds.

A top-class East might foresee the squeeze on his partner and refuse to cover the spade queen! This would give you the losing option of ruffing the spade queen and running your winners, playing West for K-J-10 of spades and the diamond guard.

Did you spot a second possibility for a squeeze on the deal? It's not very likely but East might have been dealt four diamonds and five clubs. In that case ducking a club (to rectify the count) would also isolate the club guard in the East hand. Playing the hand in the manner described above would then squeeze East in the minors.

# CHAPTER 7

# The Simple Squeeze

**D**o you remember when you first learned to drive a car? You probably found the early instruction a bit tedious. Switching on the ignition, holding the steering wheel in a particular way, looking in the mirror every five seconds — who's interested in that? What you really wanted to do was to drive the car — preferably fast and with an attractive admirer in the passenger seat.

It's the same with squeezes. I won't be offended if you found the first few chapters a bit dry and technical. However, now comes the enjoyable part, the reward for your early patience. You can take a seat at the table and enjoy yourself, inflicting pain and misery on the defenders. (There are some nice people who play bridge, but not many.)

In this chapter we will see several examples of the simple squeeze, the most common form of squeeze-play. By the end of the chapter you should be familiar with the idea and ready to benefit from any opportunities that arise in your next bridge game.

# The split two-card threat

First, we will look closely at a variant of the 'two-card threat', one where the threat card is not actually accompanied by a winner.

```
               ♠ A 7
                  N
♠ K 10 6 3     W      E     ♠ J 8 5 4 2
                  S
               ♠ Q 9
```

This spade holding represents a two-card threat against West. The ♠Q is the threat card but the winner accompanying it is not in the same hand. Suppose the North hand also contains a one-card threat in a different suit, guarded by West. You can see that it may be possible to effect a squeeze on West. If he unguards his king of spades you will score two tricks in the suit.

Such a suit combination — an accompanied winner in one hand, an accompanied threat in the other — is known as a **split two-card threat**. We have already seen it in operation in previous chapters. Here is another example in the context of a complete deal:

```
                  ♠ A 7
                  ♡ Q 10 4
                  ◇ 10 8 5 2
                  ♣ A Q 6 2
♠ K 10 6 3                        ♠ J 8 5 4 2
♡ 8 6              N              ♡ 9 5 3 2
◇ J 9 7 3     W       E          ◇ 6
♣ 10 9 7          S              ♣ 8 5 3
                  ♠ Q 9
                  ♡ A K J 7
                  ◇ A K Q 4
                  ♣ K J 4
```

North opens 1♣ and, as South, you bludgeon your way into 7NT. You win the ♣10 with the king and play two top diamonds, not overjoyed to see East show out on the second round. How would you continue?

The only remaining chance is to squeeze West in spades and diamonds. You play three more rounds of clubs, throwing the ◇4, and then run the hearts. This is the end position:

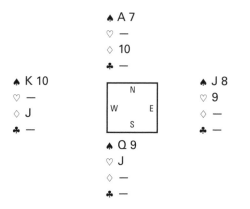

```
              ♠ A 7
              ♡ —
              ◇ 10
              ♣ —
♠ K 10                        ♠ J 8
♡ —          ┌─────────┐      ♡ 9
◇ J          │    N    │      ◇ —
♣ —          │ W     E │      ♣ —
             │    S    │
             └─────────┘
              ♠ Q 9
              ♡ J
              ◇ —
              ♣ —
```

The ♡J squeezes West in spades and diamonds. He has to give way to the one-card threat (◇10) or the split two-card threat in spades.

On that deal you had two solid four-card suits to play off — hearts and clubs. We have just seen that it worked fine to cash the clubs first, then the hearts. Suppose you played the hearts first. You would then be in dummy when you cashed the last club:

```
              ♠ A 7
              ♡ —
              ◇ 10
              ♣ Q
♠ K 10                        ♠ J 8 5
♡ —          ┌─────────┐      ♡ 9
◇ J 9        │    N    │      ◇ —
♣ —          │ W     E │      ♣ —
             │    S    │
             └─────────┘
              ♠ Q 9
              ♡ —
              ◇ Q 4
              ♣ —
```

Oh dear! To keep your diamond threat intact, you will have to throw the ♠9. West can then throw the ♠10 and you go one down.

How can you tell, in general, which suit to play first? You must visualize clearly the desired end position. You will need to end in the hand containing your intended squeeze card. This will normally be the hand opposite the entry in your two-card threat. On this deal the intended two-card threat was the split threat in spades. The spade entry (the ace) was in dummy, so you needed to be in your own hand to play the squeeze card. You had to play dummy's fourth club before running the hearts.

# The twin-entry threat

Now let's see a more powerful variant of the 'threat accompanied by a winner':

```
          ◇ A 7
        ┌─────────┐
        │    N    │
        │ W     E │
        │    S    │
        └─────────┘
          ◇ K 10 3
```

Impressed, are you? If not, you may be in a moment. Since a holding such as this contains an extra entry to the North hand, it can help you to achieve an automatic squeeze (one that wili work against both defenders) even when the one-card threat lies opposite the squeeze card.

Look at this end position, which contains the above diamond holding:

```
                  ♠ —
                  ♡ —
                  ◇ A 7
                  ♣ J 6
   ♠ —                          ♠ —
   ♡ —          ┌─────────┐     ♡ —
   ◇ 9 6 2      │    N    │     ◇ Q J 8
   ♣ 7          │ W     E │     ♣ Q
                │    S    │
                └─────────┘
                  ♠ —
                  ♡ J
                  ◇ K 10 3
                  ♣ —
```

You lead the squeeze card (♡J), throwing the small club from dummy, and will now squeeze whichever defender holds both minor-suit guards. This is the second main form of the automatic simple squeeze (to remind yourself of the first form, look back to p. 15). Again, the one-card threat (♣J) lies in a different hand from the 'threat accompanied by an entry' (◇10, accompanied by the ◇K). Since the one-card threat is now opposite the squeeze-card, an extra entry to that hand is required.

Such a diamond holding is called a **twin-entry threat**. Let's see a complete deal where it will allow you to achieve an automatic squeeze.

```
              ♠ Q 8 3
              ♡ K 8 5
              ◇ A 7
              ♣ A J 6 4 2
♠ 9 7 5 2                      ♠ 10 6
♡ 10 9 4 2     ┌─────────┐     ♡ 7 6
◇ 9 6 2        │    N    │     ◇ Q J 8 5 4
♣ 8 7          │ W     E │     ♣ K Q 10 3
               │    S    │
               └─────────┘
              ♠ A K J 4
              ♡ A Q J 3
              ◇ K 10 3
              ♣ 9 5
```

West leads the ♣8 against your contract of 6NT. Without much hope you call for a low card from dummy. Sure enough, East produces the ten. How will you play the contract when East returns the ♣K at Trick 2?

You have eleven top tricks and a minor-suit squeeze is the only real chance of bumping that total to twelve. The count has been rectified and by cashing your eight winners in the majors you will arrive at the end position we saw on the previous page. The twin-entry threat in diamonds will provide an entry to the ♣J, should East choose to abandon his guard in that suit. The squeeze is automatic, as you can see, working against East even though he is discarding after the dummy.

# Assuming the required lie of the cards

Sometimes you are forced to place a defender with certain high cards, or a particular shape, in order for a squeeze to succeed. The assumption that you make can affect the early play of the deal, in particular whether you should hold up in the suit that has been led. This is a typical such deal:

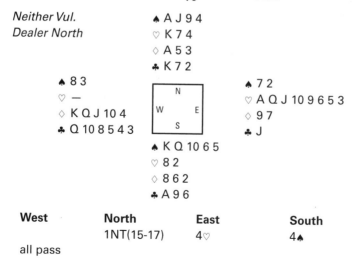

```
Neither Vul.              ♠ A J 9 4
Dealer North              ♡ K 7 4
                          ◇ A 5 3
                          ♣ K 7 2
♠ 8 3                                      ♠ 7 2
♡ —            ┌─────────┐                 ♡ A Q J 10 9 6 5 3
◇ K Q J 10 4   │    N    │                 ◇ 9 7
♣ Q 10 8 5 4 3 │ W     E │                 ♣ J
               │    S    │
               └─────────┘
                          ♠ K Q 10 6 5
                          ♡ 8 2
                          ◇ 8 6 2
                          ♣ A 9 6
```

| West | North | East | South |
|------|-------|------|-------|
|      | 1NT(15-17) | 4♡ | 4♠ |
| all pass | | | |

West leads the ◊K and partner lays out his four trumps. Great! Unfortunately the rest of the hand is not so wonderful. How can you hope to make ten tricks?

If West held a singleton heart he would have led it, so you can safely assume that hearts are 8-0. This means that East can be endplayed to give dummy a heart trick, once his non-hearts have been removed. This will bring your total to only nine tricks, however. A minor-suit squeeze on West will be needed to bump the total to ten. What shape of the East hand will permit such a squeeze to take place?

The opening lead has already removed dummy's diamond entry. Since a club honor must be in place for the minor-suit squeeze to function, East will have to hold no more than one club. If East holds three diamonds, he can guard the third round of the suit and the squeeze on West will fail. So, East must hold at most two diamonds. With hearts divided 8-0, it is unlikely that East will hold three of the four missing trumps. It looks as if you will have to play him for 2-8-2-1 shape.

How does this conclusion affect the play? You must duck the first round of diamonds! West will doubtless continue with another diamond. You win with the ace, draw trumps, and cash the ace of clubs. These cards remain:

```
                     ♠ J 9
                     ♡ K 7 4
                     ◊ 3
                     ♣ K 7
     ♠ —                            ♠ —
     ♡ —                            ♡ A Q J 10 9 6 5 3
     ◊ J 10 4          N            ◊ —
     ♣ Q 10 8 5 4   W     E         ♣ —
                       S
                     ♠ Q 10 6
                     ♡ 8 2
                     ◊ 8
                     ♣ 9 6
```

East now has only hearts in his hand. You duck a heart into his hand. If he then plays ace and another heart, you will throw your last diamond from the South hand and cash the trumps to inflict a simple squeeze on West. It won't help East to return the queen of hearts, rather than cashing the ace. You would then throw him in on the third round of hearts, discarding a diamond or a club (a loser-on-loser play), forcing him to give you a ruff-and-discard.

# Simple squeeze to resolve a blockage

Sometimes a squeeze can be used to resolve a blockage in a suit. Suppose you are playing in notrump, with no outside entry to dummy, and this is the lie of the heart suit:

$$♡ K Q 5 4 2$$

```
        N
   W         E
        S
```

♡ 10 8 7 3          ♡ 9 6

$$♡ A J$$

West's holding prevents you from overtaking the jack on the second round. However, if West holds the sole guard in another suit as well, it may be possible to squeeze him. Look at this deal:

*North-South Vul.*
*Dealer South*

```
              ♠ A 8 5
              ♡ K Q 5 4 2
              ◇ 6 5 3
              ♣ 6 3
♠ —                          ♠ 9 7 6 2
♡ 10 8 7 3        N          ♡ 9 6
◇ J 9 7 4 2   W       E      ◇ A K Q 10 8
♣ K J 9 7         S          ♣ 4 2
              ♠ K Q J 10 4 3
              ♡ A J
              ◇ —
              ♣ A Q 10 8 5
```

| West | North | East | South |
|------|-------|------|-------|
|      |       |      | 1♠    |
| pass | 2♠    | 3◇   | 4♣    |
| 5◇   | 5♡    | pass | 6♠    |
| all pass |    |      |       |

You ruff the diamond lead and play the king of spades, discovering the 4-0 break. It will not now be possible to unblock the hearts and then draw trumps ending in the dummy. What else can you try?

There is little point in taking a club finesse. You know that East has length in both spades and diamonds. If he does hold the club king it will surely fall when you take a club ruff. You play ace and another club, therefore, and West wins the second round. You ruff the diamond continuation and ruff a club with the ace, East showing out. How do you rate your chances at this stage?

You can claim the contract! You know that West guards the clubs. You know too that only he can guard the hearts (since East has shown up with four spades and introduced his diamonds at the three-level). You have already lost one club trick, rectifying the count, so absolutely nothing can stand in the way of a heart-club squeeze against West. You draw two more rounds of trumps, arriving at this end position:

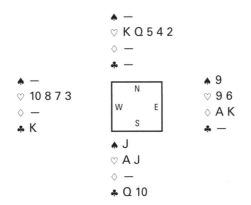

West is squeezed by the last spade. If he throws a heart, you can overtake the jack on the second round and score four tricks from the suit.

Many contracts made on squeezes can actually be defeated by attacking the suit containing the two-card menace. West had no particular reason to lead a heart here, but had he done so, and continued with a second heart when he gained the lead in clubs, the squeeze would have been broken.

Time for a coffee break. We will then see some simple squeezes played by great stars of the game.

# The stars come out to play:
## the simple squeeze

Our first real-life example of the simple squeeze illustrates the difference between a positional and an automatic squeeze. The deal arose in the inaugural World Junior Championship, played in 1987. France faced Indonesia.

```
Both Vul.              ♠ 8 7
Dealer North           ♡ 9 5 3
                       ◇ Q 9 5
                       ♣ A Q 7 6 3
        ♠ 6 4                          ♠ 9 5 3
        ♡ 10 4            N            ♡ Q J 8 7 6 2
        ◇ K 8 6 2    W       E         ◇ J 4 3
        ♣ J 10 8 4 2      S            ♣ 9
                       ♠ A K Q J 10 2
                       ♡ A K
                       ◇ A 10 7
                       ♣ K 5
```

| West | North | East | South |
|------|-------|------|-------|
| *Pancono* | *Multon* | *Wohon* | *Quantin* |
|  | pass | pass | 2◇ |
| pass | 3♣ | pass | 3♠ |
| pass | 4♣ | pass | 4◇ |
| pass | 4♠ | pass | 4NT |
| pass | 5♣ | pass | 5NT |
| pass | 6♡ | dbl | 7♠ |
| all pass | | | |

North's 3♣ bid showed the club ace. South's subsequent 4NT and 5NT were Blackwood for kings and queens respectively. East's rather pointless double of 6♡ confirmed that one of North's two queens would be where it was needed — in clubs.

Quantin won the heart lead, drew trumps, and proceeded to cash all the winners in the South hand. This end position was reached:

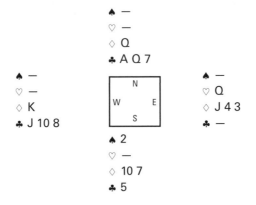

When the last trump was played, West was caught in a positional squeeze. Whatever he threw would give declarer his thirteenth trick.

Imagine now that East held the ◇K and the club length. Would the squeeze still work? Declarer would have to throw the ◇Q from dummy before East was put to his final discard. South's ten of diamonds would then become the one-card threat; a squeeze against East would succeed only if he had started with both the king and jack of diamonds as well as the long clubs.

The next deal illustrates the automatic squeeze. The deal occurred at rubber bridge in Sydney, Australia, and the declarer was the legendary Tim Seres.

*North-South Vul.*
*Dealer East*

♠ Q 10 8 6
♡ —
◇ A K 10 6 5
♣ A K 7 6

♠ J 5 4
♡ 9 7 4 2
◇ Q 9
♣ J 10 5 3

♠ 7 2
♡ K Q 10 8 6 5 3
◇ J 8 3 2
♣ —

♠ A K 9 3
♡ A J
◇ 7 4
♣ Q 9 8 4 2

| West | North | East | South |
|------|-------|------|-------|
|      |       | 3♡   | 3♠ (!) |
| pass | 5NT   | pass | 7♠    |
| pass | pass  | dbl  | 7NT   |
| all pass |   |      |       |

East made a Lightner double of 7♠, hoping for a club lead. Seres corrected the contract to 7NT and West led the ♡7, to East's queen and declarer's ace.*

---

*Notice anything strange? Yes, North bid notrump first yet South ended up as declarer. West led out of turn, in fact, and North quickly accepted the lead and put down his hand as dummy. Shrewd move when you can get Tim Seres to play the contract.

Seres played the ♣Q next. This would be the correct way to tackle the clubs even without the Lightner double, because you can pick up J-10-x-x with West but not East.

East showed out on the first round of clubs, surprising no-one, and Seres proceeded to pick up the club suit. That brought his trick total to twelve and there was one more trick to come in this end position:

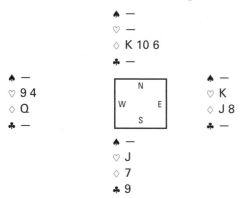

```
                    ♠ —
                    ♡ —
                    ◇ K 10 6
                    ♣ —
      ♠ —                         ♠ —
      ♡ 9 4          N            ♡ K
      ◇ Q        W     E          ◇ J 8
      ♣ —           S             ♣ —
                    ♠ —
                    ♡ J
                    ◇ 7
                    ♣ 9
```

Seres led the last club, throwing a diamond from dummy. East had to abandon one of his guards and the grand slam was made. This is the most common form of the automatic simple squeeze, with the one-card threat in the same hand as the squeeze card. The defender does not have room in one hand to retain guards against threats that declarer holds between two hands.

Our next real-life deal illustrates the other main form of the automatic squeeze, where a twin-entry threat allows you to squeeze the defender who sits over the one-card threat. England's Paul Hackett was the declarer, in a teams event played in Manchester.

```
Neither Vul.          ♠ A 7 2
Dealer East           ♡ A 10 7 3
                      ◇ A K 6 4
                      ♣ A 8
      ♠ 6                            ♠ 5 4 3
      ♡ 8 2             N            ♡ Q J 9 6
      ◇ 10 9        W     E          ◇ Q J 8 7
      ♣ Q J 10 9 5 4 3 2   S         ♣ 7 6
                      ♠ K Q J 10 9 8
                      ♡ K 5 4
                      ◇ 5 3 2
                      ♣ K
```

| West | North | East | South |
|------|-------|------|-------|
|      | Hoffman |    | Hackett |
|      |       | pass | 1♠ |
| 3♣ | 3◇ | pass | 3♠ |
| pass | 7♠ | all pass | |

The same contract was reached in both rooms and both Wests led the ♣Q. Suppose you had been the declarer. What plan would you have made?

After drawing trumps, you can throw a red card on the ♣A, then attempt to ruff good the suit you pitched. If the chosen suit does not break 3-3, you must hope for some residual squeeze chance.

The declarer at the other table chose to discard a heart. He then played the two top hearts and ruffed a heart. The suit did not break evenly and there was no squeeze chance left at all. Why was that? The red-suit lengths were likely to lie with East (who was much shorter in clubs). The two threats (♡10 and ◇ A K 6) lay in the dummy and East sat over them; he could wait to see what dummy discarded before throwing a card himself.

Paul Hackett saw that he might still catch East in a simple squeeze, provided his discard on the ♣A was a diamond rather than a heart. Three rounds of diamonds revealed the 4-2 break but the twin-entry threat in hearts was still intact. This was the end position:

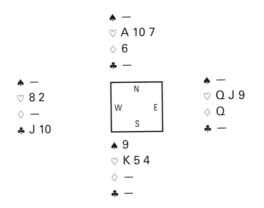

Hackett played the last spade, throwing the ♡7 from dummy. East could not defend the position and the grand slam was made. It is an instructive deal. When the one-card threat lies opposite the squeeze card, and is guarded by the defender sitting behind it, you need a twin-entry threat to provide the necessary entries.

Look back to the full diagram. Do you see another way to squeeze East, as the cards lie? You could throw a heart on the ♣A, cash the ace and king of diamonds (a Vienna Coup to set up your ◇5 as a threat) and then run the spades. East would be caught in a straightforward simple squeeze. This would be an inferior line to that chosen by Hackett, of course, because it would fail when diamonds were 3-3.

Next we will see a real-life example of a simple squeeze using a split two-card threat. Zia Mahmood is our declarer, facing American superstars, Meckstroth and Rodwell, in the 2000 Volmac Invitational.

Both Vul.
Dealer West

```
                    ♠ A Q J 6
                    ♡ Q 9 7 6 2
                    ◇ A 5
                    ♣ A 9
  ♠ K 10 5 3                        ♠ 9 8 4
  ♡ J 4          ┌─────────┐        ♡ 10
  ◇ K 4 2        │    N    │        ◇ J 10 9 8 7
  ♣ K Q 7 3      │ W     E │        ♣ J 8 4 2
                 │    S    │
                 └─────────┘
                    ♠ 7 2
                    ♡ A K 8 5 3
                    ◇ Q 6 3
                    ♣ 10 6 5
```

| West | North | East | South |
|------|-------|------|-------|
| Meckstroth | Martel | Rodwell | Zia |
| 1◇ | dbl | 2♣ | 2♡ |
| 3♣ | 3◇ | dbl | 4♣ |
| pass | 4◇ | pass | 5♡ |
| pass | 6♡ | all pass | |

Meckstroth and Rodwell did plenty of bidding on their combined 14 points but it did not deter Chip Martel and Zia Mahmood from reaching a small slam. Zia won the king of clubs lead with the ace and drew trumps with the queen and ace. A successful finesse of the spade queen was followed by a second round of clubs, won by West.

Meckstroth played a second spade, breaking declarer's link to dummy in that suit, but it did not save him from an eventual squeeze. Zia finessed the spade jack and cashed the ace, a mildly deceptive king falling on his left. He crossed to his hand with a trump and ruffed his last club. A fourth round of trumps left this end position, with the lead in the South hand:

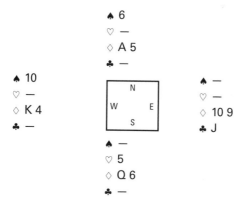

```
                    ♠ 6
                    ♡ —
                    ◇ A 5
                    ♣ —
  ♠ 10                              ♠ —
  ♡ —            ┌─────────┐        ♡ —
  ◇ K 4          │    N    │        ◇ 10 9
  ♣ —            │ W     E │        ♣ J
                 │    S    │
                 └─────────┘
                    ♠ —
                    ♡ 5
                    ◇ Q 6
                    ♣ —
```

The ♡5 was led and West was caught in a simple squeeze. When he threw the ◇4 Zia discarded dummy's ♠6 and claimed two diamond tricks with his split two-card threat.

Our final example of a real-life simple squeeze features Geir Helgemo of Norway, currently rated by many as the world's best player. The deal illustrates how several different squeeze possibilities may be combined. He sat South on this deal from the 1997 Norwegian Premier League.

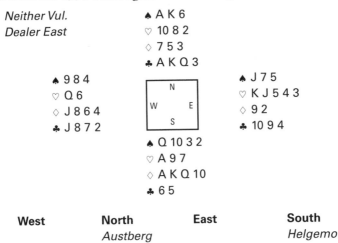

Neither Vul.
Dealer East

North hand:
♠ A K 6
♡ 10 8 2
♢ 7 5 3
♣ A K Q 3

West hand:
♠ 9 8 4
♡ Q 6
♢ J 8 6 4
♣ J 8 7 2

East hand:
♠ J 7 5
♡ K J 5 4 3
♢ 9 2
♣ 10 9 4

South hand:
♠ Q 10 3 2
♡ A 9 7
♢ A K Q 10
♣ 6 5

| West | North | East | South |
|------|-------|------|-------|
|  | Austberg |  | Helgemo |
|  |  | pass | 1NT (15-17) |
| pass | 6NT | all pass |  |

Seeking a safe lead, West placed the ♠4 on the table. Helgemo could now count eleven top tricks. Suppose you had been in the Norwegian maestro's seat. How would you have planned the play?

Helgemo captured East's ♠J with the queen and played two more rounds of the suit. He then led a low heart to the nine. The main intent behind this play was to rectify the count for a possible minor-suit squeeze. If hearts were 5-2, however, he would also isolate the heart guard in one defender's hand. West won with the ♡Q and returned another heart to East's jack and declarer's ace. When Helgemo played the last spade, West was squeezed in the minor suits. He threw a diamond, retaining a guard on the threat he could actually see (dummy's clubs). Both defenders followed to two rounds of diamonds and Helgemo played a third round to drop the jack. Slam made.

Various other simple squeezes might have arisen if the East-West cards had lain differently. If East, instead of West, had started with 3-2-4-4 shape, the last spade would have squeezed him in the minors. If East held 3-5-1-4 shape (the diamond singleton not being the jack), he would be squeezed in hearts and clubs when declarer cashed his three top diamonds. Finally, if East held 3-5-4-1 shape, West would throw a club on the last spade and both defenders would follow to two diamonds. Helgemo would then cash dummy's three club winners to squeeze East in the red suits. (In fact, with a full count on the hand once East showed out of clubs, he could take the diamond finesse.)

The reward for Helgemo's endeavors? Just another flat board!

# Quiz ✎

**A.**

$\spadesuit$ 8 7 4
$\heartsuit$ K 9 6
$\diamond$ Q 4 2
$\clubsuit$ A 9 6 2

$\clubsuit$K led

```
      N
   W     E
      S
```

$\spadesuit$ A K Q 10 3 2
$\heartsuit$ —
$\diamond$ A K J 7
$\clubsuit$ J 4 3

| West | North | East | South |
|------|-------|------|-------|
| 1$\heartsuit$ | pass | pass | dbl |
| pass | 1NT | pass | 3$\spadesuit$ |
| pass | 4$\clubsuit$ | pass | 6$\spadesuit$ |
| all pass | | | |

Plan the play in 6$\spadesuit$. What simple squeeze can you visualize? Identify the squeeze card, the one-card threat and the two-card threat.

**B.**

$\spadesuit$ K 8 4 2
$\heartsuit$ A K 6 2
$\diamond$ A 7 5
$\clubsuit$ K 6

$\diamond$K led

```
      N
   W     E
      S
```

$\spadesuit$ A Q J 10 9 6
$\heartsuit$ 7 3
$\diamond$ J 8 3
$\clubsuit$ A Q

(i) You bid to 6$\spadesuit$ and West leads the $\diamond$K. You allow this to win and he switches to a trump. How will you continue?

(ii) How would you plan the play if West had led the $\diamond$9 instead?

**C.**

```
              ♠ 10 9 6
              ♡ A K 8
              ◇ K Q 7 3
              ♣ K Q 4
                  ┌─────────┐
                  │    N    │
   ♠8 led         │ W     E │
                  │    S    │
                  └─────────┘
              ♠ K 3
              ♡ Q J 5 3
              ◇ A 9
              ♣ A 8 7 5 2
```

| West | North | East | South |
|------|-------|------|-------|
|  | 1◇ | 2♠ (weak) | 3♣ |
| pass | 3♠ | pass | 3NT |
| pass | 4NT | pass | 6NT |
| all pass |  |  |  |

East wins the spade lead with the ace and returns the spade queen. How do you plan to score twelve tricks if the clubs do not break 3-2?

**D.**

```
              ♠ 2
              ♡ K J 9 8 6 4
              ◇ 3
              ♣ Q 7 5 4 3
                  ┌─────────┐
                  │    N    │
   ♣K led         │ W     E │
                  │    S    │
                  └─────────┘
              ♠ A J 10 3
              ♡ A Q 10 5
              ◇ A Q 10 2
              ♣ J
```

| West | North | East | South |
|------|-------|------|-------|
|  |  | 2♠ | 2NT |
| 3♠ | 4◇ | pass | 6♡ |
| dbl | all pass |  |  |

East opens with a weak two-bid, showing six spades and 5-9 points. North's 4◇ is a transfer bid and you leap to 6♡, doubled by West. West leads the king of clubs, East signaling an even number with the nine and then switches to a trump. Plan the play. (You will soon discover that West started with five clubs.)

# Answers ✎

**A.** West appears to hold the king-queen of clubs and surely has the ace of hearts too. It should therefore be possible to squeeze him in these two suits. The first step is to duck the opening lead, to rectify the count. West cannot safely continue clubs, so the ace of clubs — a vital entry for the squeeze — will be left intact. You win West's diamond switch in the South hand and draw trumps. (If East has all four trumps, you can use the diamond queen as an entry to take a trump finesse.) Finally, you run all your winners in spades and diamonds. West will have to give you a trick with his final discard:

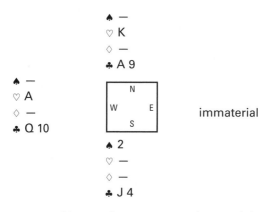

    The squeeze card is your last winner in the South hand. The one-card threat is the ♡K. You have a split two-card threat in clubs.

**B.** (i) One line would be to cash the ◇A (Vienna Coup) and run the winners in the South hand. This would squeeze West only if he held five hearts along with the diamond queen. A better idea is to leave the ace and jack of diamonds intact as a split two-card threat. Play the ace and king of hearts and ruff a heart. This will isolate the heart guard in the West hand if he started with four hearts. He can then be squeezed in the red suits.

The end position will look like this:

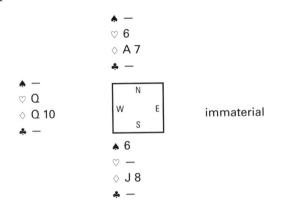

```
              ♠ —
              ♡ 6
              ◊ A 7
              ♣ —
  ♠ —                          ♠ —
  ♡ Q       ┌─────────┐        ♡ Q J
  ◊ Q 10    │    N    │        ◊ Q
  ♣ —       │ W     E │        ♣ —
            │    S    │  immaterial
            └─────────┘
              ♠ 6
              ♡ —
              ◊ J 8
              ♣ —
```

West has no answer to the ♠6.

(ii) When the ◊9 is led, you can assume that East holds the king and queen of the suit. You should again duck the first round of diamonds, thereby rectifying the count. There is no future now in attempting to isolate the heart guard with East (dummy would be left with ♡6 ◊ A 7 and would have to discard in front of East). Instead you must cash the ace of diamonds (Vienna Coup) and use hearts as the 'threat with an entry'. You will need to find East with five hearts, but that is the only chance. You hope for this end position:

```
                  ♠ —
                  ♡ K 6
                  ◊ 7
                  ♣ —
                              ♠ —
              ┌─────────┐     ♡ Q J
              │    N    │     ◊ Q
  immaterial  │ W     E │     ♣ —
              │    S    │
              └─────────┘
                  ♠ 6
                  ♡ 7
                  ◊ J
                  ♣ —
```

**C.** You can count eleven top tricks and if clubs break 3-2 the slam will be easy. You should start by cashing the king and queen of clubs, which does not remove any of your squeeze chances. If West holds a club guard, you need him to hold the diamond guard too. When you play your remaining winners in the heart suit you will reach this position:

```
              ♠ 10
              ♡ —
              ◇ K Q 7 3
              ♣ 4

♠ —              ┌─────────┐
♡ —              │    N    │
◇ J 10 5 2       │ W     E │       immaterial
♣ J 10           │    S    │
                 └─────────┘
              ♠ —
              ♡ Q
              ◇ A 9
              ♣ A 8 7
```

The ♡Q squeezes West in the minors.

If, unexpectedly, East turns up with four clubs, you can squeeze him in the black suits. You play four rounds of hearts followed by three rounds of diamonds. (You must play the hearts before the diamonds, because you need to end in dummy — alongside the one-card threat in spades). This is the three-card end position.

```
              ♠ 10
              ♡ —
              ◇ Q
              ♣ 4
                 ┌─────────┐     ♠ J
                 │    N    │     ♡ —
immaterial       │ W     E │     ◇ —
                 │    S    │     ♣ J 10
                 └─────────┘
              ♠ —
              ♡ —
              ◇ —
              ♣ A 8 7
```

The last diamond will squeeze East in the black suits.

**D.** After East's high-card signal at Trick 1 clubs are likely to break 5-2. You can ruff three clubs in the South hand, but will then need either a diamond finesse or a minor-suit squeeze against West. His double of the slam makes the squeeze the more promising line of play.

Win the trump switch in dummy and ruff a club. Cash the ace of spades and ruff a spade, continuing with a second club ruff (East showing out). You return to dummy by ruffing another spade and ruff dummy's penultimate club. You return to dummy by ruffing your last spade, draw the last trump (finally!), and these cards remain:

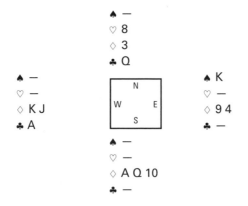

```
                    ♠ —
                    ♡ 8
                    ◇ 3
                    ♣ Q
        ♠ —                         ♠ K
        ♡ —         ┌─────────┐     ♡ —
        ◇ K J       │    N    │     ◇ 9 4
        ♣ A         │ W     E │     ♣ —
                    │    S    │
                    └─────────┘
                    ♠ —
                    ♡ —
                    ◇ A Q 10
                    ♣ —
```

You lead the ♡8, throwing the ◇10 from your hand. West cannot guard against the one-card threat in dummy (♣Q) and the two-card threat in your hand (◇A-Q).

The deal was played in the above fashion by Martin Hoffman, partnered by Arthur Lobe at the Honors Club in New York.

# CHAPTER 8

# The Show-up Squeeze

Suppose you are playing in notrump and this is the situation in the dia-mond suit:

◇ A J 7 3 2

◇ 10 9 6 4     |  N  |
               | W   E |
               |  S  |     ◇ Q 8

◇ K 5

If you need a third trick from the suit and cannot afford to surrender the lead, you have two options. After cashing the diamond king, you can finesse the jack (playing West for the missing queen) or you can rise with the ace (play-ing East for an original queen doubleton). Since the first option is around a 50% prospect and the second no better than 8%, you would doubtless choose the finesse.

When West can be brought under pressure in this suit and one other suit, however, it may be possible to squeeze him down to two diamonds. Then, if West has the queen it will 'show up' when you play the second round of the suit. When his last diamond proves not to be the queen, you can diagnose a doubleton queen with East and drop the honor offside.

Let's make this clearer by looking at a whole deal involving this diamond suit.

Both Vul.
Dealer South

```
                  ♠ K J
                  ♡ A Q 2
                  ♢ A J 7 3 2
                  ♣ K 4 2
     ♠ 9 4                          ♠ 10 8 6 5 3 2
     ♡ J 10 7 4        N            ♡ 9 5
     ♢ 10 9 6 4    W       E        ♢ Q 8
     ♣ 9 8 3           S            ♣ A 6 5
                  ♠ A Q 7
                  ♡ K 8 6 3
                  ♢ K 5
                  ♣ Q J 10 7
```

| West | North | East | South |
|------|-------|------|-------|
|      |       |      | 1NT (15-17) |
| pass | 6NT   | all pass | |

Seeking a safe lead, West reaches for the ♣9. You force out the club ace and can then count eleven top tricks. To put the defenders under pressure you next cash your winners in the black suits. This will be the position as the last black winner is led:

```
                  ♠ —
                  ♡ A Q 2
                  ♢ A J 7 3
                  ♣ —
     ♠ —                            ♠ 10 8 5
     ♡ J 10 7 4        N            ♡ 9 5
     ♢ 10 9 6     W       E         ♢ Q 8
     ♣ —              S             ♣ —
                  ♠ Q
                  ♡ K 8 6 3
                  ♢ K 5
                  ♣ —
```

If West throws a heart on the ♠Q, all your problems will be over. Let's say that he retains four hearts and throws another diamond. Before committing yourself in diamonds, you naturally test the heart suit. Three rounds, ending in your hand, reveal that West guards the fourth round. You cash the ♢K to leave this position at Trick 12:

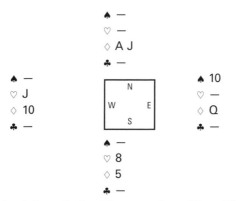

When you lead the ◇5, the 10 comes from West. This is known to be his last diamond, since he still has the ♡J. A finesse cannot possibly win, so you rise with the ace of diamonds. East was dealt a doubleton queen and this card duly tumbles to the table. The small slam is made.

Was there anything very special about that type of squeeze? Nothing at all! The term 'show-up squeeze' is used merely because you had the option of finessing in the key suit. If dummy's jack of diamonds had instead been a small diamond, the hand would qualify as the simplest of simple squeezes. West held the sole guard in both red suits and had to throw one of his stoppers when the black suits were run.

That is the beginning and end of the show-up squeeze. A simple squeeze on one opponent reveals that a finesse through him cannot succeed and you therefore play for the drop offside. There is nothing more to say about it!

# The stars come out to play:
## the show-up squeeze

A popular form of tournament, both for players and spectators, is the invitational event where sixteen world-class pairs do battle against each other. The Cap Volmac World Top tournament, played in Holland, has this format and our first real-life example of the show-up squeeze came up there in the 1995 edition of this contest.

North-South Vul.
Dealer West

```
                    ♠ 9 7
                    ♡ A 10 9 6
                    ◇ Q 10 8 7 5 2
                    ♣ 4
♠ Q J 10 6 4 3 2              ♠ A K 8 5
♡ Q 7            N            ♡ 8 3 2
◇ 3          W       E        ◇ 4
♣ J 3 2          S            ♣ A Q 10 9 6
                    ♠ —
                    ♡ K J 5 4
                    ◇ A K J 9 6
                    ♣ K 8 7 5
```

| West | North | East | South |
|------|-------|------|-------|
| *Manoppo* | *Robson* | *Lasut* | *Forrester* |
| 3♠ | pass | 4♠ | dbl |
| pass | 4NT | 5♣ | 5◇ |
| pass | 6◇ | all pass | |

Andrew Robson's bid of 4NT showed at least two places to play. The Indonesian star Lasut continued with 5♣, to suggest a lead and to help partner judge whether to sacrifice further. Tony Forrester bid his diamond suit and Robson raised bravely to six, hoping for a spade void opposite.

A club was led to the ace and Lasut tried unsuccessfully to cash a top spade. After ruffing the spade, Forrester drew the outstanding trumps and played the ♣K, throwing a heart from dummy. He then ruffed a club, isolating the club guard in the East hand. All now seemed to depend on guessing the whereabouts of the heart queen. Pressed for an immediate decision, declarer would doubtless play East for that card, since he could be counted for three hearts to his partner's two. However, Forrester could see that a show-up squeeze position would remove the need to guess. He ran dummy's remaining trumps to arrive at this ending:

```
                    ♠ —
                    ♡ A 10 9
                    ◇ 7
                    ♣ —
♠ Q J                         ♠ —
♡ Q 7            N             ♡ 8 3 2
◇ —          W       E         ◇ —
♣ —              S             ♣ Q
                    ♠ —
                    ♡ K J 5
                    ◇ —
                    ♣ 8
```

When the ◇7 was played, East had to discard a heart. Forrester threw the ♣8, which had fulfilled its role, and West threw a spade. Knowing that the hearts were now 2-2, Forrester had no temptation to finesse in the suit. He cashed the ace and king, bringing down the queen from West. A classic example of the show-up squeeze.

Our second example features the great Polish player, Piotr Gawrys. He faced England's Hackett twins, Justin and Jason, in the quarter-finals of the 2001 NEC championship in Tokyo.

*East-West Vul.*
*Dealer North*

|  | ♠ A J |  |
|---|---|---|
|  | ♡ A J 4 3 |  |
|  | ◇ J 10 5 |  |
|  | ♣ A 7 3 2 |  |

| ♠ 10 3 | | ♠ 8 7 6 5 4 2 |
| ♡ 10 7 6 5 | N | ♡ Q 9 |
| ◇ 3 | W    E | ◇ 9 8 2 |
| ♣ Q J 9 8 6 4 | S | ♣ K 5 |

|  | ♠ K Q 9 |  |
|---|---|---|
|  | ♡ K 8 2 |  |
|  | ◇ A K Q 7 6 4 |  |
|  | ♣ 10 |  |

| West | North | East | South |
|------|-------|------|-------|
|  | 1NT | pass | 4♣ |
| pass | 4♡ | pass | 5◇ |
| pass | 6◇ | pass | 7◇ |
| all pass |  |  |  |

South's 4♣ was Gerber and the response showed 0 or 3 aces. Gawrys now bid 5◇, which was nominally a sign-off if partner held no aces rather than three. He knew that North held three aces, of course, but was interested in the direction of his subsequent advance. North's removal to 6◇ indicated some degree of diamond support and Gawrys leapt to the grand slam in that suit. How would you play this contract on the ♣Q lead?

Gawrys won with the ace and drew trumps, ending in the dummy. With a show-up squeeze in mind, he ruffed a club, returned to dummy with the spade ace, and ruffed another club. The club guard was now isolated in the West hand. Declarer's next move was to cash the remaining winners in spades and diamonds. He soon reached this end position:

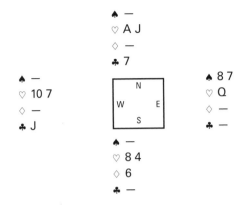

```
              ♠ —
              ♡ A J
              ◇ —
              ♣ 7
♠ —                        ♠ 8 7
♡ 10 7        ┌─────────┐   ♡ Q
◇ —          │    N    │   ◇ —
♣ J          │ W     E │   ♣ —
             │    S    │
             └─────────┘
              ♠ —
              ♡ 8 4
              ◇ 6
              ♣ —
```

When the last diamond was led, West had to release a heart in order to keep a guard on dummy's club. The ♣7 could be spared from dummy and East threw a painless spade. When Gawrys led a heart at Trick 12, he knew that the ten was West's last card in the suit. He rose with dummy's ace, toppling East's queen, and the grand slam was made. At the other table North-South stopped in 6◇, losing a big swing.

# Quiz ✐

**A.**

♠ A J 6 3
♡ 6 4
◇ K Q 5 2
♣ Q 3

```
      N
   W     E
      S
```

♡9 led

♠ K 8 2
♡ A 7
◇ A 7 6
♣ A K J 10 8

| West | North | East | South |
|------|-------|------|-------|
|      |       | 3♡   | 3NT   |
| pass | 4NT   | pass | 6NT   |
| all pass |   |      |       |

West leads the ♡9 against your small slam in notrump. Plan the play.

**B.**

♠ A 10
♡ A K 9 6
◇ A K J 6
♣ J 9 7

```
      N
   W     E
      S
```

♠9 led

♠ J 2
♡ 6 3
◇ 8 5 3
♣ K Q 10 8 5 2

| West | North | East | South |
|------|-------|------|-------|
|      |       | 2♠ (5-9) | pass |
| pass | dbl   | pass | 3♣    |
| pass | 3♠    | pass | 5♣    |
| all pass |   |      |       |

East opens with a weak two in spades and you play eventually in 5♣. You win the spade lead with dummy's ace and play a trump to the king and West's ace. West returns a spade to East's queen and back comes a trump, the suit breaking 2-2. How will you continue the play?

# Answers ✎

**A.** You have eleven top tricks. To rectify the count you should duck the first trick. Win the heart return and play the three top diamonds to discover the lie of that suit. If the diamonds break 3-3, you have twelve easy tricks. If East holds four diamonds, you will have to take the spade finesse. After East's preempt it is much more likely that West has the diamond suit guarded. What then? This is not the moment to fall back on a finesse of the ♠J. Instead you should cash your club suit. When East started with a doubleton spade queen, this end position will arise:

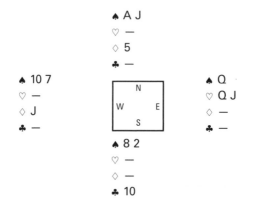

On the last club West has to throw another spade, to retain his diamond guard. You dispense with dummy's ◇5 and East throws a heart. When you lead a spade, West's ten is known to be his last card in the suit. You rise with dummy's ace, dropping East's bare queen. If instead West started with Q-x-x-x in the spade suit, his queen will appear at Trick 12.

**B.** After winning East's trump return, you should cash dummy's top hearts and ruff a heart. Suppose East follows to three rounds of hearts. It is unlikely that he has opened a weak two with 6-4 in the majors, so you can count him for 6-3-2-2 shape. When you run your remaining clubs, West will have to retain a heart and will be squeezed down to two diamonds. There is no need to take the diamond finesse. If West follows with a low diamond at Trick 12, you know that his last card is a heart. You can therefore drop the ◇Q from East. If instead East shows up with only two hearts, diamonds must be 3-3, and you will need West to hold the ◇Q.

# The Double Squeeze

A double squeeze is a combination of two simple squeezes, one on each defender. Declarer has threats in three different suits, usually two one-card threats and one two-card threat. Each defender has to guard one of the one-card threats and, as a result, neither can keep a guard on the two-card threat.

This may sound like a difficult play to recognize and perform but in fact most double squeezes are fairly straightforward. Before saying 'Oh yeah?', have a look at this diagram and then at the first full deal or two.

```
                  ♠ A 8
                  ♡ 10
                  ◇ —
                  ♣ —
   ♠ K J                        ♠ Q 9
   ♡ J          ┌─────────┐     ♡ —
   ◇ —          │    N    │     ◇ K
   ♣ —          │ W     E │     ♣ —
               │    S    │
                └─────────┘
                  ♠ 5
                  ♡ —
                  ◇ J
                  ♣ 10
```

You are playing in notrump, or clubs, and are about to lead the squeeze card (the ♣10). Dummy's ♡10 is a one-card threat against West. Your ◇J is a one-card threat against East. In spades you have a two-card threat, guarded by both defenders. In a double squeeze the two-card threat is known as the **pivot suit**.

Let's see what happens when you play the last club. West has to retain the ♡J, to guard against dummy's ♡10, so he throws a spade. You have no further use for the ♡10 and can throw it from dummy. East faces a similar dilemma to his partner. Since he has to keep the ◇K to guard against your ◇J, he too must throw a spade. You then score two spade tricks in the dummy.

As you see, West was caught in a simple squeeze in the major suits; East suffered a simple squeeze in spades and diamonds. The squeeze was positional because dummy's ♡10 would be effective only when West held the heart guard. Suppose instead that this was the ending:

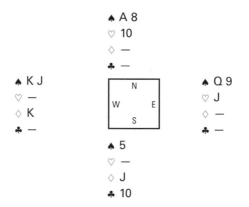

```
                    ♠ A 8
                    ♡ 10
                    ◇ —
                    ♣ —
    ♠ K J          ┌─────────┐          ♠ Q 9
    ♡ —            │    N    │          ♡ J
    ◇ K            │ W     E │          ◇ —
    ♣ —            │    S    │          ♣ —
                   └─────────┘
                    ♠ 5
                    ♡ —
                    ◇ J
                    ♣ 10
```

No good, is it? When you lead the ♣10 West will throw a spade, as before. You now have to find a discard from dummy. If you throw a spade, so will East; if you throw the ♡10, East can spare the ♡J.

This type of double squeeze, where the one-card threats are in different hands, is very common. It is time to see one in the context of a full deal:

```
                    ♠ K 8 5 3
                    ♡ A 3
                    ◇ A 8 7 2
                    ♣ A K 5
    ♠ —            ┌─────────┐          ♠ A 4
    ♡ 9 7 6 2      │    N    │          ♡ K Q 10 5 4
    ◇ Q J 10 4     │ W     E │          ◇ 9 6 5
    ♣ Q 10 7 6 2   │    S    │          ♣ J 8 3
                   └─────────┘
                    ♠ Q J 10 9 7 6 2
                    ♡ J 8
                    ◇ K 3
                    ♣ 9 4
```

You open 3♠ and are raised to 6♠. West leads the ◇Q and you win with the king. When you play on trumps, East wins with the ace and returns the king of hearts. You win with dummy's ace, draw the outstanding trump, and pause to assess your prospects. East surely guards your ♡J. If West is alone in guarding the diamonds, no-one will be able to keep a club stopper when you run the trump suit.

It is not certain that West has the sole diamond guard, however, so you play a diamond to the ace and ruff a diamond. This isolates the diamond guard in the West hand. True, he plays the jack on the third round, trying to look like a man who started with ◇QJ4, but you are not deceived by this old trick.

You return to the trump suit next, playing round after round. With one trump still to be played, these cards will remain:

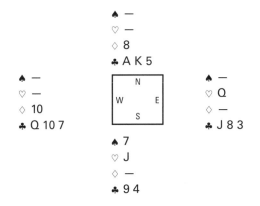

```
                   ♠ —
                   ♡ —
                   ◇ 8
                   ♣ A K 5
    ♠ —          ┌─────────┐        ♠ —
    ♡ —          │    N    │        ♡ Q
    ◇ 10         │ W     E │        ◇ —
    ♣ Q 10 7     │    S    │        ♣ J 8 3
                 └─────────┘
                   ♠ 7
                   ♡ J
                   ◇ —
                   ♣ 9 4
```

This type of position will be familiar to you by the end of the chapter. Your chant will be: 'West guards the diamonds, East guards the hearts; no-one can hold the clubs.' And so it proves. When you lead your last spade, West has to throw a club to retain his diamond guard. You can then throw the ◇8 from dummy. East is squeezed in hearts and clubs and twelve tricks are yours. Note that East's return of the ♡K assisted you. It removed dummy's ace, thereby setting up your jack as an unhindered threat card. Had East returned some other suit instead, you would have had to cash the ♡A yourself — a Vienna Coup.

There are three main types of double squeeze and this is easily the most common. We will call it the 'double squeeze with divided one-card threats.' (Yes, cool name, isn't it?) As we have already seen, it is a positional squeeze. The one-card threat in dummy must be guarded by West and not East.

Let's look now at a new type of 'threat accompanied by a winner'. For those of you interested in terminology, it is called a **recessed threat**:

```
         ♠ A K 9
       ┌─────────┐
       │    N    │
       │ W     E │
       │    S    │
       └─────────┘
         ♠ 5
```

The ♠9 is a threat accompanied by two winners. Not only that. Because the South hand has only a singleton spade, there will be room for more cards in the South hand. There will be room, in fact, for both the one-card menaces in a double squeeze!

Look at this end position:

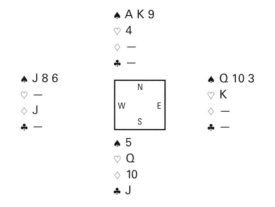

Declarer has two one-card threats (the ♡Q and the ◊10) alongside the squeeze card (the ♣J). When the club jack is led, West has to throw a spade. The redundant small heart is thrown from dummy and East is squeezed in the majors. This was possible only because of the unusual two-winner spade threat in the North hand. It created space for South to hold both one-card threats.

We need another smooth name for this position. Let's call it... a 'double squeeze with the one-card threats alongside the squeeze card'. As you see, it is an automatic squeeze. If you switch the ♡K and the ◊J the squeeze will work just as well. Here is a full-deal example of the play to cement the idea in your mind:

*Neither Vul.*
*Dealer North*

♠ K J 5
♡ A K 4
◊ A K 7
♣ A K 5 3

♠ 8 4 3　　　　　　　　　　♠ 6 2
♡ 9 2　　　　　　　　　　　♡ J 10 8 5
◊ Q 10 4　　　　　　　　　　◊ J 9 8 5 3 2
♣ Q J 10 7 2　　　　　　　　♣ 8

♠ A Q 10 9 7
♡ Q 7 6 3
◊ 6
♣ 9 6 4

| West | North | East | South |
|------|-------|------|-------|
|      | 2♣    | pass | 2♠    |
| pass | 5NT   | pass | 7♠    |
| all pass |    |      |       |

Wasting no time in the auction, you arrive in a grand slam. West leads the ♣Q and you win in the dummy. How would you give yourself the best chance? Your fourth heart is the problem. One possible line would be to draw two rounds of trumps and then cash the top hearts. Everybody and his dog would make the grand when hearts were 3-3, but on this line you would succeed also when the defender short in hearts did not hold more than two trumps. You could then ruff the fourth round of hearts in dummy. When the cards lie as in the diagram, this line would fail.

A better chance is to play for a squeeze. West's opening lead suggests that he alone may be guarding against your ♣9. If East guards the fourth round of hearts (which is more likely than normal, with West's ♣Q lead suggesting length in that suit) there will be a double squeeze, with diamonds as the pivot suit.

You draw trumps in three rounds and play a club to the king (a Vienna Coup, to free your ♣9 as a one-card threat). You then test the hearts. West shows out on the third round, leaving East's ♡J in control of the suit. 'West guards the clubs, East guards the hearts; no-one can guard the diamonds.' This will be end position as you lead the last trump:

```
              ♠ —
              ♡ —
              ◇ A K 7
              ♣ 5
  ♠ —                        ♠ —
  ♡ —          ┌───────┐     ♡ J
  ◇ Q 10 4     │   N   │     ◇ J 9 8
  ♣ J          │ W   E │     ♣ —
               │   S   │
               └───────┘
              ♠ 10
              ♡ 7
              ◇ 6
              ♣ 9
```

As you see, the recessed threat in diamonds has created extra space in the South hand. Both the one-card threats (the ♡7 and the ♣9) lie alongside the squeeze card. Each defender in turn is squeezed by the last spade and you make the grand slam.

Every double squeeze so far in this chapter has involved a two-card threat lying opposite the squeeze card. Do you recall this strange creature?

```
        ♡ A 7
       ┌───────┐
       │   N   │
       │ W   E │
       │   S   │
       └───────┘
        ♡ K 10 2
```

It's a 'twin-entry threat', which we met first in the chapter on the simple squeeze. When this is the pivot suit in a double squeeze it is possible for both the one-card threats to lie opposite the squeeze card.

Let's see a full-deal example of this:

```
                ♠ J 5
                ♡ A 7 4
                ◇ A K 7 2
                ♣ A K 8 6
 ♠ 8 4 3                        ♠ 6 2
 ♡ J 9 3         ┌─────┐        ♡ Q 8 6 5
 ◇ Q J 10 4      │  N  │        ◇ 9 8 5
 ♣ J 7 2       W │     │ E      ♣ Q 9 4 3
                 │  S  │
                 └─────┘
                ♠ A K Q 10 9 7
                ♡ K 10 2
                ◇ 6 3
                ♣ 10 5
```

Following your usual custom of overbidding by a trick (don't think I haven't noticed), you arrive in 7♠. West leads the ◇Q and you win with dummy's ace. The chance of a simple squeeze in the minors is very poor. You would need West to hold at least four cards in one minor, at least five cards in the other. A much better chance (in excess of 50%) is that the fourth-round guards in the minors are divided between the two defenders.

You draw trumps in three rounds, then cross to the ◇K and ruff a diamond. This isolates the diamond guard in the West hand. You then cash two rounds of clubs and ruff a third club. Although you cannot be certain yet from the fall of the cards, this in fact isolates the club guard in the East hand. 'West guards the diamonds, East guards the clubs; no-one will be able to guard the hearts.'

This position has been reached:

```
                ♠ —
                ♡ A 7
                ◇ 7
                ♣ 8
 ♠ —                           ♠ —
 ♡ J 9 3         ┌─────┐        ♡ Q 8 6
 ◇ J            │  N  │        ◇ —
 ♣ —           W │     │ E      ♣ Q
                 │  S  │
                 └─────┘
                ♠ 10
                ♡ K 10 2
                ◇ —
                ♣ —
```

Both the one-card threats lie opposite the squeeze card. Do you recognize the heart holding? It's the twin-entry threat that we admired earlier and it is about to deliver a grand slam bonus. You lead the last spade and West has to throw a heart. This is a positional squeeze and you now have to release from dummy the one-card threat that West was guarding. On this particular deal West has made it pretty obvious that he holds the diamond guard. You throw dummy's ◇7, therefore, and East is squeezed. He has to give way to the ♣8 (which can be reached with the ♡A, the extra entry provided by the twin-entry threat), or to the third heart in the South hand. This is the third main type of double squeeze. Our catchy name for it will the 'double squeeze with both one-card threats opposite the squeeze card'.

# Playing a single squeeze as a double squeeze

An even more powerful animal than the twin-entry threat is the fabulous **twin-entry recessed threat** (no need to remember the name!):

♠ A 6

```
        N
    W       E
        S
```

♠ K Q 9 7

This creates extra space in the North hand. On the last deal you had to discard a one-card threat from dummy on the squeeze card. You therefore had to diagnose which threat West was guarding. With the extra space provided by the twin-entry recessed threat, the squeeze will be automatic and no such guesswork will be required.

Note that such a threat contains six cards and can therefore be guarded by only one of the defenders. Nevertheless it is possible to play along double-squeeze lines, using this suit as the pivot suit. Here is a typical deal:

Both Vul.
Dealer South

```
                  ♠ A 6
                  ♡ J 7 4
                  ◇ A K Q 2
                  ♣ A 8 4 2
  ♠ 10 4 2                       ♠ J 8 5 3
  ♡ 10 9 3          N            ♡ Q 8 5 2
  ◇ 8 6 3       W       E        ◇ 10 7
  ♣ J 9 7 5         S            ♣ Q 10 3
                  ♠ K Q 9 7
                  ♡ A K 6
                  ◇ J 9 5 4
                  ♣ K 6
```

| West | North | East | South |
|------|-------|------|-------|
|      |       |      | 1NT (15-17) |
| pass | 6NT   | all pass |  |

West leads the ♡ 10 and, after a few moments of 'Why aren't we playing in diamonds?' self-commiseration, you win with the ace. What now?

The first move is to duck a round of clubs. This will have two desirable effects. It will rectify the count. It will also isolate the club guard in just one of the defenders' hands. Let's say East wins the first round of clubs and exits safely with a diamond. You cash the top winners in clubs and hearts and then run the diamond suit. This will be the end position:

```
                    ♠ A 6
                    ♡ J
                    ◇ 2
                    ♣ 8
   ♠ 10 4 2      ┌─────────┐      ♠ J 8 5 3
   ♡ 10         │    N    │      ♡ Q
   ◇ —          │ W     E │      ◇ —
   ♣ J          │    S    │      ♣ —
                └─────────┘
                    ♠ K Q 9 7
                    ♡ —
                    ◇ J
                    ♣ —
```

'West guards the clubs, East guards the hearts; no-one can hold the spades.' The double squeeze ditty still holds true, even though we know that in fact only one of the defenders can guard the spades. The technique is known as **playing a simple squeeze as a double squeeze.**

The main point of interest in this end position is that we do not have to guess which one-card threat to throw from dummy on the last diamond. The recessed threat has created space there for an idle card (the ◇ 2) and both one-card threats can be retained. Since East happens to hold the spade guard, he is squeezed in the major suits. If West had held the spade guard (with 4-2-3-4 shape, for example), he would have been squeezed in the black suits.

# Cashing winners in the right order

Until now we have looked at only some clean-cut examples of the main variants of the double squeeze. Anyone familiar with the basic idea would have found the deals fairly easy to play. Sometimes, however, the heart of a squeeze is obscured by the presence of extra winners. You may need to cash these in a particular order. Our next task is to understand the problems that may arise and to establish some guidelines to help us play such deals correctly.

Look at this notrump slam:

```
North-South Vul.            ♠ A 10 9
Dealer South                ♡ K Q J 10 2
                            ◇ K 7
                            ♣ A Q 4
        ♠ Q 5 2                              ♠ J 8 4 3
        ♡ 9 8 6           ┌─────────┐        ♡ 7 4 3
        ◇ 8 6 3           │    N    │        ◇ A J 10 4 2
        ♣ J 10 6 2        │ W     E │        ♣ 9
                          │    S    │
                          └─────────┘
                            ♠ K 7 6
                            ♡ A 5
                            ◇ Q 9 5
                            ♣ K 8 7 5 3
```

| West | North | East | South |
|------|-------|------|-------|
|      |       |      | 1♣    |
| pass | 1♡    | pass | 1NT   |
| pass | 6NT   | all pass |   |

Your partner may have overbid slightly but since you hold five clubs there is nothing at all wrong with the contract. You win the ♡9 lead with the ace and play a diamond to the king and ace. East now finds the best return of a heart, removing an entry to dummy. Suppose you test the club suit by cashing the ace and queen, discovering the bad news. This will be the position:

```
                            ♠ A 10 9
                            ♡ K Q J
                            ◇ 7
                            ♣ 4
        ♠ Q 5 2                              ♠ J 8 4 3
        ♡ 8 6             ┌─────────┐        ♡ 7 4
        ◇ 8               │    N    │        ◇ 10 4
        ♣ J 10            │ W     E │        ♣ —
                          │    S    │
                          └─────────┘
                            ♠ K 7 6
                            ♡ —
                            ◇ Q 9
                            ♣ K 8 7
```

West guards the clubs and East guards the diamonds. You have a twin-entry threat in spades, so it may seem that all you need to do is to cash the hearts.

Let's see what goes wrong if you follow this tempting line. This will be the position when you play the last heart:

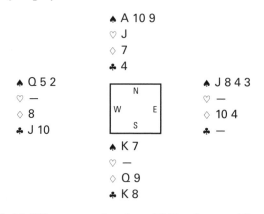

          ♠ A 10 9
          ♡ J
          ◇ 7
          ♣ 4

♠ Q 5 2                    ♠ J 8 4 3
♡ —                        ♡ —
◇ 8                        ◇ 10 4
♣ J 10                     ♣ —

          ♠ K 7
          ♡ —
          ◇ Q 9
          ♣ K 8

No good, is it? When you play the ♡K, East has an idle card to throw (his fourth spade). You will then have no good card to play from the South hand.

What went wrong? You needed to cash the ♣K (to remove East's idle card) before running the hearts. You should test the clubs by cashing the ace and king. When the suit fails to break, you return to dummy with the club queen and run the heart winners. Look at the difference it makes. This will be the ending:

          ♠ A 10 9
          ♡ J
          ◇ —
          ♣ —

♠ Q 5 2                    ♠ J 8 4
♡ —                        ♡ —
◇ —                        ◇ 10
♣ J                        ♣ —

          ♠ K 7
          ♡ —
          ◇ 9
          ♣ 8

East had to throw his idle card (the ◇4) on the ♣K. The last heart now forces him to throw a spade. The ◇9 has done its work and can be discarded. West is duly squeezed in the black suits and the slam is yours.

Are you getting a feel for these positions? The king of clubs was not needed as an entry. Your plan was to have one-card threats in clubs and diamonds, with the spade suit as the pivot. To put East under pressure, you needed to cash, at an early stage, the superfluous winner accompanying the one-card threat against West.

Here is one more example on the same theme:

*North-South Vul.*
*Dealer South*

```
                    ♠ A 9 6 3
                    ♡ J 10 6 4
                    ◇ Q 7
                    ♣ Q 4 2
♠ K J 10 8 7 5 2                        ♠ Q 4
♡ 7                                     ♡ 8 5 3
◇ J 9 6 3                               ◇ A 10 4
♣ 8                                     ♣ J 10 9 6 3
                    ♠ —
                    ♡ A K Q 9 2
                    ◇ K 8 5 2
                    ♣ A K 7 5
```

| West | North | East | South |
|------|-------|------|-------|
|      |       |      | 1♡    |
| 3♠   | 4♡    | pass | 6♡    |
| all pass |   |      |       |

Macho bidding, yes, but can you follow it with some macho play? West leads the ♣8 and you win with the ace. Since the club lead is likely to be a singleton, it is too dangerous to give up a diamond immediately, aiming to ruff two diamonds in dummy. You draw two rounds of trumps with the ace and jack, West showing out on the second round.

It is tempting to play for a minor-suit squeeze on East but in fact you can make the contract when West holds the diamond length, too. You should ruff a spade with the king and then play a diamond to the queen. East wins with the ace and returns his last trump, to stop you taking two more ruffs. You win in dummy, cash the ace of spades, and ruff another spade in the South hand. These cards remain:

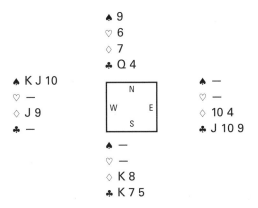

```
                ♠ 9
                ♡ 6
                ◇ 7
                ♣ Q 4
♠ K J 10                    ♠ —
♡ —                         ♡ —
◇ J 9                       ◇ 10 4
♣ —                         ♣ J 10 9
                ♠ —
                ♡ —
                ◇ K 8
                ♣ K 7 5
```

'East guards the clubs, West guards the spades; no-one can guard the diamonds.' It's true as far as it goes, but what will happen if you return to dummy with the ♣Q and play the last trump? East will be squeezed out of his diamond guard and you can throw a club from the South hand. West will not be squeezed! Because the ♣K has not yet been cashed, West has an idle card to throw (his penultimate spade).

So, in the diagrammed position you must cash both the king and queen of clubs. West throws two spades but dummy's last trump then effects a double squeeze. Diamonds was the intended pivot suit and the superfluous winners in clubs had to be cashed first.

# The non-simultaneous double squeeze

In the double squeezes we have seen up till now, both defenders were squeezed on the same trick — when the squeeze card was played. This is what happens on most double squeeze hands. Sometimes, however, the squeeze card forces one defender to release his guard on the pivot suit. Cashing your winners in the suit the first defender has retained then squeezes the other defender on a subsequent trick. Here is a typical deal:

```
        Both Vul.              ♠ Q J 2
        Dealer South           ♡ K 4
                               ◇ K 8 7 3
                               ♣ A 8 4 2
            ♠ 9 3                              ♠ 10 7 6 4
            ♡ 9 7 5 3        ┌──────────┐     ♡ Q J 10 6
            ◇ J 10 9 5 2     │ N        │     ◇ 4
            ♣ J 3            W│        E │     ♣ Q 10 9 7
                             │        S │
                             └──────────┘
                               ♠ A K 8 5
                               ♡ A 8 2
                               ◇ A Q 6
                               ♣ K 6 5
```

| West | North | East | South |
|------|-------|------|-------|
|      |       |      | 2NT   |
| pass | 6NT   | all pass |    |

West leads the ◇J against 6NT and you win with the ace. There are eleven top tricks and you duck a club, hoping for an easy twelfth trick there. East wins with the seven and switches to the queen of hearts. What now?

You should win the heart switch with dummy's king and clarify the position in the club suit. If West started with four clubs, a minor-suit simple squeeze against him is likely. If East started with the club length, your thoughts will turn towards a double squeeze with hearts as the pivot suit.

Two rounds of clubs confirm that East has the club guard. To simplify the position you play the diamond queen, discovering that West started with five cards in the suit. Three rounds of spades bring you to this end position:

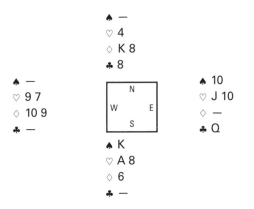

```
              ♠ —
              ♡ 4
              ◇ K 8
              ♣ 8
  ♠ —                        ♠ 10
  ♡ 9 7        ┌─────────┐   ♡ J 10
  ◇ 10 9       │ N       │   ◇ —
  ♣ —          │ W     E │   ♣ Q
               │   S     │
               └─────────┘
              ♠ K
              ♡ A 8
              ◇ 6
              ♣ —
```

Why is this end position different from those we have seen so far? The squeeze card (♠K) lies in the same hand as the length in the two-card pivot suit (♡A 8). To compensate for this deficiency, the diamond suit must be left intact — to provide an entry to dummy, in case East abandons his club guard.

When you play the spade king West has to throw a heart, abandoning his guard on the pivot suit. You throw the ◇8 from dummy, its work done. East is not squeezed on this trick. He follows suit with ♠10. However, when you cross to dummy with the ◇K it is East's turn to be squeezed. To keep a guard in the club suit he, too, has to abandon his guard on the pivot suit. You score the ace and eight of hearts for the contract.

So, the non-simultaneous double squeeze occurs when the squeeze card lies in the same hand as the two-card threat in the pivot suit. You need to retain an entry to dummy in the suit held by the left-hand opponent.

This is a long chapter, I admit, and I am happy to award you another coffee break. When you come back we will see some top-class declarers performing the double squeeze.

# The stars come out to play:
## the double squeeze

Our first real-life example of the double squeeze comes — once again — from the rubber bridge tables of Sydney's Double Bay Bridge Center. You will not be surprised to hear that the declarer was… the legendary Tim Seres.

Neither Vul.
Dealer North

```
              ♠ A Q 7 6 5 2
              ♡ Q
              ◇ 10 7 6 4
              ♣ 9 3
♠ K 9 8                        ♠ J 10 3
♡ 10 9 8        N              ♡ 5 4 2
◇ Q 9 5 3    W     E           ◇ A K J
♣ A 5 4         S              ♣ Q 10 8 6
              ♠ 4
              ♡ A K J 7 6 3
              ◇ 8 2
              ♣ K J 7 2
```

| West | North | East | South |
|------|-------|------|-------|
|      | pass  | pass | 4♡    |
| all pass |   |      |       |

Seres won the trump lead with the bare queen in dummy. Suppose you had been the declarer. What would you have done next?

One possibility is to play a club. You would then have a genuine chance of success if East held the ace and queen of the suit (and West held the spade king too!) No, such plays are for ordinary mortals. Seres preferred to play a diamond. He was hoping that West would win and make a helpful switch to clubs. In fact East rose with the diamond king and switched to the ♣10. Such a switch smelled of a Q-10-8-x holding and Seres inserted the jack. This forced West's ace and a diamond was returned to East's ace.

Seres ruffed the third round of diamonds, noting that the count had now been rectified. Three more rounds of trumps, followed by the club king, left this end position:

```
              ♠ A Q 7
              ♡ —
              ◇ 10
              ♣ —
♠ K 9 8                        ♠ J 10 3
♡ —            N               ♡ —
◇ Q          W     E           ◇ —
♣ —             S              ♣ Q
              ♠ 4
              ♡ 7
              ◇ —
              ♣ 7 2
```

Declarer's last trump completed a classic double squeeze. West had to relinquish his third-round spade guard to retain the ◇Q. The ◇10 was thrown from dummy and East likewise had to discard his spade guard. A successful finesse of the spade queen then brought in three spade tricks for the contract.

Had either defender played a spade at any time, the squeeze would have been destroyed. The link in the pivot suit would have been broken.

Our next real-life example comes from a match between Germany and Belgium, held in memory of André Lemaitre. The world junior champion of 1990, Roland Rohowski of Germany, sat South.

```
              ♠ A K J 3 2
              ♡ 8 3
              ◇ A J 7 4
              ♣ Q 3
♠ 9 6 5 4                          ♠ Q 8 7
♡ 4 2          ┌─────────┐         ♡ K J 9 7 5
◇ Q 10 6 5 2   │    N    │         ◇ K 8
♣ 10 6         │ W     E │         ♣ 5 4 2
               │    S    │
               └─────────┘
              ♠ 10
              ♡ A Q 10 6
              ◇ 9 3
              ♣ A K J 9 8 7
```

Rohowski ended in 7♣ after a Key Card Blackwood misunderstanding. The Belgian West led the ◇2, knocking out a potential entry to dummy's spade suit. Rohowski won with dummy's ace and finessed the heart queen successfully. He cashed the ace of hearts and led a third heart, overruffing West's ♣6 with the queen. He then played his remaining trumps. On the penultimate trump East released the ◇K to keep his guards in spades and hearts:

```
              ♠ A K J
              ♡ —
              ◇ J
              ♣ —
♠ 9 6 5                            ♠ Q 8 7
♡ —            ┌─────────┐         ♡ K
◇ Q            │    N    │         ◇ —
♣ —            │ W     E │         ♣ —
               │    S    │
               └─────────┘
              ♠ 10
              ♡ 10
              ◇ 9
              ♣ 8
```

On the last trump West had to throw a spade, to retain his guard in diamonds. Declarer threw the ◇J from dummy and East also had to throw a spade. Since the position of the red-suit guards was apparent to declarer, he knew that both defenders had been squeezed down to a doubleton spade. He played spades from the top and made his grand slam. The line of play would still have succeeded, of course, had the ♠J been a lower spade.

# Quiz ✏️

A.

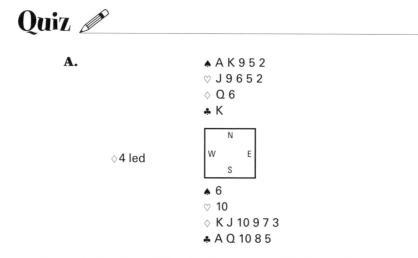

♠ A K 9 5 2
♡ J 9 6 5 2
◇ Q 6
♣ K

◇4 led

```
      N
  W       E
      S
```

♠ 6
♡ 10
◇ K J 10 9 7 3
♣ A Q 10 8 5

You arrive in 5◇ and West leads a trump to East's ace. To prevent you from discarding your heart loser on dummy's spades, East meanly cashes the ♡A. He then adds to your misery by finding a trump return, West following suit. How will you wipe the smile off East's face?

B.

♠ A K 9 8
♡ K Q
◇ K 9 6
♣ K 9 8 4

♠2 led

```
      N
  W       E
      S
```

♠ 7
♡ A J 10 8 7 6
◇ A 8 7 2
♣ A 7

| West | North | East | South |
|------|-------|------|-------|
|      |       | 3♠   | 4♡    |
| pass | 4NT   | pass | 5♣    |
| pass | 7♡    | all pass |   |

West leads the ♠2, an obvious singleton, against your grand slam. How will you play the contract?

**C.**

```
                    ♠ A 8 7 2
                    ♡ 9 3
                    ◇ A Q 9
                    ♣ A K 6 4
           ┌─────────────┐
           │      N      │
  ♣10 led  │  W       E  │
           │      S      │
           └─────────────┘
                    ♠ —
                    ♡ A K Q 7 4
                    ◇ K J 10 6 4 2
                    ♣ 5 2
```

| West | North | East | South |
|------|-------|------|-------|
|      | 1♣    | pass | 1◇    |
| 2♠   | 2NT   | 3♠   | 4♡    |
| pass | 4♠    | pass | 5♡    |
| pass | 7◇    | all pass |   |

West, who has shown long spades in the auction, leads the ♣10 against your grand slam. How will you play the contract? (West has three trumps.)

**D.**

```
                    ♠ K Q J 9 4
                    ♡ 9 7 2
                    ◇ K 3
                    ♣ 8 5 4
           ┌─────────────┐
           │      N      │
  ♣10 led  │  W       E  │
           │      S      │
           └─────────────┘
                    ♠ A
                    ♡ A K Q J 8
                    ◇ A 10 9 4
                    ♣ A 9 3
```

| West | North | East | South |
|------|-------|------|-------|
|      |       | 3♣   | dbl   |
| pass | 4♠    | pass | 4NT   |
| pass | 5◇    | pass | 5♡    |
| pass | 6◇    | pass | 7NT   |
| all pass |   |      |       |

The Roman Key Card Blackwood 5♡ follow-up locates the spade queen and the diamond king. If one of the majors breaks badly, can you visualize a possible double squeeze?

**E.**

                    ♠ 5 4 2
                    ♡ A K Q 8 4 3
                    ◊ 7 3
                    ♣ 8 3

```
        N
    W       E
        S
```

◊ 10 led

                    ♠ A Q 7
                    ♡ 5 2
                    ◊ A K Q J 6 4
                    ♣ A J

| West | North | East | South |
|------|-------|------|-------|
|      |       |      | 2♣    |
| pass | 3♡    | 5♠   | 7NT   |
| all pass |   |      |       |

Expecting partner to hold a solid heart suit, you bid a confident 7NT. East follows to the diamond lead and you win with the ace. What now?

**F.**

                    ♠ Q 9 7
                    ♡ A Q 8 7
                    ◊ 7 6
                    ♣ J 9 8 4

```
        N
    W       E
        S
```

♣ 6 led

                    ♠ K 3
                    ♡ K 3 2
                    ◊ A K 4
                    ♣ A K Q 10 2

| West | North | East | South |
|------|-------|------|-------|
| 2♠ (5-9) | pass | pass | dbl |
| pass | 3♡ | pass | 4NT |
| pass | 5◊ | pass | 6NT |
| all pass |  |  |  |

North's 3♡ shows intermediate values, since you are playing the Lebensohl convention (2NT by North would indicate a weak hand). Yes, 6♣ would have been a better contract, but how will you play 6NT on a club lead? West will subsequently show up with three clubs.

# Answers ✏

**A.** If the ♣J does not fall in three rounds, you will need a double squeeze. This can operate only if West, rather than East, holds the sole heart guard (because East discards after the dummy). 'West will guard the hearts, East will guard the clubs; no-one can guard the spades.' To maximize the chance that West is alone in guarding the hearts, you should take two heart ruffs. Win the trump return with the queen and ruff a heart. You can then return to dummy with the ♣K and ruff another heart. If East started with fewer than four hearts (or West started life with the ♡KQ), West will now guard the heart suit. Cash the top clubs and then the remaining trumps. You have this end position in mind:

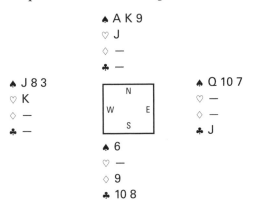

> ♠ A K 9
> ♡ J
> ◇ —
> ♣ —
>
> ♠ J 8 3        ♠ Q 10 7
> ♡ K           ♡ —
> ◇ —           ◇ —
> ♣ —           ♣ J
>
> ♠ 6
> ♡ —
> ◇ 9
> ♣ 10 8

When you play the last diamond, neither defender can retain a spade guard. If instead West holds the club stopper, you will need him to hold five spades, or Q-J-10(-x), for a simple black-suit squeeze to succeed.

**B.** If East holds four clubs, you cannot make the contract; there is no black-suit squeeze because East sits over the threats. If West holds four or more clubs (and the trumps are not 5-0), you can make the grand even if diamonds are 3-3. A double squeeze will be possible. 'West guards the clubs, East guards the spades; no-one can guard the diamonds.' Win the spade lead, draw trumps, and play the club ace and king. Cash the other spade, throwing a diamond, and ruff a club to isolate the club guard in the West hand. When you run the trumps you will reach an end position something like this:

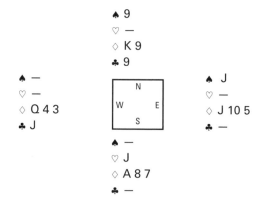

When you play the final trump, West has to abandon diamonds to keep his last club. You throw dummy's club and East is squeezed in spades and diamonds. Actually, a more likely scenario is that West holds at least four cards in both minors. This line ('a single squeeze played as a double') will win in that case too.

**C.** Suppose you win the club lead and play the ace and king of trumps. When West shows up with three trumps in addition to his spade length, he may well hold fewer than two hearts. If you play for a heart ruff, you run a substantial risk that West will ruff one of your top hearts.

There is no need to walk such a tightrope. Aim for: 'West guards the spades, East guards the hearts; no-one can guard the clubs.' Draw just one round of trumps, with the ace, cash the ♠A and ruff a spade. Return to dummy with the trump queen, exposing the 3-1 break, and ruff another spade. You hope that this will isolate the spade guard with West. When you run all your red winners, neither defender can keep a club guard. The ending will be something like this:

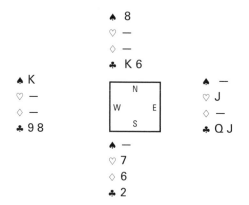

When you play the last trump, each defender will be squeezed in turn.

**D.** If West holds five hearts but the spades come in, you will need to find East with the sole guard in diamonds. A minor-suit simple squeeze would then be possible. When hearts are not 5-0, a double squeeze will come into the reckoning if West holds five of the six outstanding spades. 'West guards the spades, East guards the clubs; no-one can guard the diamonds.' Win the club lead and play five rounds of hearts. To keep five spades, West will have to abandon the diamonds. Play the ♠A and cross to the ♦K to play the three spade winners in dummy. The last of these will squeeze East in the minors. It is a non-simultaneous double squeeze.

**E.** The spade finesse — a certainty on the bidding — will bring your total to twelve tricks. If West holds four or more hearts you can then make the contract with a double squeeze, using clubs as the pivot suit. 'West guards the hearts, East guards the spades; no-one can retain a club guard.'

After winning the diamond lead, cross to the ♡A and take the spade finesse. Then cash the ♠A and run your diamonds. To keep his heart guard, West will have to reduce to one club. When you subsequently cash dummy's two remaining heart winners, East has to retain his spade guard. He, too, will have to reduce to one club and you will then make two club tricks.

**F.** West has nine black cards and would doubtless not have opened with a weak two if he held four hearts too. You should aim for a double squeeze with diamonds as the pivot suit. 'West guards the spades, East guards the hearts; no-one can guard the diamonds.' Since the diamonds lie in the same hand as the squeeze card (the last club), the squeeze will be non-simultaneous. To rectify the count, lead the ♠K from hand. West cannot duck or you will score two spade tricks. West's most awkward return is a diamond. You must then cash three hearts before running the clubs.

```
              ♠ Q 9
              ♡ 8
              ♦ 7
              ♣ —
♠ J 10                      ♠ —
♡ —          ┌─────────┐    ♡ J
♦ Q 5        │   N     │    ♦ J 8 3
♣ —          │ W     E │    ♣ —
             │   S     │
             └─────────┘
              ♠ 3
              ♡ —
              ♦ A 4
              ♣ 2
```

West has to throw a diamond when you play the last club and you can now release your low spade from dummy. East will be squeezed in the red suits when you cash the ♠Q.

# Squeeze Without the Count

In the squeezes we have seen so far, it was necessary to rectify the count before the squeeze card was played. In a small slam, for example, you had to surrender one trick to tighten the end position. On some deals this is not possible, for practical reasons. Ducking a trick might result in an adverse ruff or the immediate cashing of a second defensive trick. Nevertheless, a squeeze may still be possible. You may be able to surrender a trick *after* the squeeze has taken place.

It's not an easy concept to visualize, so let's look straight away at an example of this play:

```
 Neither Vul.            ♠ Q J 6
 Dealer South            ♡ A 8 4 2
                         ◇ A J 8 5
                         ♣ A 7
        ♠ 3                              ♠ 9 7 4
        ♡ K Q J 7 5 3        N           ♡ 9
        ◇ K Q 4         W         E      ◇ 10 7 6 3
        ♣ J 8 3              S           ♣ Q 9 6 5 4
                         ♠ A K 10 8 5 2
                         ♡ 10 6
                         ◇ 9 2
                         ♣ K 10 2
```

| West | North | East | South |
|------|-------|------|-------|
|      |       |      | 1♠    |
| 2♡   | 3♡    | pass | 4♠    |
| pass | 4NT   | pass | 5♡    |
| pass | 6♠    | all pass |   |

West leads the ♡K against your spade slam and you see straight away that you will need a red-suit squeeze to provide a twelfth trick. How can you rectify the count, though? If you duck the first trick there is a serious risk that East will ruff the second round of hearts. Suppose instead that you win the first heart, cash two clubs and take a club ruff, draw trumps, and give up a heart. That's no good. West will switch to the ◇K, killing the necessary entry to the two-card threat. No squeeze will then be possible.

The only solution is to run your winners without rectifying the count. You win the first heart, take your two club winners and ruff a club. Then you play the remaining trumps, arriving at this end position:

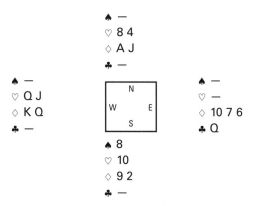

When you lead the last spade West is in trouble, even though the count has not been rectified. If he discards a diamond, you will throw a heart from dummy and score two diamond tricks. If instead he throws another heart, you will release the ◇J from dummy and surrender a heart to set up dummy's ♡8. Do you see what happened? To keep the diamonds guarded, West had to throw away a heart winner. It was then safe to knock out his remaining top card in hearts.

To become more familiar with this idea, let's look at another deal along the same lines:

```
              ♠ K J 9 7
              ♡ A 6 5
              ◇ A J 4 3
              ♣ 9 3
♠ A Q 8 2                      ♠ 10 6 5 4
♡ Q J 3          N             ♡ 8 7 2
◇ 7          W       E         ◇ 9 6 5
♣ K Q J 7 5      S             ♣ 8 6 2
              ♠ 3
              ♡ K 10 9 4
              ◇ K Q 10 8 2
              ♣ A 10 4
```

West opens 1♣ and, sitting South, you arrive in 3NT. West attacks in clubs and you win the third round. At this stage West has enough top cards to beat the contract. You, meanwhile, have only eight tricks. West holds the heart guard, however, and when you run your diamonds he will come under pressure. This will be the position when you lead your last diamond:

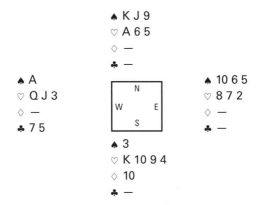

West has scored two tricks already and has three further winners in his hand. When you cash the last diamond he will have to throw another club winner, to keep the hearts guarded. It will then be safe for you to play a spade, setting up the ♠K as your ninth trick.

Look back at the end position. The defender under pressure has holdings in three different suits. It does not affect the squeeze in the slightest that the winners accompanying his heart guard are in two different suits (spades and clubs) rather than in one.

Back in the chapter on the simple squeeze, problem C (page 64) gave the North-South hands on this next deal:

*North-South Vul.*
*Dealer North*

♠ 10 9 6
♡ A K 8
◇ K Q 7 3
♣ K Q 4

♠ 8 5
♡ 10 6 2
◇ J 10 4 2
♣ J 10 6 3

♠ A Q J 7 4 2
♡ 9 7 4
◇ 8 6 5
♣ 9

♠ K 3
♡ Q J 5 3
◇ A 9
♣ A 8 7 5 2

| West | North | East | South |
|------|-------|------|-------|
| | 1◇ | 2♠ | 3♣ |
| pass | 3♠ | pass | 3NT |
| pass | 4NT | pass | 6NT |
| all pass | | | |

West led the ♠8, East winning the spade ace and returning a spade. You tested the clubs, then played to squeeze West in the minors (or East in the black suits, depending on how the clubs lay). But suppose that East plays the ♠J at Trick 1, refusing to assist you by rectifying the count. Now what?

You should play three rounds of hearts, to test the lie of that suit. When East shows up with three hearts, the odds are enormous that West will guard the clubs, if anyone. You therefore play a fourth round of hearts, throwing a spade from dummy. On this trick West is squeezed out of his remaining spade. The ace, king and queen of clubs confirm that West does indeed guard the club suit but it is now safe to concede a club to West. He no longer has a spade to play.

Suppose instead that the cards lie like this:

```
                 ♠ 10 9 6
                 ♡ A K 8
                 ◊ K Q 7 3
                 ♣ K Q 4
  ♠ 8 5                          ♠ A Q J 7 4 2
  ♡ 10 6 4 2        N            ♡ 9 7
  ◊ J 10 6 5 4 2  W   E          ◊ 8
  ♣ 6               S            ♣ J 10 9 3
                 ♠ K 3
                 ♡ Q J 5 3
                 ◊ A 9
                 ♣ A 8 7 5 2
```

You win the first round of spades again but this time East shows out on the third heart. Assuming spades are 2-6, which is likely on the bidding, West has only seven spaces remaining in the minors and cannot therefore guard both minor suits. A spade-diamond squeeze on East is not possible because he sits over the lengths in dummy. So, if clubs do not break 3-2 the only possible squeeze remaining is a black-suit squeeze on East. You play the last heart, throwing a diamond from dummy, followed by one top club and three top diamonds. This will be the position as the last diamond winner is led:

```
                 ♠ 10 9
                 ♡ —
                 ◊ Q
                 ♣ Q 4
  ♠ 5                            ♠ A Q
  ♡ —               N            ♡ —
  ◊ J 10 6 5      W   E          ◊ —
  ♣ —               S            ♣ J 10 9
                 ♠ 3
                 ♡ —
                 ◊ —
                 ♣ A 8 7 5
```

The last diamond squeezes East without the count. If he throws a spade, you will establish a second spade trick in the dummy. If he keeps two spades, throwing a club, you will play for the clubs to be good instead.

# The ducking threat

It's time to look at a new type of threat. What do you make of these?

| **A.** | ♡ A K 8 2 | **B.** | ♡ A K 8 2 |
|---|---|---|---|

A.
```
        ♡ A K 8 2
        ┌─────────┐
        │    N    │
        │ W     E │
        │    S    │
        └─────────┘
        ♡ 7 5
```

B.
```
        ♡ A K 8 2
        ┌─────────┐
        │    N    │
        │ W     E │
        │    S    │
        └─────────┘
        ♡ J 5
```

We will suppose that the North holding lies in an otherwise entryless dummy. What use can such suits be as threats in a squeeze?

There is no point in cashing two rounds and ruffing a third round, isolating the guard, because there is no outside entry to dummy. Nor will it be profitable to duck a round, with the same aim. If you try that, the defenders can smartly return a second round of the suit, killing your last entry to dummy. Two sensible possibilities remain. You can play for a defender to hold five cards in the suit, and therefore the sole guard. Alternatively you can play for a squeeze without the count. You plan to reduce the defender with four or more hearts to just three hearts. You can then duck a round of hearts after the squeeze has taken place. If you have holding (b) rather than (a), you can duck the first round to a particular defender — the one who holds the queen.

Let's see this ducking play in the context of a full deal.

```
North-South Vul.          ♠ 7 4
Dealer East               ♡ A K 4 2
                          ◇ 7 6 5 4
                          ♣ 9 3 2
        ♠ 10 8 5 3                      ♠ 9 2
        ♡ Q 9 8 3      ┌─────────┐      ♡ 10 6 5
        ◇ J 9 8 2      │    N    │      ◇ 10
        ♣ 6           │ W     E │      ♣ K Q J 10 8 5 4
                       │    S    │
                       └─────────┘
                          ♠ A K Q J 6
                          ♡ J 7
                          ◇ A K Q 3
                          ♣ A 7
```

| West | North | East | South |
|---|---|---|---|
|  |  | 3♣ | dbl |
| pass | 3♡ | pass | 4♠ |
| pass | 5♠ | pass | 6♠ |
| all pass |  |  |  |

West leads his singleton club against your small slam in spades. You win with the ace and draw trumps in four rounds. Two rounds of diamonds reveal the unfortunate split there. What can be done?

This is the position around the table:

```
                    ♠ —
                    ♡ A K 4 2
                    ◇ 7 6
                    ♣ —
    ♠ —                           ♠ —
    ♡ Q 9 8 3        ┌──────┐     ♡ 10 6 5
    ◇ J 9            │   N  │     ◇ —
    ♣ —             │ W   E │     ♣ K Q J
                    │   S  │
                    └──────┘
                    ♠ 6
                    ♡ J 7
                    ◇ Q 3
                    ♣ 7
```

If you lead the ♡J and duck when West covers, West will play another heart, cutting you off from dummy. Instead, you must play your last trump. West cannot release his diamond guard and will have to throw a heart. Now is the time to lead the ♡J. When West covers, you allow his queen to win. You can then score three heart tricks in the dummy.

The same play may succeed when West started with three spades and two clubs. He is likely to throw his second club, to keep both red suits guarded, and the same ending will result. Double-dummy, in this layout, he could defeat you by keeping a club and abandoning hearts, since his partner's ten can guard the third round of hearts.

# The see-saw squeeze

Suppose you have in your armory a suit like this:

```
    ♣ A 7 2
    ┌──────┐
    │   N  │
    │ W   E │
    │   S  │
    └──────┘
    ♣ K Q J
```

Totally useless for a squeeze, would you say? Once in a while, such a holding may prove useful. You cash the king and lead the queen on the second round. Suppose that West has double guards in two other suits and must find a discard on the second club. If he reduces to a single guard in the suit held by the dummy, you will win the trick with the queen. You can then set up dummy's suit, conceding a trick to West, and the ♣A will remain as an entry. If instead West weakens his guard in a suit held in your own hand, you will overtake the second round of clubs and clear this suit instead.

Let's see a full deal on this theme:

```
Neither Vul.              ♠ A K 6 5 2
Dealer North              ♡ 4
                          ◇ Q J 8 7
                          ♣ A 7 2
        ♠ Q J 10 9 4            N           ♠ 3
        ♡ Q 10 9 7      W              E    ♡ J 6 5
        ◇ 4 2                  S           ◇ 10 9 6 3
        ♣ 9 3                               ♣ 10 8 6 5 4
                          ♠ 8 7
                          ♡ A K 8 3 2
                          ◇ A K 5
                          ♣ K Q J
```

| West | North | East | South |
|------|-------|------|-------|
|      | 1♠    | pass | 2♡    |
| pass | 2♠    | pass | 6NT   |

West leads the ♠Q against your small slam in notrump. How would you tackle the deal?

After this opening lead there is little chance of a 3-3 spade break. Nor will prospects of a major-suit squeeze be at all good if you duck the opening lead. You would need West to hold five hearts. What if you take the first spade and duck a heart instead? West would win and fire back a second spade, leaving you with no entry in either of your threat suits.

To make the slam, you must win the opening lead and play four rounds of diamonds, throwing a heart from your hand. You then play a club to the king to leave this position:

```
                          ♠ K 6 5 2
                          ♡ 4
                          ◇ —
                          ♣ A 7
        ♠ J 10 9              N           ♠ —
        ♡ Q 10 9 7      W              E    ♡ J 6 5
        ◇ —                    S           ◇ —
        ♣ —                                 ♣ 10 8 6 5
                          ♠ 8
                          ♡ A K 8 3
                          ◇ —
                          ♣ Q J
```

At this stage West holds a double guard in both of the major suits. When you lead the ♣Q, he must reduce to a single guard in one of the suits. If he chooses to throw a heart, you will aim for an extra heart trick. You overtake the ♣Q with the ace (to leave your ♣J as an entry) and play three rounds of hearts. Whichever defender wins, you will have an entry to the long heart.

Suppose instead that West throws a spade. You will drop dummy's ♣7 under your queen and then play king and another spade. The ♣A remains in dummy as an entry to the established spade winner.

This fancy maneuver is known as a **see-saw squeeze** or an **entry-shifting squeeze**.

# The stars come out to play:
## the squeeze without the count ☆

You will surely permit a writer from England to show you one deal from the 1955 world championship final (the one and only such final that Great Britain has ever won). It is a meaty deal with plenty of interest. Adam 'Plum' Meredith occupies the hot seat for Great Britain against USA.

```
Neither Vul.              ♠ A Q 8 4
Dealer North              ♡ J 9 5
                          ◊ 5 4 2
                          ♣ K 10 7

    ♠ J 9 7 5 3       ┌─────────┐       ♠ 10
    ♡ 10 4            │    N    │       ♡ Q 8 7 3 2
    ◊ A Q 10 3        │ W     E │       ◊ K 7 6
    ♣ Q 8             │    S    │       ♣ J 9 6 4
                      └─────────┘
                          ♠ K 6 2
                          ♡ A K 6
                          ◊ J 9 8
                          ♣ A 5 3 2
```

| West | North | East | South |
|------|-------|------|-------|
| Ellenby | Dodds | Rosen | Meredith |
|  | pass | pass | 1NT |
| pass | 3NT | all pass | |

West led the ♠5, Meredith taking East's 10 with the king. Prospects are poor, despite the presence of 25 points. What would you do next?

Meredith led the jack of diamonds. This was not so much a deceptive move, feigning strength in the suit; he was starting the long process of rectifying the count, hoping to apply pressure in the end-game. West won with the diamond queen and persevered with the ♠J, won in the dummy. A second diamond went to the nine and ten and West played another spade, Meredith taking the marked finesse of the eight. When declarer led a third round of diamonds, Ellenby overtook his partner's king with the ace. This was the position with West on lead:

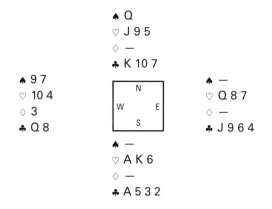

```
              ♠ Q
              ♡ J 9 5
              ◇ —
              ♣ K 10 7
♠ 9 7                        ♠ —
♡ 10 4        ┌─────────┐    ♡ Q 8 7
◇ 3          │ N       │    ◇ —
♣ Q 8        │ W     E │    ♣ J 9 6 4
             │   S     │
             └─────────┘
              ♠ —
              ♡ A K 6
              ◇ —
              ♣ A 5 3 2
```

What would most defenders do next? They would cash the long diamond. Ellenby could see that this would be a poor idea, almost certain to set up a squeeze on his partner. (East would have had to throw a club and dummy's ♠Q would subsequently catch him in a simple squeeze.) The American West showed a fine understanding of the situation when he exited instead with a spade. East discarded a club and declarer threw a heart.

Meredith crossed to a heart honor and led a club to the eight, ten and jack. The safe hand was on lead and he had established a ninth trick in the club suit, making his game. It would have done West no good to insert the club queen because declarer would then have played clubs from the top, forcing East to win the third round.

A fine hand, don't you agree? South did his best to rectify the count but West thwarted him. When that little battle was over, East was still caught in a squeeze without the count.

The next deal comes from the 1970 Lederer Memorial, played in London. North was Dr. Rockfelt, a famous international of the day, and his partner was Dr. Alan Manch, a consistently heavy winner at rubber bridge. At both tables, the final contract was six diamonds by South.

```
Both Vul.              ♠ 4 3 2
Dealer South           ♡ 5 4 2
                       ◇ 7 2
                       ♣ A J 9 7 6
♠ 10 7 6                            ♠ J 9 8 5
♡ K Q J 9 8   ┌─────────┐          ♡ 7 6
◇ 8 3        │ N       │          ◇ 6 5 4
♣ K Q 10     │ W     E │          ♣ 8 5 4 3
             │   S     │
             └─────────┘
                       ♠ A K Q
                       ♡ A 10 3
                       ◇ A K Q J 10 9
                       ♣ 2
```

The opening lead was the ♡K. Manch won the trick with the ace and ran the trump suit, followed by the spades. This end position resulted:

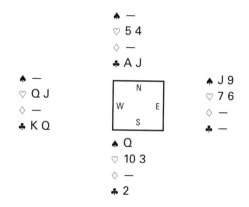

```
                    ♠ —
                    ♡ 5 4
                    ◇ —
                    ♣ A J
  ♠ —                              ♠ J 9
  ♡ Q J         ┌──────────┐       ♡ 7 6
  ◇ —           │    N     │       ◇ —
  ♣ K Q         │ W     E  │       ♣ —
                │    S     │
                └──────────┘
                    ♠ Q
                    ♡ 10 3
                    ◇ —
                    ♣ 2
```

When the last spade was led, West had to keep both clubs to guard against dummy's holding in the suit. He released the ♡J which allowed Manch to throw the ♣J from dummy. A heart was ducked to the bare queen, setting up South's ♡10, and declarer claimed the last two tricks.

At the other table of this match declarer ducked the opening ♡K lead, to rectify the count. It could hardly have been clearer to West that a squeeze was impending. He switched smartly to the ♣K, removing the only entry to dummy. East discarded all his clubs when the diamonds were run and West then knew which card to keep for Trick 13. One down.

You want some big names from the modern game next? How about Bob Hamman playing with Zia Mahmood? This deal arose in the 1994 Macallan International Pairs, played in London's White House Hotel.

```
Neither Vul.          ♠ A 8 3
Dealer South          ♡ 10 8
                      ◇ A 10 8 6 5
                      ♣ 9 6 3
  ♠ 10 9 6                             ♠ 5 4 2
  ♡ A Q J 7 4     ┌──────────┐         ♡ 6 5 3 2
  ◇ K J 3 2       │    N     │         ◇ 9 7 4
  ♣ 2             │ W     E  │         ♣ 10 8 7
                  │    S     │
                  └──────────┘
                      ♠ K Q J 7
                      ♡ K 9
                      ◇ Q
                      ♣ A K Q J 5 4
```

| West | North | East | South |
|------|-------|------|-------|
| Ata-Ullah | Zia | Sheehan | Hamman |
| | | | 1♣ |
| 1♡ | dbl | pass | 4NT |
| pass | 5♡ | pass | 6♠ |
| all pass | | | |

Six clubs would have been a better contract but Hamman expected Zia to hold four spades for his negative double. In that case, playing in spades might allow discards to be taken on the long club suit.

Hamman won the trump lead and drew trumps in three rounds. West's overcall placed him with the ♡A. If he held all the missing honors in the red suits a squeeze might be possible, but there was no way to rectify the count. Hamman ran his black-suit winners anyway, realizing that West would still come under pressure. This was the eventual end position:

```
                    ♠ —
                    ♡ 10 8
                    ◇ A 10
                    ♣ —
      ♠ —                        ♠ —
      ♡ A Q          N           ♡ 6 3
      ◇ K J      W     E         ◇ 9 7
      ♣ —            S           ♣ —
                    ♠ 7
                    ♡ K 9
                    ◇ Q
                    ♣ —
```

If West threw a diamond on the last spade the ◇10 would score, so he chose to throw the ♡Q. Hamman discarded the ◇10 from dummy and then played a low heart. When the heart ace appeared, South's king was good for a twelfth trick. Note that it was important to keep two hearts in dummy. Otherwise West could exit with the ◇K, scoring the final trick with the ◇J.

Our next example comes from the 1991 Bermuda Bowl in Yokohama. Poland faces Brazil.

```
Both Vul.            ♠ A 9 8 2
Dealer East          ♡ 10 5 2
                     ◇ A 5 3
                     ♣ J 8 2
  ♠ Q J 7 5 4                        ♠ 10 3
  ♡ 6              N                 ♡ A 9 8
  ◇ K J 7      W       E             ◇ 10 8 4
  ♣ Q 9 5 3          S               ♣ A K 10 7 6
                     ♠ K 6
                     ♡ K Q J 7 4 3
                     ◇ Q 9 6 2
                     ♣ 4
```

| West | North | East | South |
|------|-------|------|-------|
| Lasocki | Mello | Gawrys | Branco |
| | | 1♣ | 1♡ |
| 1♠ | 2♡ | pass | 3◇ |
| pass | 4♡ | pass | pass |
| dbl | all pass | | |

The Polish West led a club, his partner winning with the king and continuing with the club ace. Branco ruffed and led the jack of trumps to East's ace. When a third round of clubs was played, Branco ruffed and drew East's remaining trumps. This was the position as East's last trump was drawn:

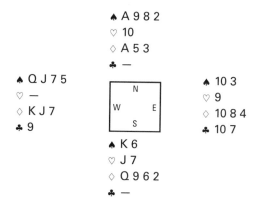

&spades; A 9 8 2
&hearts; 10
&diams; A 5 3
&clubs; —

&spades; Q J 7 5     &spades; 10 3
&hearts; —     &hearts; 9
&diams; K J 7     &diams; 10 8 4
&clubs; 9     &clubs; 10 7

&spades; K 6
&hearts; J 7
&diams; Q 9 6 2
&clubs; —

*'Branco plays his remaining trumps, which brings Lasocki more pressure than he can bear. He has to throw his vital fourth club, then a diamond, and now Branco can build a second diamond trick for +790.'*

This is the analysis from the 1991 world championship book. What do you make of it? It seems that neither Lasocki (West) nor the writer counted declarer's tricks. Branco had only eight top tricks and therefore needed two more for his contract. West could beat the contract by keeping a club and throwing a spade on the penultimate trump! Declarer could ruff a long spade good, for a ninth trick, but there would be no route to a tenth. If instead declarer persisted with his last trump, West could throw a diamond.

Finally we will look at a real-life example of the **losing card squeeze**, where declarer rectifies the count and plays his squeeze card on the same trick. It comes from the 1993 Forbo International tournament in Scheveningen, Holland. Johan Sylvan of Sweden, is the declarer and the contract is six spades.

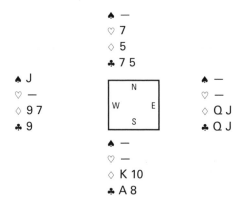

♠ Q
♡ A 7 6 4 2
◇ A 5 3
♣ K 7 5 2

♠ J 10 5 3
♡ K Q J 5
◇ 9 7 6
♣ 9 3

♠ 9 6
♡ 10 8 3
◇ Q J 8 2
♣ Q J 10 4

♠ A K 8 7 4 2
♡ 9
◇ K 10 4
♣ A 8 6

West led the ♡K, won in the dummy. Aiming to set up a long heart, Sylvan ruffed a heart immediately. A trump to the queen permitted a second heart ruff and Sylvan then played the ace and king of trumps, discovering that he had a trump loser. Battling on regardless, he crossed to the ♣K and ruffed a fourth round of hearts. This was doubly beneficial — he scored the last of his small trumps; he also set up a long heart. A diamond to dummy's ace left this position:

♠ —
♡ 7
◇ 5
♣ 7 5

♠ J
♡ —
◇ 9 7
♣ 9

♠ —
♡ —
◇ Q J
♣ Q J

♠ —
♡ —
◇ K 10
♣ A 8

The count had not been rectified but, even so, East was caught in a simple squeeze when the ♡7 was led. He threw a diamond, hoping that West held the ◇10, and Sylvan released a club. West ruffed the trick but declarer claimed the balance, making his slam.

# Quiz ✎

**A.**

      ♠ 6 3
      ♡ J 9
      ◇ 7 5 3
      ♣ A 10 8 7 6 2

♠K led

|   | N |   |
|---|---|---|
| W |   | E |
|   | S |   |

      ♠ A 8 5 2
      ♡ K 7
      ◇ A K Q J 4
      ♣ K 4

| West | North | East | South |
|------|-------|------|-------|
| 1♠ | pass | pass | 2NT |
| pass | 3NT | all pass | |

West leads the ♠K against your notrump game. Plan the play. (West, who holds five spades, will continue the suit if you hold up the ace.)

**B.**

      ♠ A Q 7 2
      ♡ 10 5
      ◇ A K 6
      ♣ A K Q 5

◇J led

|   | N |   |
|---|---|---|
| W |   | E |
|   | S |   |

      ♠ K J 6 3
      ♡ K J
      ◇ Q 7 5 2
      ♣ 9 7 4

| West | North | East | South |
|------|-------|------|-------|
| 2♡ (5-9) | dbl | pass | 3♠ |
| pass | 5♠ | pass | 6♠ |
| all pass | | | |

You win the diamond lead in dummy and cash the king and jack of trumps, West showing out on the second round. How will you continue?

**C.**

      ♠ 8 4
      ♡ 8 6 5
      ◇ K 6 5
      ♣ K Q J 9 4

                    ┌─────────┐
                    │    N    │
      ♡7 led        │ W     E │
                    │    S    │
                    └─────────┘

      ♠ Q J 6
      ♡ A 10 4
      ◇ A 8 4 2
      ♣ A 10 5

| West | North | East | South |
|------|-------|------|-------|
|      |       | 1♡   | 1NT   |
| pass | 3NT   | all pass |   |

West leads the ♡7 to East's jack. Can you see any chance of making 3NT? (If you duck in hearts, East will continue the suit.)

**D.**

      ♠ A K Q 4
      ♡ 5
      ◇ A K J 10 4
      ♣ A 10 6

                    ┌─────────┐
                    │    N    │
      ♣7 led        │ W     E │
                    │    S    │
                    └─────────┘

      ♠ 10 9 6 3
      ♡ A J 6
      ◇ Q 6 5
      ♣ J 8 3

| West | North | East | South |
|------|-------|------|-------|
|      |       | 1♡   | pass  |
| pass | dbl   | 2♣   | 2♠    |
| pass | 4NT   | pass | 5◇    |
| pass | 6♠    | all pass |   |

We are not here to admire the bidding! How do you plan the play? (When you play the ♠AK you will find that West has jack fourth in the suit.)

# Answers ✎

**A.** You should hold up the spade ace until the third round. When spades prove to be 5-2, your best chance is that West holds three or more clubs in addition to the ♡A and his spades. You cash your diamonds, watching West's discards carefully. This is the ending you are looking for:

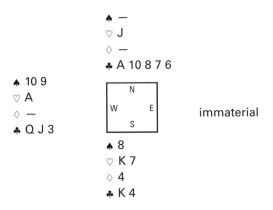

```
                    ♠ —
                    ♡ J
                    ◇ —
                    ♣ A 10 8 7 6
    ♠ 10 9
    ♡ A              ┌─────────┐
    ◇ —              │    N    │
    ♣ Q J 3          │ W     E │         immaterial
                     │    S    │
                     └─────────┘
                    ♠ 8
                    ♡ K 7
                    ◇ 4
                    ♣ K 4
```

If West throws a spade at any stage, you must hope that his remaining cards are one spade, the heart ace and three clubs. You will play a low heart to set up your king. If instead West throws a club, you must play on clubs, hoping that the suit is now running.

**B.** Unless clubs are 3-3 you will need a club ruff to bring your trick total to eleven. If the clubs do break evenly, West's shape is likely to be 1-6-3-3 and you will have no problem. When West has 1-6-4-2 distribution, you must ruff the fourth round of clubs in the South hand and draw East's remaining trumps. On the last round of trumps you throw the ♡J. This will be the position:

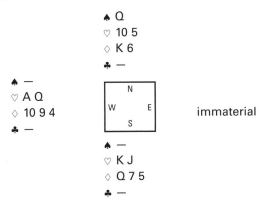

```
                    ♠ Q
                    ♡ 10 5
                    ◇ K 6
                    ♣ —
    ♠ —
    ♡ A Q            ┌─────────┐
    ◇ 10 9 4         │    N    │
    ♣ —              │ W     E │         immaterial
                     │    S    │
                     └─────────┘
                    ♠ —
                    ♡ K J
                    ◇ Q 7 5
                    ♣ —
```

You lead dummy's last trump, throwing the ♡J. West cannot afford to discard a diamond and if he throws the ♡Q you will set up a heart trick.

**C.** You can make 3NT if East holds all the guards (♠A K and four diamonds) in addition to his hearts. Win the second or third round of hearts and run five rounds of clubs, throwing two diamonds from your hand.

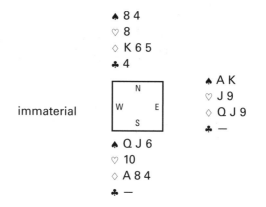

immaterial

```
          ♠ 8 4
          ♡ 8
          ◇ K 6 5
          ♣ 4
                         ♠ A K
                         ♡ J 9
                         ◇ Q J 9
                         ♣ —
          ♠ Q J 6
          ♡ 10
          ◇ A 8 4
          ♣ —
```

The last club leaves East with no good discard. If he throws another diamond, you will score three diamond tricks. If instead he throws a heart or a spade, you will have time to set up a spade trick.

**D.** If trumps are 3-2 you will be able to ruff one heart and discard two of the three remaining losers on the diamonds. If West has jack fourth in the trump suit you will not be able to take a heart ruff and must rely on a squeeze. Win the first club (otherwise East can switch to hearts, killing a vital entry). Play the trump ace-king, East showing out on the second round. Cross to the diamond queen and run the ♠10 through the jack. After drawing trumps, run the diamonds.

```
          ♠ —
          ♡ 5
          ◇ 10
          ♣ 10 6
                         ♠ —
                         ♡ K Q
                         ◇ —
                         ♣ K Q
          ♠ —
          ♡ A J
          ◇ —
          ♣ J 8
```

immaterial

When you lead the ◇ 10 you will score an extra trick in whichever suit East discards.

# CHAPTER 11

# The Strip and Endplay

In the previous chapter we studied the basic form of the squeeze without the count. A defender who needed to retain a guard in one of declarer's suits was forced to throw one or more winners. Since declarer could then afford to lose the lead, he was able to set up an extra trick.

We look now at a variant where a defender, after he has been squeezed, is thrown in to concede a trick in the suit where he has retained a guard. The play is known as a 'strip and endplay' in North America, as a 'strip squeeze' in Britain. Here is an example of the basic end position:

```
                    ♠ —
                    ♡ 5
                    ◊ A 8 2
                    ♣ —
      ♠ —                          ♠ —
      ♡ Q J         ┌─────────┐    ♡ 9
      ◊ K 5         │    N    │    ◊ J 10 6
      ♣ —           │ W     E │    ♣ —
                    │    S    │
                    └─────────┘
                    ♠ 9
                    ♡ 10
                    ◊ Q 9
                    ♣ —
```

You are in 6NT and have not yet lost a trick. When you play the squeeze card (the ♠9) West has to throw one of his heart winners to retain his diamond guard. You then throw him in with a heart and he has to surrender two diamond tricks.

As declarer, you will often have to read which cards the defender has chosen to retain. For example, if West sees the strip-and-endplay approaching, he may reduce to ♡QJ6 ◊K. When you play the squeeze card he will throw a casual ♡J, giving the impression that he is ripe for a throw-in. Yes, there are such cool customers around!

Reading the cards creates no difficulty on our first full-deal example.

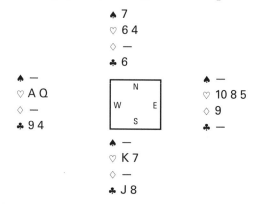

Both Vul.
Dealer West

North
♠ A K J 7 3
♡ 6 4
◇ A 7 4
♣ 6 5 3

West
♠ 5
♡ A Q J 9 3 2
◇ 10 6
♣ 9 7 4 2

East
♠ 10 9 4
♡ 10 8 5
◇ 9 8 5 3 2
♣ K 10

South
♠ Q 8 6 2
♡ K 7
◇ K Q J
♣ A Q J 8

| West | North | East | South |
|------|-------|------|-------|
| 2♡ (5-9) | 2♠ | pass | 4NT |
| pass | 5♣ | pass | 6NT |
| all pass | | | |

Roman Key Card Blackwood reveals that North holds three key cards (two aces and the spade king) and you decide to bid the slam in notrump, to protect the ♡K. West leads the ♣7 to the king and ace. The queen of clubs fetches the two and the ten. West's lead of the ♣7, followed by the ♣2 on the next round of the suit, is consistent in his methods with a four-card holding. When you play two rounds of spades, West shows out on the second round. How will you continue?

West must hold the ♡A for his vulnerable weak two-bid, so the only real chance for twelve tricks is a strip-and-endplay. You cash three diamonds and West shows out on the third round, confirming that his shape is 1-6-2-4. You then play the remaining spades, arriving at this end position:

North
♠ 7
♡ 6 4
◇ —
♣ 6

West
♠ —
♡ A Q
◇ —
♣ 9 4

East
♠ —
♡ 10 8 5
◇ 9
♣ —

South
♠ —
♡ K 7
◇ —
♣ J 8

You play dummy's last spade and throw the ♡7 from your hand. What can West do? If he discards a club, your last two clubs will be good. If instead he discards the ♡Q, you will throw him in with the heart ace to lead back into your club tenace. The slam is yours.

Sometimes you are forced to assume a particular distribution:

*Neither Vul.*
*Dealer South*

```
                  ♠ A 5
                  ♡ 9 2
                  ◇ A Q 9 8 5
                  ♣ A J 5 4
♠ Q 10 9 7 3          N           ♠ 6 4
♡ A Q J 8 4                       ♡ 10 7 6
◇ 3        W              E       ◇ 7 6 4
♣ 9 8            S                ♣ Q 10 7 3 2
                  ♠ K J 8 2
                  ♡ K 5 3
                  ◇ K J 10 2
                  ♣ K 6
```

| West | North | East | South |
|------|-------|------|-------|
|      |       |      | 1◇ |
| 2◇[1] | 2♠ | pass | 2NT |
| pass | 4◇ | pass | 4♡ |
| pass | 6◇ | all pass | |

1. Michaels.

West gives nothing away with his ♣9 lead, won with the king. The major-suit finesses are likely to fail after West's vulnerable Michaels cuebid (showing at least 5-5 in spades and hearts). What can be done?

You should aim to ruff two clubs in the South hand and then run dummy's trumps to catch West in a strip and endplay. West has advertised considerable length in the majors. How will his minor suits have to be distributed for your plan to succeed?

Suppose first that West holds two diamonds and one club. You would have to draw a second round of trumps, then play ace of clubs, club ruff. A spade to the ace would permit a second club ruff, but you would then be stuck in the South hand. You could return to dummy, to run the trumps, only by ruffing a spade; this would destroy the spade tenace that you need for the endplay.

You must therefore assume that West has only one diamond. Win the club lead with the king and draw one round of trumps. Play the ace of clubs, trusting that West cannot ruff, and ruff a club high. You return to dummy with a trump and ruff the last club. After this careful management of your entries you can reach dummy with a spade to the ace. This will be the position when you lead the last of dummy's trumps:

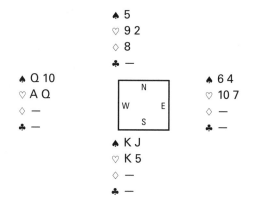

```
              ♠ 5
              ♡ 9 2
              ◇ 8
              ♣ —
   ♠ Q 10              ♠ 6 4
   ♡ A Q              ♡ 10 7
   ◇ —                ◇ —
   ♣ —                ♣ —
              ♠ K J
              ♡ K 5
              ◇ —
              ♣ —
```

On the last trump you throw the ♡5. West has had no opportunity to fool you since you know his exact shape. If he discards the ♡Q you will throw him in with a heart for a spade return into the tenace. If instead West throws the ♠10, you will play a spade to the king, dropping the bare queen. Twelve tricks are yours.

# Squeezing a defender out of an exit card

In our examples so far, the defender has been squeezed out of winners (or a guard on one of your suits). Another common form of this squeeze is where a defender is squeezed out of an exit card in a suit where his partner holds one or more winners. The form of the play is exactly the same, as you would expect. Look at this deal:

*Neither Vul.*
*Dealer West*

```
                     ♠ A 8 3
                     ♡ J 10 4
                     ◇ A 6 4 3
                     ♣ A 9 5
   ♠ K J 10 9 6 5 2            ♠ —
   ♡ 2                        ♡ 8 7 6 3
   ◇ 10 9                     ◇ J 8 7 2
   ♣ 8 4 3                    ♣ Q J 10 7 6
                     ♠ Q 7 4
                     ♡ A K Q 9 5
                     ◇ K Q 5
                     ♣ K 2
```

| West | North | East | South |
|------|-------|------|-------|
| 3♠ | pass | pass | 3NT |
| pass | 4NT | pass | 6NT |
| all pass | | | |

Accepting the slam try was a risky move, with your spades being only queen-high. You are pleased to see West lead the ◇10 (rather than laughing openly and leading a top spade). How will you tackle the deal?

If diamonds are 3-3, there are twelve tricks immediately available. If West has four diamonds, it will be easy to remove his hearts and clubs and throw him in with the fourth diamond. It is unlikely that West has many diamonds, however, with the spades marked as 7-0. You should direct your attention to the case where East holds the diamond length.

If you had three clubs in the South hand, you could play a double squeeze with clubs as the pivot suit. That will not work here because both minor-suit lengths lie in the dummy, with East sitting over them. You should aim instead to reduce the West hand to just spades. You can then duck a spade to force a lead away from the king.

Win the diamond lead and play two more rounds of the suit. It is no surprise to find that East holds four diamonds. Next you run your heart suit. West will be feeling the pinch in this end position:

```
                     ♠ A 8 3
                     ♡ —
                     ◇ —
                     ♣ A 9 5
    ♠ K J 10                          ♠ —
    ♡ —           ┌─────────┐         ♡ —
    ◇ —           │    N    │         ◇ J
    ♣ 8 4 3       │ W     E │         ♣ Q J 10 7 6
                  │    S    │
                  └─────────┘
                     ♠ Q 7 4
                     ♡ Q
                     ◇ —
                     ♣ K 2
```

What can West discard on the ♡Q? If he throws a spade, you will play ace and another spade, setting up a twelfth trick in that suit. He is therefore forced to throw a club. He has no guard in the club suit but his cards there do at least give him a safe exit, if he gets thrown in. You discard a club from dummy and remove West's remaining clubs by cashing the ace and king. West is down to his three spade honors and you now play a low spade from both hands. He wins the trick and has to lead from the spade king at Trick 12, giving you the slam.

Such a squeeze is called a non-material squeeze, because West's key discard does not surrender a trick directly; it merely restricts his future mobility and communications.

Suppose now that you are planning an endplay in this suit:

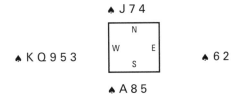

```
                  ♠ J 7 4
                 ┌─────────┐
                 │    N    │
♠ K Q 9 5 3      │ W     E │      ♠ 6 2
                 │    S    │
                 └─────────┘
                  ♠ A 8 5
```

For one reason or other — perhaps from the bidding, perhaps through necessity — you place West with both top spades and plan to endplay him by leading low towards dummy's jack. This will not be effective unless you can strip West of his non-spades. Nor will it be any good to reduce him to ♠KQ9 and one non-spade and to expect your squeeze card to extract the non-spade. West will throw a spade instead and defeat you. No, you must force West to reduce his other holdings while you still retain a master card in each suit.

This deal illustrates the technique:

```
Neither Vul.              ♠ A 10 5 2
Dealer South              ♡ A 9 7
                          ◇ K 7
                          ♣ 8 5 4 3
        ♠ 9 7 3                          ♠ Q J 8 4
        ♡ 8 6 5 3        ┌─────────┐     ♡ Q J 10 2
        ◇ 8 5            │    N    │     ◇ 9 6 4 2
        ♣ J 10 9 7       │ W     E │     ♣ Q
                         │    S    │
                         └─────────┘
                          ♠ K 6
                          ♡ K 4
                          ◇ A Q J 10 3
                          ♣ A K 6 2
```

| West | North | East | South |
|------|-------|------|-------|
|      |       |      | 2NT   |
| pass | 4NT   | pass | 6◇    |
| pass | 6NT   | all pass |   |

West has read all the textbooks and knows he should seek a safe lead against your 6NT. Much good does it do him! His ♣J lead proves to be a disaster, drawing the queen from partner and setting up a possible endplay in the suit.

Aiming to extract West's non-clubs, you start on the diamond suit straight away. West cannot spare a club and must therefore throw three cards in the majors. To cause any sort of guess for you, he must keep three cards in one of the majors. Let's say that he throws two spades and one heart. These cards remain:

```
                    ♠ A 10
                    ♡ A 9
                    ◇ —
                    ♣ 8 5 4
    ♠ 9                            ♠ Q J 8
    ♡ 8 6 5          ┌─────────┐   ♡ Q J 10 2
    ◇ —             │    N    │    ◇ —
    ♣ 10 9 7        │ W     E │    ♣ —
                    │    S    │
                    └─────────┘
                    ♠ K 6
                    ♡ K 4
                    ◇ —
                    ♣ K 6 2
```

You must now cash your winners in the major suit in which West has two cards or fewer remaining. In this case you must play the ace and king of spades (the obvious guess, since West has thrown more cards from that suit). The second spade squeezes West out of his third heart and the ace-king of hearts then reduce West to the desired ♣ 10 9 7. A club towards dummy's eight completes the job.

Suppose instead that declarer plays the two top hearts. He will go down. When he continues with his two top spades, West will retain the 10-9 of clubs and a heart.

# Near-rectification of the count

One feature of the strip-and-endplay is that the count is not rectified. However, when you are attempting to squeeze a defender out of an exit card, the count does need to be 'nearly rectified'. In other words, you must be within a single trick of having rectified the count.

Let's look first at an extreme illustration of a hand where the count does not have to be rectified — the type of squeeze where the defender has a bundle of winners alongside a guard to a tenace:

Neither Vul.
Dealer South

|  |  |  | ♠ Q 7 |  |  |
|  |  |  | ♡ 9 8 6 5 |  |  |
|  |  |  | ◊ 10 8 5 |  |  |
|  |  |  | ♣ K Q 9 7 |  |  |

♠ K J 9 8　　　　　　　　　　♠ 10 6 5 2
♡ A K　　　　　　N　　　　　♡ 10 7 2
◊ K Q J 7 3 2　W　　E　　　◊ 9 6
♣ 5　　　　　　　　S　　　　♣ 10 6 4 3

　　　　　　　♠ A 4 3
　　　　　　　♡ Q J 4 3
　　　　　　　◊ A 4
　　　　　　　♣ A J 8 2

| West | North | East | South |
|------|-------|------|-------|
|  |  |  | 1NT |
| dbl | pass | pass | pass |

West leads the ◊K against your contract of 1NT doubled and we will say, for our purposes, that you win the first trick. Is the count rectified? Nowhere near! To rectify the count in a 1NT contract, you would have to lose six tricks and you have actually lost none. Nevertheless, when you play four rounds of clubs, West will be subjected to a strip and endplay (a strip squeeze). He holds seven winners in his hand alongside his spade guard. He can afford two spade discards but on the last club he will have to release one of his winners. When you then throw him in, with a red card, he can cash six winners but will have to lead away from the spade king at Trick 12.

So, rectifying the count to any extent is quite unnecessary when you are squeezing a defender out of winners. Now let's see a deal where you plan to squeeze him out of an exit card. In fact, this is a slight modification of the 6NT deal from Page 118.

　　　　　　　♠ A 8 3
　　　　　　　♡ K Q 8
　　　　　　　◊ K Q 8 5
　　　　　　　♣ K 9 5

♠ K J 10 9 5 2　　　　　　　♠ —
♡ 9 2　　　　　　N　　　　　♡ J 10 7 6 5
◊ 4　　　　　　W　　E　　　◊ 10 9 3 2
♣ 8 6 4 3　　　　　S　　　　♣ Q J 10 2

　　　　　　　♠ Q 7 6 4
　　　　　　　♡ A 4 3
　　　　　　　◊ A J 7 6
　　　　　　　♣ A 7

Suppose that West again opens 3♠ but this time you stop short of a slam in 5NT. West leads the ♣6 to his partner's ten. What now?

If you simply win and run your winners, making no attempt to adjust the count, you will reach this end position:

```
                    ♠ A 8 3
                    ♡ —
                    ◇ Q
                    ♣ K 9
   ♠ K J 10                        ♠ —
   ♡ —          ┌─────────┐        ♡ J 9
   ◇ —          │    N    │        ◇ 10
   ♣ 8 4 3      │ W     E │        ♣ Q J 2
                │    S    │
                └─────────┘
                    ♠ Q 7 6 4
                    ♡ —
                    ◇ 7
                    ♣ 7
```

The ◇Q draws one club from West but he is immune to a throw-in. You cannot remove his last club, which is a link to the club winners held by his partner.

The only way to make the contract is to duck the first trick, allowing East's ♣10 to win! West will then have a club fewer in the end position above. He will have to throw his penultimate club on the ◇Q and the ♣K will then strip him of his non-spades, permitting a throw-in.

So, when you are planning to squeeze a defender out of an exit card you must 'nearly rectify' the count. Here you are hoping to lose just two tricks in your contract of 5NT. You must therefore deliberately lose one trick, to bring the count to within one trick of being rectified.

# The stars come out to play:

We will start with a Golden Oldie, from the 1961 World Championship. American ace Norman Kay was in the hot seat as the USA faced Argentina.

```
Both Vul.              ♠ K J 10
Dealer North           ♡ K 7 6
                       ◊ J 7 6
                       ♣ A 10 8 2
        ♠ 7 3 2                        ♠ A 8 6 5
        ♡ Q 8 2        ┌─────────┐     ♡ A J 9
        ◊ 9 8 4 3      │    N    │     ◊ K 10 5 2
        ♣ J 6 5        │ W     E │     ♣ 7 4
                       │    S    │
                       └─────────┘
                       ♠ Q 9 4
                       ♡ 10 5 4 3
                       ◊ A Q
                       ♣ K Q 9 3
```

| West | North | East | South |
|------|-------|------|-------|
| Rocchi | Silodor | Calvente | Kay |
| | 1♣ | dbl | 3NT |
| all pass | | | |

West led a spade to his partner's ace and back came the ♠5 to dummy's jack. Kay finessed the queen of diamonds successfully, cashed three rounds of clubs, and then returned to his hand with the diamond ace. This position had been reached:

```
                       ♠ K
                       ♡ K 7 6
                       ◊ J
                       ♣ 10
        ♠ 3                           ♠ 8 6
        ♡ Q 8          ┌─────────┐    ♡ A J
        ◊ 9 8 4        │    N    │    ◊ K 10
        ♣ —            │ W     E │    ♣ —
                       │    S    │
                       └─────────┘
                       ♠ Q
                       ♡ 10 5 4 3
                       ◊ —
                       ♣ 9
```

The last club tightened the noose around East's neck (as the more dramatic bridge writers like to say). If he threw a spade or the ◊ 10, keeping two heart winners, declarer would cash the ♠K and throw him in with a diamond. If instead he threw the ♡J, declarer would duck a heart immediately. Calvente's actual discard was the ♠6 and he was caught in an endplay a few seconds later.

**124 • Bridge Squeezes for Everyone**

Did you spot any 'extras' on that deal? Firstly, East could have escaped the endplay by keeping ◊ K 5 rather than ◊ K 10. Secondly, declarer does better if he cashes four rounds of clubs before taking the diamond finesse. There is no defense to this line. If East throws a heart on the last club, declarer can duck two rounds of hearts (his protection in diamonds is still intact). Thirdly, East can always beat the hand by switching to a diamond at Trick 2.

The next real-life deal was played by Joe Moskal in 1971, at the Grand Slam Bridge Club (then in Bayswater, London).

```
Both Vul.              ♠ 4
Dealer South           ♡ A Q J 10 8 7
                       ◊ A 4 3
                       ♣ 7 3 2

         ♠ 3 2                          ♠ 8 6 5
         ♡ K 9 6 4        N             ♡ 5 3
         ◊ K Q J 6    W       E         ◊ 9 8 5 2
         ♣ 8 6 5          S             ♣ K Q J 9

                       ♠ A K Q J 10 9 7
                       ♡ 2
                       ◊ 10 7
                       ♣ A 10 4
```

| West | North | East | South |
|------|-------|------|-------|
|      | Hoffman |    | Moskal |
|      |       |      | 1♠ |
| pass | 2♡ | pass | 3♠ |
| pass | 4◊ | pass | 4NT |
| pass | 5♡ | pass | 6♠ |
| all pass |   |      |       |

Moskal won the ◊ K lead and proceeded to run his trumps. West first threw a diamond, then his three small clubs, then a heart. These cards remained:

```
                       ♠ —
                       ♡ A Q J
                       ◊ 4
                       ♣ 7

         ♠ —                            ♠ —
         ♡ K 9 6        N               ♡ —
         ◊ Q J      W       E           ◊ 8 5
         ♣ —            S               ♣ K Q J

                       ♠ —
                       ♡ 2
                       ◊ 10
                       ♣ A 10 4
```

When Moskal continued with the ♣A West was embarrassed for a discard. If he threw a heart, a single finesse would bring in the suit. When he chose to throw a diamond instead, Moskal finessed the heart queen, then threw West in with ◇Q. West was forced to lead into dummy's ♡A-J and twelve tricks were made.

The next deal is slightly unusual because declarer loses the lead twice after the squeeze has taken place. The declarer was Dirk Schroeder, playing for Germany against Ireland in the 1982 Europa Cup.

```
Neither Vul.              ♠ 6 5 4
Dealer South             ♡ J 9 8 5 2
                         ◇ K 6
                         ♣ 4 3 2

       ♠ A 3 2                          ♠ 7
       ♡ 7 4 3            ┌──────┐      ♡ K Q 10 6
       ◇ 7 2              │  N   │      ◇ J 10 9 8 5 4 3
       ♣ K J 9 8 7        │W    E│      ♣ 5
                          │  S   │
                          └──────┘
                         ♠ K Q J 10 9 8
                         ♡ A
                         ◇ A Q
                         ♣ A Q 10 6
```

| West | North | East | South |
|------|-------|------|-------|
| Walshe | Fr. Schroeder | Jackson | Schroeder |
|  |  |  | 2♣ |
| dbl | pass | pass | 2♠ |
| pass | 3♠ | pass | 4♠ |
| all pass |  |  |  |

West, whose earlier double had announced good clubs, led the ◇7 against South's spade game. Declarer won with the ace and knocked out the ace of trumps. He captured the diamond continuation and played three more rounds of trumps to reach this position:

```
                         ♠ —
                         ♡ J 9 8 5
                         ◇ —
                         ♣ 4 3 2

       ♠ —                              ♠ —
       ♡ 7 4 3            ┌──────┐      ♡ K Q 10 6
       ◇ —               │  N   │      ◇ J 10
       ♣ K J 9 8          │W    E│      ♣ 5
                          │  S   │
                          └──────┘
                         ♠ 9 8
                         ♡ A
                         ◇ —
                         ♣ A Q 10 6
```

The penultimate trump forced West to throw a heart (otherwise declarer could give up two clubs). Schroeder then cashed the ♡A and led the ♣Q, throwing West on lead. West exited with his last heart, ruffed by South, but was then thrown in with ♣6. At Trick 12 he had to lead into the ♣A 10 and the game was made. Clyde Love, the famous American writer, called this play the 'Double Delayed Duck' because declarer concedes two tricks after the squeeze takes place.

Alfredo Versace of Italy played the following deal in the 2000 Reisinger:

```
East-West Vul.              ♠ 8
Dealer North               ♡ A 4 3
                           ◇ A K J 7 6 3
                           ♣ 5 3 2

      ♠ Q J 5 4 3      ┌──────────┐      ♠ K 9 6 2
      ♡ K J 7 5        │    N     │      ♡ 10 8
      ◇ Q 2            │ W     E  │      ◇ 5 4
      ♣ A 9            │    S     │      ♣ Q J 8 6 4
                       └──────────┘
                           ♠ A 10 7
                           ♡ Q 9 6 2
                           ◇ 10 9 8
                           ♣ K 10 7
```

| **West** | **North** | **East** | **South** |
|----------|-----------|----------|-----------|
| *Treber* | *Lauria* | *Woolf* | *Versace* |
|          | 1◇        | pass     | 1♡        |
| 1♠       | 2◇        | 2♠       | 2NT       |
| pass     | 3♡        | pass     | 3NT       |
| all pass |           |          |           |

Frank Treber led the ♠4 to his partner's king and Keith Woolf switched to the queen of clubs, a play that would have been vital had his partner held three clubs instead of two. When the seven and nine of clubs appeared from the closed hands, East switched back to spades. Suppose you had been South. How would you have played from this point?

Versace captured the third round of spades and then ran dummy's diamond suit. West had to keep the ♣A. Since he also needed to keep a guard on the ♡K, he had to throw both his remaining spades. In the three-card ending Versace exited with a club to the king and ace. West was left with ♡K J in his hand and had to lead into the split tenace. Game made.

The play was a strip and endplay where West was squeezed out of an exit card (his fourth spade). Declarer had lost three tricks (two spades and a club), thereby near-rectifying the count. Had he not done this — by winning the second round of spades, for example — the strip and endplay would have failed.

What would have happened if East had played back a spade at Trick 2 instead of switching to clubs? Declarer would still succeed. After winning the third spade, he would again run the diamonds. This would be the end position:

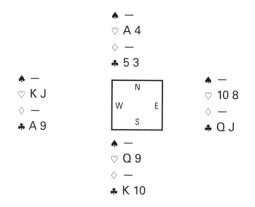

♠ —
♡ A 4
◊ —
♣ 5 3

♠ —
♡ K J
◊ —
♣ A 9

♠ —
♡ 10 8
◊ —
♣ Q J

♠ —
♡ Q 9
◊ —
♣ K 10

A club exit would lead to defeat now. Instead declarer would play ace and another heart, forcing West to concede a trick to the ♣K.

In the very same event, the 2000 Reisinger, another strip-and-endplay arose. The young Norwegian star, Boye Brogeland, was at the helm.

*Both Vul.*
*Dealer South*

♠ A K 5
♡ 7
◊ K Q 10 9 7 4
♣ 8 6 3

♠ 8 4
♡ A Q 6 5 4
◊ J 5 3
♣ A J 10

♠ J 9 7 3 2
♡ 10 9 3 2
◊ —
♣ Q 9 7 2

♠ Q 10 6
♡ K J 8
◊ A 8 6 2
♣ K 5 4

| West | North | East | South |
|------|-------|------|-------|
| *Robson* | *Saelensminde* | *Shugart* | *Brogeland* |
| | | | 1◊ |
| 1♡ | 2♡ | 3♡ | pass |
| pass | 5◊ | all pass | |

3NT would have been easy, as you can see. Brogeland might have bid 3NT at his second turn, but partner's 2♡ promised no more than a sound raise to 3◊ and the playing strength for 3NT was not evident. Brogeland's own view is that North might have invited 3NT by bidding 3♠ at his second turn.

Andrew Robson launched the defense with the ace of hearts, Rita Shugart playing a discouraging two. Brogeland won the trump switch, East throwing the ♡3, and now had some reading of the cards to do. How would you have played the contract?

It looks as if declarer needs the ♣A to be onside, but Brogeland saw that he could succeed also if West held both the ♣A and the ♡Q. East's discouraging signal at Trick 1 suggested that West might indeed hold the heart queen. There was no clear-cut indication as to the position of the ♣A but Brogeland placed it with the overcaller. ('My only clue was that Shugart, with four card support, a void and the ace of clubs might have bid 4♡ or 3◇ instead of a competitive 3♡,' he tells me by email.)

The young Norwegian ran six rounds of diamonds, throwing two clubs from the South hand. He then turned to the spade suit, arriving at this end position:

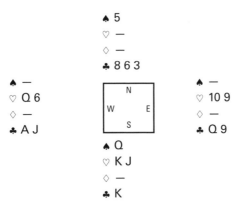

When the spade queen was led Robson could see that he would be endplayed if he kept ♡Q 6 ♣A as his last three cards. He therefore discarded the club ace, retaining the jack. This would have saved the day if East held the club king but there was no such luck on this occasion. Brogeland faced the ♣K and claimed his game.

**A.**

♠ Q 5
♡ J 6 3
◇ 10 6 2
♣ A K Q 10 4

♠7 led

```
      N
   W     E
      S
```

♠ K 6 2
♡ A Q 5
◇ K J 9 4
♣ J 9 3

| West | North | East | South |
|------|-------|------|-------|
|      |       | 1♠   | pass  |
| pass | 2♣    | pass | 3NT   |
| all pass |   |      |       |

East's opening bid promised at least five spades. West leads the ♠7 against 3NT and East takes dummy's queen with the ace. He continues spades and you win the third round, West following suit. How will you play the hand?

**B.**

♠ A Q 7 5
♡ 9 7 6
◇ K 7 4
♣ 6 5 3

♡8 led

```
      N
   W     E
      S
```

♠ K J 10 9 8 6 2
♡ Q 2
◇ A 10 9
♣ A J

| West | North | East | South |
|------|-------|------|-------|
|      |       | 2♡ (5-9) | 3♠ |
| pass | 4♠    | all pass |   |

East wins the heart lead with the king and continues with the heart ace. He then switches to the ♣9. How will you play the hand? (Trumps are 2-1.)

**C.**

♠ K Q J 9 8 3
♡ 10 7
◇ 2
♣ A 10 8 3

```
      N
  W       E
      S
```

♣9 led

♠ A 5
♡ K J 6
◇ A K Q 10 4
♣ K 7 5

| West | North | East | South |
|------|-------|------|-------|
| 2♡ (5-9) | 2♠ | pass | 4NT |
| pass | 5♠ | pass | 6NT |
| all pass | | | |

The ♣9 opening lead is covered by the ten, jack and king. You play two rounds of spades and West throws a heart on the second round. (i) How will you continue? (ii) How would you play if West showed up with two spades instead of one?

**D.**

♠ Q 5 4
♡ 8 6 5
◇ K J 8 5
♣ K 9 6

```
      N
  W       E
      S
```

♡K led

♠ A 7 6
♡ A 7 4 3
◇ A Q 10 2
♣ A 7

| West | North | East | South |
|------|-------|------|-------|
| | | 3♠ | 3NT |
| all pass | | | |

East follows to the first heart, which you duck. On the second round of hearts East throws a spade. Plan the play.

# Answers ✎

**A.** After winning the third spade, you should cross to dummy with a club and finesse the ♡Q. If this wins, play off the rest of dummy's club suit, watching East's discards. If he throws a spade, it will be safe to lead a diamond to the king (East must hold the diamond ace unless he has opened on a 10-count). If instead East throws two red cards, play a heart to the ace in the expectation that the ♡K is now bare.

**B.** East has already shown up with eight points in hearts and can hold at most the ◊J in the minors. When West holds the sole diamond guard (◊QJxx or ◊Qxxxx) he will have to reduce to three diamonds and the bare ♣K when you run the spades. You can then throw him in with a club to open the diamond suit. If he exits with a diamond honor, you will play him for both honors. If he exits with a low diamond instead, win East's honor with the ace and run the ◊10 through West.

**C.** (i) West's ♣9 lead is a likely doubleton. Although defenders do not always stick to their standard leading conventions against a slam, they are unlikely to lead the nine from a holding such as 9-6-2. In Europe most players would start with the six. In North America the two would be a popular choice. When you start to play the spades, West shows out on the second round. His most likely shape is now 1-6-4-2. Three more spades will bring you to a position similar to this:

```
                    ♠ 8
                    ♡ 10 7
                    ◊ 2
                    ♣ A 8 3
   ♠ —                                   ♠ —
   ♡ A Q          ┌──────────┐           ♡ 8 3
   ◊ J 7 6 3      │    N     │           ◊ 9 8 5
   ♣ 4           W│        E │           ♣ Q 6
                  │    S     │
                  └──────────┘
                    ♠ —
                    ♡ K J
                    ◊ A K Q 10
                    ♣ 7
```

When you play the sixth spade, throwing the ♡J, West will doubtless mark time by throwing his club. He will then show out on the ace of clubs, confirming his count as 1-6-4-2. If he bares the heart ace on this trick you will throw him in with it, forcing a lead into your diamond tenace. If instead West throws a diamond, you will play for the remaining cards in the suit to break 3-3.

**C.** (ii)When West has two spades, his most likely shape is 2-6-3-2. By playing dummy's spade suit you may reach a position like this:

```
                   ♠ 8
                   ♡ 10 7
                   ◇ 2
                   ♣ A 8 3
   ♠ —                            ♠ —
   ♡ A Q 9        ┌─────────┐     ♡ 8
   ◇ 7 6 3        │ W   E   │     ◇ J 9 8 5
   ♣ 4           │    S    │     ♣ Q 6
                   └─────────┘
                   ♠ —
                   ♡ K
                   ◇ A K Q 10 4
                   ♣ 7
```

The last spade draws the ♡8 from East. You next cash the three top diamonds. If the jack does not drop, you throw East in with a diamond to lead into dummy's club tenace.

**D.** If East holds only two clubs you will be able to strip him of his non-spades and throw him in with a spade. If East started with three or more clubs, though, you will need a strip and endplay. To prepare for this you must 'nearly rectify' the count, by ducking three rounds of hearts. (If West switches at Trick 3, you will win and duck a third heart yourself.) Your last diamond will then remove a club from East and you can extract his other clubs before throwing him in.

# The Suicide Squeeze

The suicide squeeze is a variant of the simple squeeze. Its particular characteristic is that the squeeze card is played by one of the defenders, rather than declarer. Such squeezes can sometimes be avoided, if the defender notices that his partner is beginning to squirm (!) and resists the temptation to cash all his top cards. It's not always the case, though. On many deals declarer will be able to establish the tricks he needs, should the defender not cash his winners.

Look at this end position:

```
                    ♠ A Q 9 6
                    ♡ —
                    ◇ —
                    ♣ A 2
    ♠ 7 5 2        ┌──────────┐        ♠ J 10 8 3
    ♡ 5            │    N     │        ♡ —
    ◇ —            │ W     E  │        ◇ —
    ♣ 8 6 4        │    S     │        ♣ Q J 7
                   └──────────┘
                    ♠ K 4
                    ♡ —
                    ◇ —
                    ♣ K 10 9 5 3
```

Declarer is playing in notrump and needs six of the last seven tricks with West on lead. If West cashes his last heart he will inflict a suicide squeeze on his partner. If instead he resists the temptation and switches to a spade, declarer will win with dummy's ace and play three rounds of clubs, setting up the South hand.

Let's see a suicide squeeze in the context of a whole deal:

```
              ♠ 9 6 4
              ♡ A J 6
              ◇ J 7 3
              ♣ A Q 8 2
♠ K Q J 10 3      ┌─────────┐      ♠ 8 5 2
♡ 5 2             │    N    │      ♡ K Q 8 3
◇ 9 8 6        W  │         │  E   ◇ K 10 5 2
♣ 9 7 3           │    S    │      ♣ 6 5
                  └─────────┘
              ♠ A 7
              ♡ 10 9 7 4
              ◇ A Q 4
              ♣ K J 10 4
```

You arrive in 3NT with no adverse bidding and West leads the king of spades, his partner playing the two to suggest an odd number of cards in the suit. Spades appear to be 5-3, so you will not be able to play on hearts. Even if the diamond king is onside, you have only eight available tricks. How will you tackle the play?

You should duck the first spade and win the second. The general idea then is to give West the lead with dummy's third spade. If he cashes all his winners in the suit, you hope that this will apply pressure to East.

You play four rounds of clubs and exit with the ♠9. West wins and cashes a fourth round of spades to leave these cards still out:

```
              ♠ —
              ♡ A J
              ◇ J 7 3
              ♣ —
♠ 3               ┌─────────┐      ♠ —
♡ 5               │    N    │      ♡ K Q
◇ 9 8 6        W  │         │  E   ◇ K 10 5
♣ —               │    S    │      ♣ —
                  └─────────┘
              ♠ —
              ♡ 10 9
              ◇ A Q 4
              ♣ —
```

If West cashes his last spade, you will throw the ♡J from dummy and East will be caught in a suicide squeeze. Nor can West prevent this by retaining his last spade and switching to a heart instead. You will win with the heart ace and exit in hearts, forcing East to give you three diamond tricks.

Could the defenders have beaten you, do you think? It doesn't help for West to switch to hearts immediately after the throw-in, when he still has two spades in his hand. At that stage you will have A-J-6 of hearts in dummy and 10-9-7 in your hand. You will play a low heart from dummy and East will win and be endplayed. The only successful defense is for West to switch to a red suit at Trick 2. Bob Hamman might find it!

# The stars come out to play:
## the suicide squeeze

We start our real-life action at the 1986 Reykjavik Festival of Bridge. Had the organizers invited a few big names to boost the reputation of their tournament? Yes, indeed. The mighty Zia Mahmood will be our declarer.

```
Both Vul.                 ♠ A Q 9 4 2
Dealer South              ♡ K 9 7
                          ◊ K 9 4 2
                          ♣ 2
        ♠ J 8 5                            ♠ K 10 7
        ♡ Q 8            ┌─────────┐        ♡ J 10 4 3
        ◊ 7 6 3         │ N       │        ◊ A 8
        ♣ J 9 5 4 3     │ W     E │        ♣ Q 10 7 6
                         │    S    │
                         └─────────┘
                          ♠ 6 3
                          ♡ A 6 5 2
                          ◊ Q J 10 5
                          ♣ A K 8
```

| West | North | East | South |
|------|-------|------|-------|
|      | Myers |      | Zia |
|      |       |      | 1NT (12-14) |
| pass | 2♣ | pass | 2♡ |
| pass | 3♠ | pass | 3NT |
| all pass | | | |

West led a fourth-best ♣4 against 3NT. There was no purpose in a hold-up and Zia won East's queen with the king. When East took the diamond ace and returned a club, it seemed that the contract would depend on the spade finesse, doomed to fail. Zia won the second round of clubs with the ace and marked time by cashing his three diamond winners. East chose the ♠10 as his first discard (letting partner — and, more importantly, Zia — know that he held the king). Suppose you had been East. What would your second discard have been?

Recalling that Zia had shown four hearts during the auction, East retained his holding there and threw an apparently valueless club. Big mistake! These cards now remained:

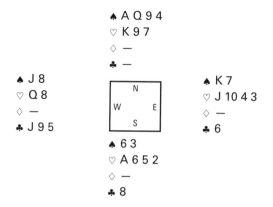

```
                    ♠ A Q 9 4
                    ♡ K 9 7
                    ◇ —
                    ♣ —
  ♠ J 8                              ♠ K 7
  ♡ Q 8           ┌──────────┐       ♡ J 10 4 3
  ◇ —             │    N     │       ◇ —
  ♣ J 9 5         │ W      E │       ♣ 6
                  │    S     │
                  └──────────┘
                    ♠ 6 3
                    ♡ A 6 5 2
                    ◇ —
                    ♣ 8
```

Zia now exited with a club. When West cashed all three club winners, East was squeezed in the majors to concede the contract. If instead West had cashed fewer than three clubs, declarer would have been able to set up the spade suit.

This ending would not have been possible if East had kept both his clubs, throwing a heart. West could then have won the club exit and switched to a spade while club communication between the defenders was still intact. How could East have known that a heart discard was safe? By counting declarer's points! Zia had opened a weak notrump and had shown up already with ten points in the minors. He could not therefore hold A-Q-x-x in the heart suit. Alternatively, East could count declarer's tricks. He had five winners in the minors plus the ♠A. If he also held A-Q-x-x in hearts he would have nine tricks.

The next example comes from the 1972 Olympiad, played at Miami Beach. The eventual winners, the magnificent Italian Blue Team, were humbled 17-3 by Switzerland in the qualifying rounds, partly as a result of this amazing deal:

*East-West Vul.*
*Dealer West*

```
                    ♠ 4
                    ♡ Q 9 5 4
                    ◇ J 9 6 3
                    ♣ 10 9 8 6
  ♠ K 10 8 7 6 3                    ♠ A 2
  ♡ K 7           ┌──────────┐       ♡ J 10 6 3 2
  ◇ K             │    N     │       ◇ 10 8 7 4
  ♣ Q J 5 4       │ W      E │       ♣ 7 3
                  │    S     │
                  └──────────┘
                    ♠ Q J 9 5
                    ♡ A 8
                    ◇ A Q 5 2
                    ♣ A K 2
```

| West | North | East | South |
|------|-------|------|-------|
| *Belladonna* | *Besse* | *Avarelli* | *Fenwick* |
| 1♠ | pass | pass | 2NT (20-22) |
| pass | 3♣ | pass | 3♠ |
| pass | 3NT | all pass | |

Belladonna led ♠7, won by East's ace. The spade return was covered by the queen and king, leaving West with no good return. He tried the ♡7 but Tom Fenwick (good old Swiss name!) could place him with the remaining high cards and called for dummy's queen. When this card won, he continued with a diamond to the ace. More good news — the singleton king fell from West.

When declarer turned to clubs next, East threw a heart on the third round. Belladonna cashed his remaining club winner, drawing another heart discard from his partner. Declarer threw the ♠9 and these cards remained:

```
                    ♠ —
                    ♡ 9 5
                    ◇ J 9 6
                    ♣ —
  ♠ 10 8 6 3                        ♠ —
  ♡ K            ┌─────────┐        ♡ J 10
  ◇ —           │    N    │        ◇ 10 8 7
  ♣ —           │ W     E │        ♣ —
                │    S    │
                └─────────┘
                    ♠ J
                    ♡ A
                    ◇ Q 5 2
                    ♣ —
```

When West returned a spade, a diamond was thrown from dummy and East was caught in a suicide squeeze. He threw the ♡10 and Fenwick won with the spade jack. The ace of hearts drew the outstanding cards in that suit and dummy's ♡9 gave declarer the game-going trick. There was no defense to the contract.

Our final real-life example comes from high-stakes rubber bridge at the Town Club in New York. The declarer is Martin Hoffman and West is a top New York player, Jimmy Rosenblum. See if you can spot any inaccuracies in the play.

Both Vul.
Dealer South

```
                    ♠ K Q 10
                    ♡ Q 10 2
                    ◇ Q 9 8 7
                    ♣ 10 6 4
      ♠ A 9 8 7 5      ┌─────────┐      ♠ 6 4 3
      ♡ 8 5 4 3        │    N    │      ♡ K J 6
      ◇ 6 2           │ W     E │      ◇ A 5 4
      ♣ Q 8            │    S    │      ♣ J 7 5 2
                       └─────────┘
                    ♠ J 2
                    ♡ A 9 7
                    ◇ K J 10 3
                    ♣ A K 9 3
```

| West | North | East | South |
|------|-------|------|-------|
| Rosenblum | | | Hoffman |
| | | | 1NT (15-17) |
| pass | 3NT | all pass | |

West led the ♠7 and Hoffman won with dummy's king, continuing with a diamond. East rose with the ace and returned a second spade, ducked by West. Hoffman cashed the rest of the diamonds ending in dummy and then exited with a spade. Rosenblum took his three spade tricks and the last of these squeezed East in hearts and clubs — a suicide squeeze. Nine tricks resulted.

What did you make of that? First of all, this was the position when West was about to cash his last spade:

```
                    ♠ —
                    ♡ Q 10 2
                    ◇ —
                    ♣ 10 6
      ♠ 8            ┌─────────┐      ♠ —
      ♡ 8 5          │    N    │      ♡ K J
      ◇ —           │ W     E │      ◇ —
      ♣ Q 8          │    S    │      ♣ J 7 5
                     └─────────┘
                    ♠ —
                    ♡ A 9
                    ◇ —
                    ♣ A K 9
```

If West had switched to a heart, instead of cashing his last spade, the game would have been defeated.

A second point is that declarer made a slight error by cashing all the diamonds before exiting. Suppose he cashes only one winning diamond before putting West in with a spade. This would then have been the ending when West was ready to take his last winner.

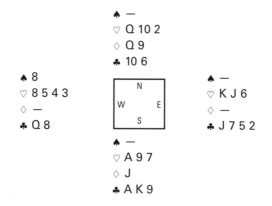

The contract cannot be defeated. If West plays the last spade, the discards are club-club-heart around the table. West can exit with a heart to the jack and ace, but two rounds of diamonds then squeeze East.

Suppose instead that West refuses to cash the last spade. A club exit, high or low, will give declarer three club tricks. On a heart exit, declarer can win and set up a heart. A complex deal, indeed!

# Quiz

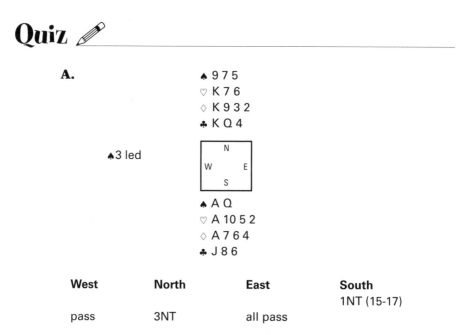

**A.**

♠ 9 7 5
♡ K 7 6
◇ K 9 3 2
♣ K Q 4

♠3 led

♠ A Q
♡ A 10 5 2
◇ A 7 6 4
♣ J 8 6

| West | North | East | South |
|------|-------|------|-------|
|      |       |      | 1NT (15-17) |
| pass | 3NT | all pass | |

West leads a fourth-best ♠3 against your 3NT. You win East's jack with the queen and play a club to the king and ace. How will you continue when East returns the ♠8 to your ace, West playing the ♠2?

**B.**

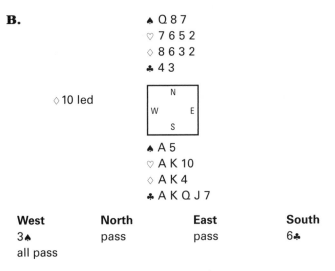

♠ Q 8 7
♡ 7 6 5 2
◇ 8 6 3 2
♣ 4 3

◇ 10 led

```
      N
  W       E
      S
```

♠ A 5
♡ A K 10
◇ A K 4
♣ A K Q J 7

| West | North | East | South |
|------|-------|------|-------|
| 3♠ | pass | pass | 6♣ |
| all pass | | | |

After an everyday auction you arrive in 6♣. West leads the ◇ 10 to your ace and you draw trumps, surprised to find West with four. Can you see any chance of making the contract?

# Answers ✏

**A.** The spade suit appears to be 5-3. If you give up a trick in one of the red suits, the defenders will surely score three tricks in spades to beat the contract. Instead you should cross to dummy and exit with the ♠9. If West cashes all his spade winners, your last club will squeeze East — should he hold the sole guard on both red suits. If instead West refuses to cash all his spades, the link between the defenders will be broken. You will have the chance to play ace, king and another diamond, hoping to lose a trick to the safe East hand and set up an extra diamond winner.

**B.** West's most likely shape is 7-0-2-4 because if his shape had been 7-1-1-4 he might have chosen to lead the heart singleton instead (an interesting application of the Principle of Restricted Choice). In any case, as we will see, you need West's shape to be 7-0-2-4 to make the contract against best defense. After five rounds of trumps, you should play your remaining high diamond, hoping to strip West of his last red card and arrive at this position:

```
                    ♠ Q 8 7
                    ♡ 7 6
                    ◇ 8
                    ♣ —
♠ K J 10 9 6 4                        ♠ 3
♡ —          ┌─────────────┐         ♡ Q J 3
◇ —          │      N      │         ◇ Q J
♣ —          │  W       E  │         ♣ —
             │      S      │
             └─────────────┘
                    ♠ A 5
                    ♡ A K 10
                    ◇ 4
                    ♣ —
```

You then play ace and another spade. If West wins with the king he will have to play a spade to dummy's queen and this will squeeze East in the red suits — a suicide squeeze.

If instead, West allows dummy's ♠Q to win the second round of spades, East will be caught in a strip-and-endplay, as he will have to throw a diamond honor on this trick. You play a heart to East's queen and your ace, and exit with a diamond to East's remaining diamond honor. He will then have to lead into your ♡K-10.

You may wonder what could possibly go wrong with the same play if West has 7-1-1-4 distribution. This would be the ending instead:

```
                    ♠ Q 8 7
                    ♡ 7 6
                    ◇ 8
                    ♣ —
♠ K J 10 9 6                          ♠ 3
♡ 4          ┌─────────────┐         ♡ Q J 3
◇ —          │      N      │         ◇ Q J
♣ —          │  W       E  │         ♣ —
             │      S      │
             └─────────────┘
                    ♠ A 5
                    ♡ A K 10
                    ◇ 4
                    ♣ —
```

Surely you could remove his singleton heart and then play ace and another spade? The answer is that West can defeat you this time if he refuses to rise with the spade king! Dummy's ♠Q would be good for an eleventh trick but no squeeze would follow. The count has not been rectified, and East is under no pressure. As we have seen, when West has 7-0-2-4 shape this defense does not work.

(This deal took me a while to construct but I'm quite proud of it. Sorry if it gave you a headache!)

# The Trump Squeeze

A trump squeeze is one where a suit can be ruffed good after the squeeze has taken place. Suppose you are playing in a spade contract with this diamond side suit:

$\diamond$ A K 8 2

$\diamond$ J 9 4

$\diamond$ Q 10 6 5

$\diamond$ 7 3

If you took a diamond ruff, to isolate the diamond guard with one defender, this would be merely a preliminary to some other sort of squeeze. It would not make the hand a trump squeeze. If instead you squeezed East out of one of his diamonds and then ruffed dummy's last diamond good, that would be a trump squeeze!

Such a squeeze is necessary only when the alternative of taking the ruff first (isolating the guard) would leave you with inadequate threats or entries. Let's look straight away at the type of deal where a trump squeeze is necessary.

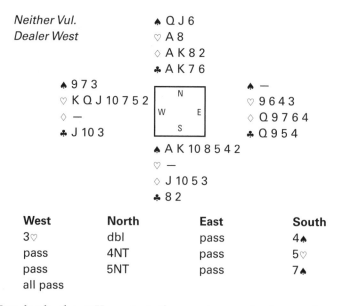

Neither Vul.
Dealer West

```
                        ♠ Q J 6
                        ♡ A 8
                        ◇ A K 8 2
                        ♣ A K 7 6
    ♠ 9 7 3                              ♠ —
    ♡ K Q J 10 7 5 2                     ♡ 9 6 4 3
    ◇ —                                  ◇ Q 9 7 6 4
    ♣ J 10 3                             ♣ Q 9 5 4
                        ♠ A K 10 8 5 4 2
                        ♡ —
                        ◇ J 10 5 3
                        ♣ 8 2
```

| West | North | East | South |
|------|-------|------|-------|
| 3♡ | dbl | pass | 4♠ |
| pass | 4NT | pass | 5♡ |
| pass | 5NT | pass | 7♠ |
| all pass | | | |

West leads the ♡K against the spade grand slam and you win with dummy's ace, throwing a diamond. You draw the outstanding trumps and are surprised to find that West holds all three of them. Seeking further information, you lead a diamond. When West shows out you have a complete map of the hand. West has 3-7-0-3 shape. But... can you take advantage of this knowledge? How will you continue?

Suppose you play two rounds of clubs and ruff a club, isolating the guard in the East hand. No good, is it? This will be the end position:

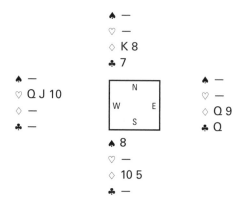

```
                        ♠ —
                        ♡ —
                        ◇ K 8
                        ♣ 7
    ♠ —                                ♠ —
    ♡ Q J 10                           ♡ —
    ◇ —                                ◇ Q 9
    ♣ —                                ♣ Q
                        ♠ 8
                        ♡ —
                        ◇ 10 5
                        ♣ —
```

When you play the last spade, dummy will have to discard before East. If you throw the ◇8 East can also throw a diamond. You will have no way to reach the established ◇10. You have set up a positional squeeze and the two guards lie with the wrong defender.

How can you reach this ◇10, which (as we have just seen) can be established by squeezing East? There is only one answer. You must delay taking the club ruff until after the squeeze! The club ruff itself will then give you an entry to the ◇ 10. Let's play the hand again, leaving the club holding intact while we run some trumps. This, much more promising, ending arises:

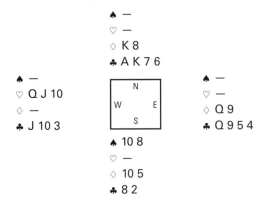

You play the penultimate spade, throwing dummy's ◇ 8 and East has no answer. If he throws a club, you will ruff a club good and reach it with the ◇ K. If instead East bares the ◇ Q, you will cash the blocking ◇ K and reach the established ◇ 10 by playing the top clubs and ruffing a club. This is the essence of a trump squeeze. Your diamond threat is blocked (because dummy has to find a discard before East). You then resolve the blockage by using the ruffing entry to hand.

To reinforce this idea, which may be new to you, let's look at a similar deal.

*Both Vul.*
*Dealer West*

♠ K 8 4 2
♡ A 4 2
◇ A K 9 6 2
♣ 6

♠ Q 10 3          ♠ J 9 7 5
♡ 7              ♡ 8 6 5
◇ 10 4           ◇ Q J 7
♣ K Q J 10 9 8 5  ♣ 7 3 2

♠ A 6
♡ K Q J 10 9 3
◇ 8 5 3
♣ A 4

| West | North | East | South |
|------|-------|------|-------|
| 3♣ | dbl | pass | 4NT |
| pass | 5♡ | pass | 5NT |
| pass | 6♡ | pass | 7♡ |
| all pass | | | |

You don't like the bidding? Well, I had to get them to 7♡ somehow! West leads the ♣ K and you win with the ace. You ruff a club with the ace and draw trumps in three rounds. What next?

Perhaps your plan is to cash the ◊A K (a Vienna Coup), setting up the ◊8 as a threat against East, and to run the trumps. East will be squeezed only if he holds five spades and three diamonds, which would give West an unlikely 2-1-2-8 shape.

A better idea is to play for a trump squeeze, which will require East to hold only four spades. Nothing interesting happens when you try a diamond to the ace and you return to the ♠A to play some more trumps. This is the position as you lead your penultimate heart:

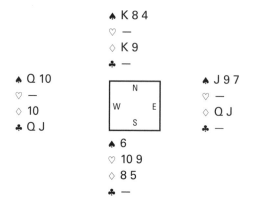

West throws a club and you release dummy's ◊9 (blocking your diamond threat, as on the previous deal). East is not a happy man. What is more, you will be able to read the situation whatever he throws.

Suppose he throws the ♠7. If you have been watching the discards you will know that there are still three diamonds out. It cannot be right, therefore, to cross to the ◊K in the hope that this will establish your last diamond. Instead you will cross to the spade king and ruff a spade, succeeding when the remaining four spades break 2-2.

Suppose instead that East throws the ◊J. You will know now that there are still five spades out. Since there is no chance of ruffing a spade good, you will chance your arm in the diamond suit, cashing dummy's king. When the two outstanding diamonds appear on the table, you will claim the remainder, reaching the established ◊8 with a spade ruff.

It may seem that West assisted you to read the position by unnecessarily retaining his cards in spades and diamonds. You would still have been able to read the situation, even if he discarded one of these cards. If he threw the ◊10, and East subsequently threw a spade, you would know that West would not keep a useless club to throw from a diamond guard (he could have beaten the contract simply by retaining the guard). You would therefore play for the remaining spades to be 2-2. Similarly, if West threw a spade and East then threw a diamond, you would know that West was not throwing a spade from a three-card holding. He could have beaten the contract by retaining it in that case. You would read the ending correctly, as before, playing for the outstanding diamonds to be 1-1.

Although a trump squeeze ending does sometimes require you to guess which suit has been unguarded, there are usually sufficient clues available to those who look for them. See what you make of this deal:

East-West Vul.
Dealer South

```
                        ♠ A 7 6
                        ♡ A 10 7 2
                        ◇ A 4 3
                        ♣ K J 3
        ♠ J 9 5                           ♠ 8 2
        ♡ 9 8              N              ♡ K Q J 6 4 3
        ◇ 9 8 7 6     W         E         ◇ K Q 10
        ♣ 9 6 5 4          S              ♣ 10 7
                        ♠ K Q 10 4 3
                        ♡ 5
                        ◇ J 5 2
                        ♣ A Q 8 2
```

| West | North | East | South |
|------|-------|------|-------|
|      |       |      | 1♠ |
| pass | 2♣ | 2♡ | 3♣ |
| pass | 3♡ | pass | 3♠ |
| pass | 4◇ | pass | 4♡ |
| pass | 6♠ | all pass | |

West leads the ♡9 against your small slam in spades. How would you play the contract?

If the trumps in the North hand were better (A-J-6), a dummy reversal might work well. You could ruff three hearts in your hand, ruffing with high trumps on the third and fourth rounds; you could then draw trumps and discard one of dummy's diamond losers on the clubs.

That's no good with dummy's actual trump holding and you should try something different. After winning with the heart ace, you should lead a low diamond towards the jack. East wins with the queen and plays a top heart, which you ruff low, West following suit.

What will happen now if you draw two rounds of trumps with the ace and king, then play four rounds of clubs to discard a diamond? The cards lie well for you and you can ruff a diamond in dummy successfully. However, you will run into a trump promotion when you try to return to hand by ruffing a third round of hearts with the ten. You must look for some other plan.

East appears to hold the guards in both red suits. Can he be squeezed? It's rather awkward, since you will need to cash the four clubs first, relying on the trump ace as a late entry to dummy. Let's play it through. You cash the king and queen of trumps, all following. You then play four rounds of clubs, throwing a diamond from dummy. These cards will remain:

```
                    ♠ A
                    ♡ 10 7
                    ◇ A
                    ♣ —
    ♠ J                              ♠ —
    ♡ —          ┌─────────┐         ♡ Q J
    ◇ 9 7 6      │    N    │         ◇ K 10
    ♣ —          │  W   E  │         ♣ —
                 │    S    │
                 └─────────┘
                    ♠ 10 4
                    ♡ —
                    ◇ J 5
                    ♣ —
```

It works! You cross to the ace of trumps and East has no good card to play. If he throws a heart, you will ruff a heart good and reach it with the ◇A. If he throws a diamond, you will cash the ◇A and reach the established ◇J with a ruff. A classic trump squeeze with the unusual feature that you had to cash four rounds of clubs before drawing the last trump.

# Ruffing good one of two suits

Sometimes you have two suits which both have the potential to be ruffed good. When the same defender holds length in these suits, you may be able to squeeze him out of the necessary guard in one of them. You will then proceed to ruff that suit good. Look at this deal:

```
North-South Vul.        ♠ K J 6 5 3
Dealer West             ♡ A
                        ◇ A Q 7 5 4
                        ♣ K 10
    ♠ 10 9                              ♠ 2
    ♡ K Q 10 8 5 4   ┌─────────┐        ♡ J 9 3
    ◇ J 3            │    N    │        ◇ K 10 9 6 2
    ♣ Q 7 4         │  W   E  │        ♣ J 9 8 2
                    │    S    │
                    └─────────┘
                        ♠ A Q 8 7 4
                        ♡ 7 6 2
                        ◇ 8
                        ♣ A 6 5 3
```

| West | North | East | South |
|------|-------|------|-------|
| 2♡ (5-9) | 3♡ | pass | 4NT |
| pass | 5♣ | pass | 5NT |
| pass | 7◇ | pass | 7♠ |
| all pass | | | |

Your partner's 3♡ overcall is a Michaels cuebid, showing a two-suiter in spades and a minor. Roman Key Card Blackwood gets you to a grand slam in spades and West leads the ♡K. How will you seek thirteen tricks?

If you head for a cross-ruff, you will run into a trump promotion. A better idea is to attempt to set up dummy's diamonds. You win the heart lead and draw trumps in two rounds, East throwing a heart on the second round. After ace of diamonds and a diamond ruff, you ruff a heart and ruff another diamond, revealing the 2-5 break. You are only halfway through the hand but already East is in trouble:

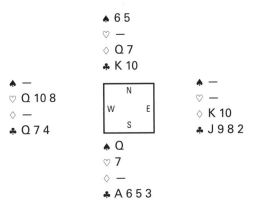

When you ruff your last heart in dummy, what can East throw? A diamond discard will allow you to set up a long diamond in dummy, so East will doubt-less throw a club. You then play the king and ace of clubs, proceeding to ruff a long club good. You can reach it by ruffing a diamond in the South hand.

# A trump squeeze without the count

Let's look now at a trump squeeze 'without the count'. A trick will be lost after the squeeze has taken effect.

*Neither Vul.*
*Dealer East*

|  | ♠ A K 5 |  |
|---|---|---|
|  | ♡ 9 |  |
|  | ◇ K 9 6 2 |  |
|  | ♣ A K 8 6 5 |  |

| ♠ 10 9 6 |  | ♠ Q J 8 7 4 2 |
|---|---|---|
| ♡ 7 6 3 2 | N | ♡ 10 |
| ◇ 10 7 5 4 | W E | ◇ A Q J |
| ♣ J 9 | S | ♣ Q 7 4 |

|  | ♠ 3 |  |
|---|---|---|
|  | ♡ A K Q J 8 5 4 |  |
|  | ◇ 8 3 |  |
|  | ♣ 10 3 2 |  |

| West | North | East | South |
|---|---|---|---|
|  |  | 1♠ | 4♡ |
| pass | 4NT | pass | 5♠ |
| pass | 6♡ | all pass |  |

After East's 1♠ opening and your 4♡ overcall, partner drives to 6♡. How will you play the contract when West gives you a chance by leading the ♠10?

You win the spade lead and cash a second spade, throwing a diamond (as East shakes his head!). The ◇A is surely offside, after East's opening bid, so the only real chance of success is to ruff that card out. This will be an easy task if East started with ace doubleton in the diamond suit. If he started with three or more diamonds, a trump squeeze will be required.

You play five rounds of trumps to reach this position:

```
                    ♠ —
                    ♡ —
                    ◇ K 9 6 2
                    ♣ A K
   ♠ —                              ♠ —
   ♡ —           ┌─────────┐        ♡ —
   ◇ 10 7 5 4    │    N    │        ◇ A Q J
   ♣ J 9         │ W     E │        ♣ Q 7 4
                 │    S    │
                 └─────────┘
                    ♠ —
                    ♡ 5 4
                    ◇ 8
                    ♣ 10 3 2
```

On the next round of trumps you throw a diamond from dummy and East is squeezed without the count. If he throws a club, you can untangle three club tricks. Suppose instead that he throws a diamond. You now duck a round of diamonds (conceding a trick after the squeeze has taken effect). East wins with the queen and returns a club to dummy. A second round of diamonds brings down East's ace and the slam is made.

As is common in a trump squeeze, you needed to read which cards East had kept. This is not in the least bit difficult against 95% of the world's defenders. They will throw the 'easy' cards first then — at the crucial moment — sit back in their chair and spend ages thinking which suit to unguard. Against such opponents it is safe to assume that the final discard is the one that has unguarded a suit.

When the key defender is a strong player, he is more likely to foresee any pressure that is coming his way. He may well make the critical, unguarding discard a trick or two before the squeeze card is played. Against such an opponent it is a good idea to look at the signals made by his partner. Without such a clear idea of what is looming, the partner of your intended victim may well signal his distribution in an honest way.

# Double trump squeeze

It is possible to catch both defenders in a trump squeeze simultaneously. Unusually for a double squeeze, the threats span only two suits. Look at this deal:

```
Both Vul.                  ♠ Q 10 9
Dealer North               ♡ A 7 6
                           ◇ A 8 2
                           ♣ A Q 7 6
        ♠ J 6 3                              ♠ A K 8 7 4 2
        ♡ 9 5 4 2          ┌─────────┐       ♡ 8
        ◇ J 5 4         W  │ N       │ E     ◇ Q 10 9 3
        ♣ 10 8 4           │    S    │       ♣ 9 3
                           └─────────┘
                           ♠ 5
                           ♡ K Q J 10 3
                           ◇ K 7 6
                           ♣ K J 5 2
```

| West | North | East | South |
|------|-------|------|-------|
|      | 1NT (15-17) | 2♠ | 3♡ |
| pass | 4♡ | pass | 4NT |
| pass | 5♣ | pass | 6♡ |
| all pass | | | |

Six clubs would have proved an easy make (a diamond can be thrown on the hearts) but it was difficult to reach after the intervention. How would you tackle the less secure contract of six hearts on a low spade lead?

You play the ♠9 from dummy and East wins the first trick with the spade king. He returns the ◇10 and you must consider carefully where to win this trick. Your general line of play will be to cash four trumps and four clubs. Since you will certainly need the ace of diamonds later, as the sole entry to dummy, you must win this diamond switch with the king.

Four rounds of trumps and three rounds of clubs leave this position:

```
                           ♠ Q 10
                           ♡ —
                           ◇ A
                           ♣ Q
        ♠ J 6                                ♠ A 8
        ♡ —                ┌─────────┐       ♡ —
        ◇ J 5           W  │ N       │ E     ◇ Q 10
        ♣ —                │    S    │       ♣ —
                           └─────────┘
                           ♠ —
                           ♡ 10
                           ◇ 7 6
                           ♣ 5
```

You now play dummy's queen of clubs. It is fairly clear how the spade suit lies. If East throws another spade on the club queen, you will lead the ♠10, ruffing out East's ace. Let's suppose that East throws a diamond instead. West is then in a similar dilemma. If he throws the ♠6 you will lead the spade queen, pinning West's jack. West's only alternative is to discard a diamond but in that case you will cash the diamond ace and reach the established diamond in the South hand by ruffing a spade.

The bidding, the opening lead, and the play to the first trick made the lie of the spade suit obvious. There was nothing much more to it, provided you had the technical know-how to visualize the required play.

This chapter has been hard work and once again we both need a coffee break before watching the stars in action. See you in a few minutes!

# The stars come out to play:
## the trump squeeze ☆

Our first real-life deal comes from what many regard as the Golden Age of bridge, the period of the Blue Team's ascendancy and their many great battles with the USA. The 1973 World Championship was played in Guaruja, Brazil, and this deal comes from the final with (how did you guess?) Italy facing the USA.

```
North-South Vul.        ♠ Q J
Dealer South            ♡ A J 7 2
                        ◇ J 9 4
                        ♣ A K 10 9

    ♠ 9 5 4 2                       ♠ 7
    ♡ 10 9 5          N             ♡ K Q 8 6
    ◇ K Q 2       W       E         ◇ A 10 6 5 3
    ♣ 6 5 2          S             ♣ Q 8 4

                        ♠ A K 10 8 6 3
                        ♡ 4 3
                        ◇ 8 7
                        ♣ J 7 3
```

| West | North | East | South |
|------|-------|------|-------|
| Jacoby | Garozzo | Wolff | Belladonna |
| | | | 2♠ |
| pass | 2NT | pass | 3♠ |
| pass | 4♠ | all pass | |

Jacoby led the ◇K against the spade game, Wolff signaling his count with the ◇3. When the ◇Q was led at Trick 2 East contributed the ten. He trusted his partner to read him for five diamonds, rather than three, and intended the ten as a suit-preference signal for a heart switch. Message received! Jacoby duly switched to the ♡10 and the Americans had found the only start to trouble declarer. 'Play the jack,' said Belladonna.

Wolff won with the king, a minor deception, and played back the ace of diamonds, ruffed by declarer. Belladonna drew two rounds of trumps, East throwing a diamond on the second round. The serious options at this stage are just two in number. Declarer can take an eventual club finesse through West. Alternatively, he can play for one of the defenders to hold the queen of clubs and at least four hearts.

Perhaps Belladonna had sensed some vibes from around the table. Perhaps he read East for only three diamonds, after the appearance of the ◇ 10, in which case the odds would be greater that he held length in hearts and clubs. Anyway, the great man proceeded to demonstrate his almost supernatural bridge powers by playing for a trump squeeze. He drew a third round of trumps, throwing a club from dummy, and this position had been reached:

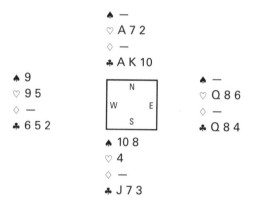

On the fourth round of trumps Belladonna threw the ♣10 from dummy. East was caught in a trump squeeze. He chose to throw a club, hoping that West held the ♣J, but Belladonna then cashed dummy's two club winners. Ace and another heart, ruffed in the South hand, allowed him to score the ♣J as his tenth trick.

The same declarer made a grand slam via a trump squeeze, playing in a 1976 exhibition match in Australia sponsored by the Lancia automobile company. The contract was 7♣ and this was the layout:

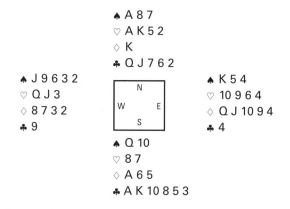

```
              ♠ A 8 7
              ♡ A K 5 2
              ◇ K
              ♣ Q J 7 6 2
♠ J 9 6 3 2        N        ♠ K 5 4
♡ Q J 3                     ♡ 10 9 6 4
◇ 8 7 3 2      W       E    ◇ Q J 10 9 4
♣ 9                S        ♣ 4
              ♠ Q 10
              ♡ 8 7
              ◇ A 6 5
              ♣ A K 10 8 5 3
```

David Watkins led a trump against the grand slam. A diamond ruff will bring the total to twelve tricks. How many different major-suit squeeze possibilities can you see for a thirteenth trick?

The first would be to cash the ace of spades (Vienna Coup), and then play for an automatic simple squeeze. This would succeed if either defender held the ♠K and five hearts. Alternatively, you could cash the top hearts and ruff a heart, attempting to isolate the heart guard in the West hand. A positional squeeze on West would arise if West held the ♠K and four or more hearts. Belladonna chose a third option, playing for a trump squeeze. This would succeed if either defender held the ♠K and four or more hearts, but he might have to read which cards had been kept.

A diamond to the king was followed by a second round of trumps to the South hand. Belladonna played the ace of diamonds, throwing a spade, and continued with a diamond ruff. Two more rounds of trumps brought the position to:

```
              ♠ A 8
              ♡ A K 5 2
              ◇ —
              ♣ —
♠ J 9 6           N        ♠ K 5
♡ Q J 3                    ♡ 10 9 6 4
◇ —           W       E    ◇ —
♣ —               S        ♣ —
              ♠ Q 10
              ♡ 8 7
              ◇ —
              ♣ 10 8
```

The penultimate trump drew the ♠6 from West, the ♠8 from dummy, and the ♠5 from East. Since there were still seven hearts out, it was not possible to ruff a heart good. The Italian maestro was therefore spared a guess. He played a spade to the ace, toppling East's king, and claimed the grand slam.

**A.**

♠ A 5
♡ A 9 7 6
◇ 10 2
♣ A K 9 6 5

```
      N
  W       E
      S
```

♡3 led

♠ K Q J 9 8 6 4
♡ 2
◇ A K
♣ 8 7 2

| West | North | East | South |
|------|-------|------|-------|
|      |       | 3♡   | 4♠    |
| pass | 4NT   | pass | 5♠    |
| pass | 5NT   | pass | 7♠    |
| all pass |    |      |       |

West leads the ♡3 against your grand slam in spades. East shows out on the first round of trumps. Plan the play.

**B.**

♠ A 10 8 3
♡ K 9 6
◇ A K 5
♣ J 8 3

```
      N
  W       E
      S
```

♣A led

♠ K 6
♡ A Q J 10 7
◇ J 8 3
♣ Q 6 2

| West | North | East | South |
|------|-------|------|-------|
|      |       |      | 1♡    |
| pass | 1♠    | pass | 1NT   |
| pass | 2♣[1] | pass | 2♡    |
| pass | 4♡    | all pass |   |

1. Checkback.

West cashes two top clubs and gives his partner a club ruff — not the best of starts for you. How will you attempt to recover the situation when East returns a trump? (You will find that trumps started 2-3.)

# Answers ✎

**A.** If East holds three or more clubs, which is not such a long shot after he has shown up void in trumps, you can catch him in a trump squeeze. Play all the trumps except one, followed by the diamonds. This is the position as you play the second diamond:

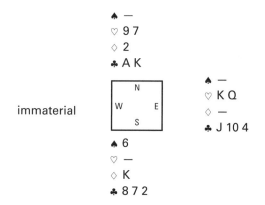

```
                    ♠ —
                    ♡ 9 7
                    ◇ 2
                    ♣ A K
                          N                   ♠ —
immaterial          W         E               ♡ K Q
                          S                   ◇ —
                                              ♣ J 10 4
                    ♠ 6
                    ♡ —
                    ◇ K
                    ♣ 8 7 2
```

If East started with three or more clubs, he is squeezed on this trick. If he reduces to a singleton heart, you will cross to a club and ruff dummy's last heart good. If instead he keeps two hearts and two clubs, you will cash the ♣AK and return to your hand with a ruff to enjoy the established club. No guesswork is required since West's ♡3 lead (along with East's preempt in the suit) marks East with seven hearts.

**B.** Suppose you draw trumps, cash the ace and king of diamonds (Vienna Coup), return to the ♠K, and play the remaining trumps. When will a squeeze result? A squeeze will arise only when a defender holds the diamond queen and five spades. Since West started with five clubs, there is barely room for him to hold these cards. So, you must aim to squeeze East. If you employ a trump squeeze you can do this even when he holds only four spades rather than five.

Cash the ◇A (just in case West holds ♠ Jxxxx ♡ xx ◇Q ♣AKxxx and chose not to bid). Play four rounds of trumps, throwing the ◇5 from dummy. If East holds the two guards he will have to find a further discard from a holding such as ♠Qxxx ◇Qx. If he throws a spade, you will ruff a spade good. If instead he throws a diamond, you will play the second top diamond and return to hand with the ♠K to score the ◇J. You may need to guess which cards East has kept.

# CHAPTER 14

# The Criss-Cross

# Squeeze

In the previous chapter, while discussing the trump squeeze, we encoun-
tered the idea of a blocked threat, a holding such as a doubleton queen facing a bare ace. The criss-cross squeeze is a rare form of the simple squeeze
that employs two blocked threats. By way of a gentle introduction, look at
the following deal:

```
                    ♠ A 5
                    ♡ Q 4
                    ◇ A J 9 8 2
                    ♣ K J 7 3
   ♠ K J 10 7 2                      ♠ 9 6 4 3
   ♡ K 10 9 8 6 2      N             ♡ J 5 3
   ◇ 10            W       E         ◇ 7 4 3
   ♣ 4                  S            ♣ 8 6 2
                    ♠ Q 8
                    ♡ A 7
                    ◇ K Q 6 5
                    ♣ A Q 10 9 5
```

You open 1♣ on the South cards and West overcalls 2♣, a Michaels cuebid
showing both majors. A few masterly bids later, you arrive in 7♣. How would
you plan the play when West leads the ◇10?

Not very difficult, is it? You can place West with the two major-suit kings
and a positional simple squeeze will deliver the slam. After winning the lead
and drawing trumps, you will cash the remaining diamonds, throwing a heart,
then play the ♡A and the remaining trumps. On your last trump West will have
to discard from ♠K J ♡K, giving way to either the one-card threat in dummy
(♡Q) or the split two-card threat in spades.

Suppose instead that North was the dealer and had opened 1◇, with East
(rather than West) making a Michaels cuebid of 2◇ to show the majors. Playing
a grand slam in diamonds from the North hand, you would catch East in a sim-

ple squeeze. After cashing the ♠A, you would draw trumps and play the clubs followed by the rest of the diamonds.

It was easy when you knew which defender held the two kings. Now for something more difficult and much more interesting — what is the best play when you have no idea which defender holds the two kings?

If you follow the first line, you will succeed only when West holds the missing honors. Choose the second line and you will need East to hold them. Instead, let's see what happens if you leave both major-suit aces in play. Cash the diamonds, throwing the ♡7, then play the clubs. When East started with the two kings, the ending will be like this:

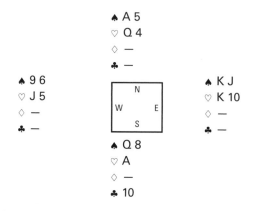

```
              ♠ A 5
              ♡ Q 4
              ◇ —
              ♣ —
♠ 9 6                        ♠ K J
♡ J 5          N            ♡ K 10
◇ —        W       E        ◇ —
♣ —            S            ♣ —
              ♠ Q 8
              ♡ A
              ◇ —
              ♣ 10
```

You lead the ♣10, throwing the ♠5 from dummy. East must bare one of his kings. If you judge that the spade king is now bare, you will cross to the ♠A, dropping the king, then return to the ♡A to score the established ♠Q. If instead you reckon that the heart king is bare, you will cash the heart ace and cross to dummy to enjoy the ♡Q. You would face exactly the same guess when West held the two kings.

Following this line allows you to squeeze either defender! Is there a price to be paid for this luxury? There sure is. You have to guess which king has been bared. However, this is much better than a 50-50 guess. Most of the world's defenders will reduce to two doubleton kings and make the key discard, baring a king, only at the last moment. Other pointers may be available to the keen-eyed declarer. Firstly, when the defenders are playing 'count' discards, the partner of the defender under stress will often give a true count — revealing the situation. Secondly, most defenders will choose to retain a guard against the Q-x that they can actually see (the one in dummy). That's because there is a chance that their partner can guard against declarer's highest card in the other suit.

On the deal we have just seen, the criss-cross squeeze removed the need to guess between two simple squeezes. The same type of squeeze may be necessary when you have just one victim in mind but the entries do not permit a simple squeeze. Look at this deal:

```
            ♠ A K 5
            ♡ 9 7 2
            ◇ K J 4
            ♣ Q 9 5 3
♠ 10 9 6 3    ┌─────────┐    ♠ Q 8 2
♡ 8 5         │    N    │    ♡ K J 10 6 4 3
◇ 9 7 6 3     │ W     E │    ◇ 10 8 2
♣ 8 4 2       │    S    │    ♣ 7
              └─────────┘
            ♠ J 7 4
            ♡ A Q
            ◇ A Q 5
            ♣ A K J 10 6
```

East opens a weak 2♡ and — trying to impress the kibitzers — you reach an ambitious 7♣. West leads the ♡8 and you win with the queen. What chance can you see of thirteen tricks?

Unless the spade queen falls in two rounds, you will have to squeeze East in the major suits. He is certain to hold the sole guard on dummy's ♡9. You must hope that he holds the spade queen, too. A simple squeeze cannot work, because East is sitting over the major-suit lengths in dummy. Only a criss-cross squeeze will be good enough. You cash your winners in the minor suits, arriving at this end position:

```
            ♠ A K 5
            ♡ 9 7
            ◇ —
            ♣ —
♠ 10 9 6 3    ┌─────────┐    ♠ Q 8 2
♡ 5           │    N    │    ♡ K J
◇ —           │ W     E │    ◇ —
♣ —           │    S    │    ♣ —
              └─────────┘
            ♠ J 7 4
            ♡ A
            ◇ —
            ♣ 10
```

You lead the last club and throw the ♠5 from dummy. Whichever major suit East unguards, you be able to disentangle your extra trick.

After these two examples, you can see how the two blocked threats interact. The blocking honors in both suits may be needed as entries, to reach the winner established by the defender's final discard.

Before the stars step forward to dazzle us, we will see one more example —something a bit more exotic.

East-West Vul.
Dealer North

```
                    ♠ A
                    ♡ Q J 8 6 5 3 2
                    ◇ 9 7 4 3
                    ♣ 7
    ♠ 9 3 2                              ♠ J 8 7 6 4
    ♡ 10 7 4          N                  ♡ K 9
    ◇ Q J 6 5     W       E              ◇ 10 8 2
    ♣ 8 4 3          S                   ♣ 10 5 2
                    ♠ K Q 10 5
                    ♡ A
                    ◇ A K
                    ♣ A K Q J 9 6
```

| West | North | East | South |
|------|-------|------|-------|
|      | 3♡    | pass | 4NT   |
| pass | 5◇    | pass | 7♣    |
| all pass | | | |

By agreement, on this sequence, South was playing ordinary Blackwood rather than Roman Key Card Blackwood. (With a heart fit he would have started with a cuebid.) On any lead but a trump, declarer could arrange a spade ruff. West reached for a trump, however. Put yourself in the South seat now. How would you seek thirteen tricks?

Unless the ♠J falls in three rounds, you will need a criss-cross squeeze in the major suits. You run your winners in the minor suits, arriving at this ending:

```
                    ♠ A
                    ♡ Q J 8 6
                    ◇ 9
                    ♣ —
    ♠ 9                                  ♠ J 8 7 6
    ♡ 10 7 4         N                   ♡ K 9
    ◇ Q J         W       E              ◇ —
    ♣ —              S                   ♣ —
                    ♠ K Q 10 5
                    ♡ A
                    ◇ K
                    ♣ —
```

When you play the ◇K, East has no good discard. If he throws a spade, you will cross to the spade ace and return to the ♡A to score three more spade tricks. If instead he bares the ♡K, you will cash the heart ace and cross to dummy with the ♠A. The king and queen of spades will wither on the vine but you will enjoy four tricks in the heart suit!

# The stars come out to play:
## the criss-cross squeeze

Nothing but the best in the world for you now, as Helgemo and Helness take on Meckstroth and Rodwell in the 1994 Europe versus USA match, played in Italy. Geir Helgemo occupies the hot seat.

```
Neither Vul.              ♠ A 8 4
Dealer North              ♡ 10 7 4
                          ◇ Q 8 6 4 3
                          ♣ 9 2
        ♠ 9 3                             ♠ Q J 7 5 2
        ♡ J 9 8 6 2           N           ♡ Q 5 3
        ◇ J              W         E       ◇ 10 9 7 2
        ♣ K 8 7 5 3           S           ♣ 6
                          ♠ K 10 6
                          ♡ A K
                          ◇ A K 5
                          ♣ A Q J 10 4
```

| West | North | East | South |
|------|-------|------|-------|
| Meckstroth | Helness | Rodwell | Helgemo |
| | pass | pass | 2♣ |
| pass | 3◇ | pass | 4◇ |
| pass | 4♠ | pass | 4NT |
| pass | 5◇ | pass | 5NT |
| pass | 6◇ | pass | 6NT |
| all pass | | | |

Meckstroth led the ♡9, Helgemo winning East's queen with the king. The diamond ace and queen revealed the 4-1 split in that suit. When the ♣9 was run to West's king, Meckstroth did the best he could by returning the ♠9. This broke up the twin-entry threat (♠A8 opposite ♠K106), which would have permitted a simple spade-diamond squeeze against East.

Helgemo won East's ♠J with the king and ran the club suit, leaving:

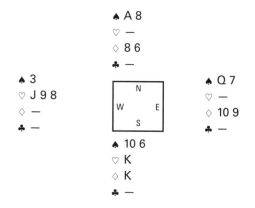

```
              ♠ A 8
              ♡ —
              ◊ 8 6
              ♣ —
♠ 3                          ♠ Q 7
♡ J 9 8        ┌─────────┐   ♡ —
◊ —            │    N    │   ◊ 10 9
♣ —            │ W     E │   ♣ —
               │    S    │
               └─────────┘
              ♠ 10 6
              ♡ K
              ◊ K
              ♣ —
```

Helgemo now cashed the king of hearts, throwing the ♠8 from dummy. Rodwell (East) was caught in a criss-cross squeeze. When East threw the ♠7, Helgemo crossed to the bare ace of spades and returned to the diamond king to enjoy the established ♠10.

It had been a great performance by both sides. Note how right Helgemo was to play the slam in notrump, rather than diamonds. He could see that in notrump he might be able to survive a bad break in the diamond suit.

The next example of the play comes from a 1974 international tournament in Marbella. Fighting it out for the main prize were the legendary Italian Blue Team and a French squad including the great Omar Sharif. This deal decided the matter:

```
Neither Vul.        ♠ A Q J 10 7 6 3
Dealer South        ♡ 6 2
                    ◊ Q 8
                    ♣ A K
        ♠ 8                          ♠ 4 2
        ♡ Q 8 3        ┌─────────┐   ♡ J 10 7 4
        ◊ K J 9 6 4    │    N    │   ◊ 7 5 3 2
        ♣ Q 8 7 6      │ W     E │   ♣ 10 3 2
                       │    S    │
                       └─────────┘
                    ♠ K 9 5
                    ♡ A K 9 5
                    ◊ A 10
                    ♣ J 9 5 4
```

| West | North | East | South |
|------|-------|------|-------|
| | Chemla | | Sharif |
| | | | 1NT (15-17) |
| pass | 3♠ | pass | 4◊ |
| pass | 4NT | pass | 5♡ |
| pass | 5NT | pass | 6♡ |
| pass | 7NT | all pass | |

Paul Chemla could count twelve tricks for certain after the two Blackwood responses. Since Sharif's opening bid placed him with another 1-3 points, it seemed there was likely to be some play for a grand — if only a finesse.

With no obvious safe lead, West chose ♣6. Sharif won in the dummy and saw that he had a choice of squeezes before him. If East held ♣Q and ◇K, he could be caught in a positional simple squeeze in the minors. If East held ♣Q and West held ◇K, a Vienna Coup of the diamond ace would lead to a double squeeze with hearts as the pivot suit.

Sharif chose instead to play for a criss-cross squeeze in the minors. Unlike the other two chances, this would succeed against two different placements of the missing minor-suit honors — both with East or both with West. To pay for this privilege, declarer would have to read which cards the key defender had chosen to keep.

Sharif cashed the two heart honors in his hand, followed by one of dummy's club honors. He then ran dummy's spade suit to bring about this end position:

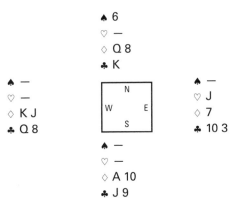

```
                      ♠ 6
                      ♡ —
                      ◇ Q 8
                      ♣ K
        ♠ —                           ♠ —
        ♡ —                           ♡ J
        ◇ K J      ┌──────────┐       ◇ 7
        ♣ Q 8      │    N     │       ♣ 10 3
                   │ W      E │
                   │    S     │
                   └──────────┘
                      ♠ —
                      ♡ —
                      ◇ A 10
                      ♣ J 9
```

On the last spade, declarer threw the ◇10 from his hand and West chose to throw a club. (As I mentioned a page or two back, it was natural for West to retain a guard against the threat he could actually see, dummy's ◇Q 8.) Sharif duly read the position correctly. He cashed the club king, dropping West's queen, and crossed to the diamond ace to score the jack of clubs. As a result the French team finished a single VP ahead of the Italians to win the championship.

One of your friends may tell you that it's not worth mastering the criss-cross squeeze because it doesn't come up very often. Let him try to persuade Omar Sharif on the matter!

# Quiz ✎

**A.**

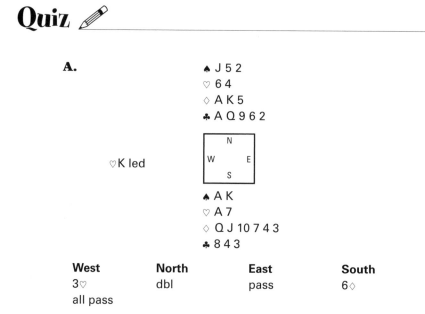

♠ J 5 2
♡ 6 4
◇ A K 5
♣ A Q 9 6 2

♡K led

N
W　　E
S

♠ A K
♡ A 7
◇ Q J 10 7 4 3
♣ 8 4 3

| West | North | East | South |
|------|-------|------|-------|
| 3♡ | dbl | pass | 6◇ |
| all pass | | | |

West leads the ♡K against your small slam in diamonds. Plan the play. (Yes, yes, I realize you will head immediately for a criss-cross squeeze. How will the play go, though?) You will soon discover that West holds one trump to East's three.

**B.**

♠ A 6
♡ A Q J
◇ Q 7 5 2
♣ 9 7 6 4

◇A led

N
W　　E
S

♠ K Q J 10 4 3
♡ 10 7 4 2
◇ —
♣ A K 8

| West | North | East | South |
|------|-------|------|-------|
| | | 3◇ | 4♠ |
| 5◇ | 6♠ | all pass | |

West leads the ◇A against your small slam in spades. Plan the play. (Surprisingly, East will turn up with four trumps. West holds the ♡K.)

# Answers ✏

**A.** Since there is a remote chance that West holds eight hearts, you should win the first trick (rather than ducking to rectify the count). You draw trumps in three rounds, noting that West has a singleton. Clearly, you need the ♣K onside. If West held ♠Q-x-x and ♣K-x-x, you could catch him in a simple squeeze. This is most unlikely, since his preempt suggested seven hearts and he has showed up with one trump. No, you must aim to squeeze East. Since he will be discarding after the dummy, only a criss-cross squeeze will be good enough.

You should now concede a heart trick, to rectify the count. Let's say that West wins and exits with a spade. You will then run the trump suit to arrive at this type of ending:

```
              ♠ J 5
              ♡ —
              ◇ —
              ♣ A Q 9
  ♠ 10 7                      ♠ Q 9
  ♡ Q          ┌──────┐       ♡ —
  ◇ —          │  N   │       ◇ —
  ♣ K 7      W │      │ E     ♣ J 10 5
               │  S   │
               └──────┘
              ♠ A
              ♡ —
              ◇ 7
              ♣ 8 4 3
```

You play the last diamond, throwing the ♣9 from dummy. East must give way to one of your black-suit threats. If he throws a club, you will finesse the club queen, cash the ace of clubs, and return to the spade ace to score the established club. If instead he throws a spade, you will cash the ace of spades before taking the club finesse.

There was a pitfall to be avoided on this deal. Suppose you unwisely took a club finesse before ducking a heart trick. The defenders could then return a second club, killing the entry that you needed in the end game. It would be similarly disastrous to take the club finesse in the five-card ending shown. You would then have to use your last spade entry to reach the diamond squeeze card. Not that you would even think of committing such atrocities, having soldiered through to this point in the book!

**B.** You ruff the diamond lead and draw trumps, finding East (the preemptor) with four. You discard two diamonds from dummy, meanwhile, and plan to squeeze West in hearts and clubs. After finessing the ♡Q successfully, you duck a round of clubs. Whichever defender wins, and whatever card is returned, you will able to play two rounds of both hearts and clubs, obtaining a complete count on the hand. A criss-cross squeeze on West will result. The ending will be similar to this:

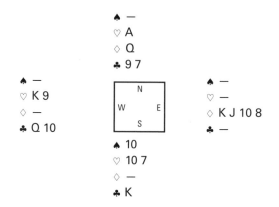

When you lead the last trump (or ruff the ◇Q if the chosen defense has left you in dummy) West will have to abandon hearts or clubs. No guesswork will be required on your part since you will know West's distribution.

# CHAPTER 15

# The Stepping Stone Squeeze

In several of the more unusual squeeze positions, declarer has enough winners for his contract but a blockage prevents him from scoring them all. The elegantly named stepping stone squeeze is one of these. Suppose declarer has no outside entry to dummy and among his assets is this club holding:

♣ A 9 7 6 4 2

♣ J 8 3

```
      N
  W       E
      S
```

♣ 10 5

♣ K Q

West has to retain all three of his clubs or declarer will be able to overtake on the second round. To achieve a stepping stone squeeze here, declarer must reach a position where West is reduced to one or more winners and his ♣J83. Declarer can then cash the king and queen of clubs and throw West in with a winner. At Trick 13 West will have to lead his last club to dummy's ♣A. It is a special form of the strip and endplay, which we introduced in Chapter 11. Instead of leading into a tenace after the throw-in, the defender has to lead to a winner in an entryless dummy.

Let's see this spectacular play in the context of a full deal:

```
              ♠ A 10 6
              ♡ 8
              ♦ 8 6 2
              ♣ K 9 7 6 4 2
♠ K Q J 9 2        N          ♠ 8 3
♡ A K 6                       ♡ 10 9 7 4 3 2
♦ 7 5          W     E        ♦ 10 9 4
♣ J 8 3            S          ♣ 10 5
              ♠ 7 5 4
              ♡ Q J 5
              ♦ A K Q J 3
              ♣ A Q
```

You open 2NT and partner raises to game. West attacks with spades and you win the third round, East showing out. All would be easy if East held the ♡AK — you could simply lead a heart from dummy at this stage. There is no hurry to do this, however (you can lead the ♡Q from hand later, if need be, after cashing your minor-suit winners). Nothing can be lost by playing off the diamonds first. West follows to two rounds, then throws a low heart and his two spade winners.

How do you think the cards lie? The odds are high that West is keeping three clubs accompanied by two top hearts. You cash the ace and queen of clubs, both defenders following, to leave this position:

```
              ♠ —
              ♡ 8
              ♦ —
              ♣ K 9
♠ —                N          ♠ —
♡ A K                         ♡ 10 9 7
♦ —            W     E        ♦ —
♣ J                S          ♣ —
              ♠ —
              ♡ Q J 5
              ♦ —
              ♣ —
```

Now you exit with the queen of hearts. West can score two heart tricks but then has to concede the final trick to dummy's ♣K. You have used the West hand as a stepping stone to the blocked club winner in dummy.

Note that this line of play will still land the contract when West holds the club stopper and East has both top hearts (East's last three cards will be ♡AKx and he will have to give you a heart trick at the end). The stepping stone squeeze itself will work equally well against East, when that defender holds both the club stopper and the ♡AK.

The next deal has an unusual aspect to it — the key defender is given a choice of poisons.

```
                    ♠ 7 5 3
                    ♡ 7 3 2
                    ◇ Q 6 3
                    ♣ K 8 4 2
  ♠ Q J 10 8 4    ┌─────────┐    ♠ 9 6
  ♡ 10 8 5 4      │    N    │    ♡ 9
  ◇ J 8           │ W     E │    ◇ A 10 9 5 4 2
  ♣ 7 5           │    S    │    ♣ 10 9 6 3
                  └─────────┘
                    ♠ A K 2
                    ♡ A K Q J 6
                    ◇ K 7
                    ♣ A Q J
```

Having checked that it was not just a dream, picking up that South hand, you bid unopposed to 6♡. West leads the ♠Q to your ace and you draw trumps in four rounds, noting the 4-1 division. West's honor-sequence lead in spades suggests length there, as well as in hearts. The odds are well against a 3-3 club break (which would allow you to overtake on the third round). What can be done?

There is not much point in playing the king of diamonds at this stage. Even if a defender were tempted to take the ace immediately, he could then return a second diamond — removing the entry to dummy while the clubs were still blocked. A better idea is to play East (who is known to be short in both majors) for both the club length and the ◇A.

After drawing trumps, you should cash the ace and queen of clubs, followed by your second spade winner. These cards will be left:

```
                    ♠ —
                    ♡ —
                    ◇ Q 6 3
                    ♣ K 8
  ♠ J 10 8       ┌─────────┐    ♠ —
  ♡ —            │    N    │    ♡ —
  ◇ J 8          │ W     E │    ◇ A 10 9
  ♣ —            │    S    │    ♣ 10 9
                 └─────────┘
                    ♠ 2
                    ♡ 6
                    ◇ K 7
                    ♣ J
```

On the last heart you throw a diamond from dummy. East must throw a diamond too, since a club discard would allow you to overtake the ♣J. You now play the last club honor. If West were to surprise you by following suit, you would overtake in dummy, playing for the suit to be 3-3. Here West shows out and you play low from dummy. Next you play the king of diamonds. East has a choice of losing plays. If he wins this trick, dummy's queen will serve as an entry to the stranded ♣K. If instead East ducks the first round of diamonds, he will have to win the second round. It will then be his dubious privilege to lead a club to dummy's king at Trick 13. Very enjoyable!

# The double stepping stone squeeze

When both defenders hold a guard on declarer's blocked suit it may be possible to effect a double stepping stone squeeze. At least one of them will have to retain a guard on the blocked suit — otherwise declarer can overtake one honor with another. That defender (or perhaps both defenders) will then be subject to an endplay.

Let's see a full-deal example of this pretty play.

```
North-South Vul.          ♠ 6 5
Dealer West               ♡ 7 4
                          ◇ 9 7 6 5
                          ♣ K 8 7 4 2
          ♠ 9                              ♠ 8 7 3 2
          ♡ K Q J 8 6 3 2   ┌─────────┐    ♡ 9 5
          ◇ 8 4             │    N    │    ◇ Q J 10 2
          ♣ 10 9 5          │ W     E │    ♣ J 6 3
                            │    S    │
                            └─────────┘
                          ♠ A K Q J 10 4
                          ♡ A 10
                          ◇ A K 3
                          ♣ A Q
```

| West | North | East | South |
|------|-------|------|-------|
| 3♡ | pass | pass | 6♠ |
| all pass | | | |

South belonged to the 'practical' school of bidding. He leapt to 6♠ on the first round of bidding ("I wanted to be sure that we reached a slam," he said later) and West led the king of hearts. Take the South cards now. How would you play the contract?

There are twelve tricks on view, in a sense, but the club suit is blocked. Finding the diamonds 3-3 will not help you, of course, because if you ducked a diamond the defenders would cash a heart. When you run the trumps, however, at least one defender must retain three clubs to prevent you from overtaking the queen on the second round. Anyone keeping three clubs may become vulnerable to an endplay.

After winning the ♡K lead, you should play five rounds of trumps. Let's say that both defenders keep their options open by retaining a club guard. When you cash the ace and king of diamonds, to clear the air there, these cards will remain:

```
              ♠ —
              ♡ —
              ◇ 9 7
              ♣ K 8 7
  ♠ —                      ♠ —
  ♡ Q J        N           ♡ —
  ◇ —       W     E        ◇ Q J
  ♣ 10 9 5     S           ♣ J 6 3
              ♠ 4
              ♡ 10
              ◇ 3
              ♣ A Q
```

It's an elegant end position and when you play the last trump, the defenders will have to surrender. First, what can West discard? If he throws a heart, you will cash the ace and queen of clubs and throw him in with his remaining heart. He will have to surrender the last trick to dummy's ♣K. Let's say that West abandons his club guard instead. You throw a diamond from dummy and East faces the same dilemma as his partner. He must either abandon the club suit too, allowing you to overtake on the second round, or throw a diamond and submit himself to an endplay.

There it is, then. The double stepping stone squeeze!

# The stars come out to play:
## stepping stone squeeze ⸻ ☆

Our real-life example of this unusual form of squeeze was played by Henky Lasut of Indonesia, in the 1993 Far Eastern Teams.

```
Neither Vul.        ♠ 2
Dealer West         ♡ K 10 9 8 6 4
                    ◇ A 9 8 6 5
                    ♣ 4
     ♠ 9 7                          ♠ 10 8 4
     ♡ Q 5            N             ♡ A J 3
     ◇ 10 2        W     E          ◇ J 7 4 3
     ♣ K Q 10 9 7 5 2   S           ♣ 8 6 3
                    ♠ A K Q J 6 5 3
                    ♡ 7 2
                    ◇ K Q
                    ♣ A J
```

| West | North | East | South |
|------|-------|------|-------|
|      | Sacul |      | Lasut |
| 3♣   | pass  | pass | dbl   |
| pass | 4♡    | pass | 4NT   |
| pass | 5♡    | pass | 6♠    |
| all pass |   |      |       |

The 4NT bid was Roman Key Card Blackwood in hearts and if North had shown three key cards (♡AK ◇A) Lasut would have bid the grand slam. As it was, he stopped in the small slam and West led the ♣K, East playing the three to suggest three cards in the suit. The lead of either major suit would have spelled defeat. If you had been the declarer, how would you have taken advantage of your reprieve?

West's preempt makes it unlikely that the ♡A is onside. If diamonds are 3-3, you can make the contract by unblocking the two high diamonds in your hand and then crossing to dummy with a club ruff to score the diamond ace. With West holding seven clubs to his partner's three, it is more likely that diamonds are 2-4. (If West held a singleton diamond he might have led it.)

Lasut won the club lead, ruffed his club loser and then returned to the South hand with the ◇K. Six rounds of trumps brought him to this end position:

```
              ♠ —
              ♡ K 10
              ◇ A 9
              ♣ —
  ♠ —                        ♠ —
  ♡ Q 5        ┌─────────┐   ♡ A J
  ◇ 10      W  │    N    │ E ◇ J 7
  ♣ Q          │    S    │   ♣ —
              └─────────┘
              ♠ 5
              ♡ 7 2
              ◇ Q
              ♣ —
```

On the last spade Lasut threw the ♡10 from dummy. East had no escape. If he released a diamond, declarer would be able to overtake the diamond queen. He chose instead to throw the ♡J, but Lasut then cashed the diamond queen and used East's ♡A as a stepping stone to the stranded ace of diamonds. Twelve tricks!

# Quiz ✎

**A.**

                    ♠ A J 6 4 3 2
                    ♡ 10 7
                    ◇ 8 5
                    ♣ 8 7 2

```
        N
    W       E
        S
```

◇K led

                    ♠ K
                    ♡ A K Q 9 5 4 2
                    ◇ A J
                    ♣ A K 5

| West | North | East | South |
|------|-------|------|-------|
|      |       |      | 2♣    |
| pass | 2◇    | pass | 3♡    |
| pass | 3♠    | pass | 4♣    |
| pass | 4♡    | pass | 6♡    |
| all pass |    |      |       |

West leads the ◇K and an unhelpful dummy hits the deck. Plan the play.

**B.**

                    ♠ A 2
                    ♡ K 8 6 3
                    ◇ 10 6 4 3 2
                    ♣ A 2

```
        N
    W       E
        S
```

♣9 led

                    ♠ K Q J 10 7 3
                    ♡ A Q J
                    ◇ A 5
                    ♣ Q 3

| West | North | East | South |
|------|-------|------|-------|
|      |       |      | 1♠    |
| pass | 2◇    | pass | 3♠    |
| pass | 4♣    | dbl  | 4NT   |
| pass | 5♡    | pass | 6♠    |
| all pass |    |      |       |

West leads the ♣9 against your small slam in spades. Plan the play.

# Answers ✏

**A.** West's ◇K lead marks him with the ◇Q. If he also holds the ♠Q, you can catch him in a stepping stone squeeze. Win the first trick and cash the ace of trumps. If the jack falls singleton, you can unblock the ♠K and cross to dummy with a trump to enjoy the spade ace. Otherwise run your winners in trumps and clubs, aiming for this position:

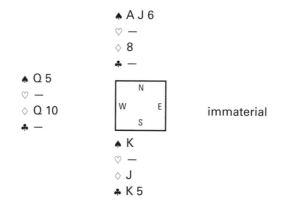

```
                    ♠ A J 6
                    ♡ —
                    ◇ 8
                    ♣ —
     ♠ Q 5          ┌──────────┐
     ♡ —            │    N     │
     ◇ Q 10         │ W     E  │      immaterial
     ♣ —            │    S     │
                    └──────────┘
                    ♠ K
                    ♡ —
                    ◇ J
                    ♣ K 5
```

West has no good discard on the ♣K. If he throws a diamond, you can unblock the ♠K and throw him in with a diamond to give dummy the last trick in spades. If instead he throws a spade, you will overtake the spade king with the ace and score the ♠J. There is no guess involved in the end position, since you can lead the ♠K, playing low from dummy unless the queen appears from West.

There is a second, less likely, chance of success — that East holds five clubs and the spade queen. If the fall of the cards allows you to diagnose that situation, you can play for a stepping stone squeeze on East instead. He will be reduced to ♠Qx ♣Q. You can then cash the spade king and exit with a club.

**B.** West's lead of the ♣9 would make East a very strong favorite to hold the club king, even if he had forgotten to double the 4♣ cuebid. You should win the opening lead with the ace of clubs and play all six rounds of trumps. If East started with four or more hearts, this will reduce him to four hearts and the club king. After cashing the ace and queen of hearts, you will lead the heart jack. If West shows out, you will play low from dummy and attempt to endplay East with the ♣Q to give dummy the last trick in hearts. If instead West follows to the third heart, you will overtake in dummy, playing for a 3-3 heart break.

# CHAPTER 16

# The Vice Squeeze

The vice squeeze is a further variant of the squeeze without the count. The victim does not hold a direct guard on one of the suits; he has two intermediate cards that prevent declarer from establishing an extra winner. Look at this end position, played at notrump:

```
                    ♠ A 9
                    ♡ —
                    ◇ K 10
                    ♣ —
    ♠ K 10                          ♠ J 8
    ♡ —            ┌─────────┐      ♡ —
    ◇ Q J          │    N    │      ◇ A 8
    ♣ —            │ W     E │      ♣ —
                   │    S    │
                   └─────────┘
                    ♠ Q 4
                    ♡ —
                    ◇ 6
                    ♣ 7
```

West's diamond holding is valuable, since it prevents declarer from establishing a diamond trick. He has the sole guard in the spade suit, too. When the last club is played, West has to discard a diamond to retain his spade guard. Declarer throws the ♠9 from dummy and proceeds to establish a diamond trick. Think of North's ◇ K 10 as the jaws of the vice and West's ◇ Q J as being caught in it.

Let's see an example of this play in the setting of a complete deal:

North-South Vul.      ♠ K J 7
Dealer South         ♡ K 10 9 3 2
                       ◇ K 5 2
                       ♣ 6 3

```
♠ 6 3                           ♠ 10 8 4 2
♡ 8 6 4            N            ♡ 5
◇ 9 8 3       W        E        ◇ Q J 7 6
♣ A 9 7 5 4        S            ♣ Q J 8 2
```

                     ♠ A Q 9 5
                     ♡ A Q J 7
                     ◇ A 10 4
                     ♣ K 10

| West | North | East | South |
|------|-------|------|-------|
|      |       |      | 2NT   |
| pass | 3◇[1] | pass | 4♡    |
| pass | 4NT   | pass | 5♣    |
| pass | 6♡    | all pass |   |

1. Transfer.

You break partner's transfer response and arrive in a borderline slam, West leading the ◇ 8. How should you plan the play?

At first glance it may seem that you will need the ♣A to be onside. West's opening lead is revealing, though. Surely it is a second-best card from a poor suit and East holds both the queen and jack of diamonds. In that case you can make the slam when East holds either the ♣A or ♣Q J.

You win the opening lead with dummy's king of diamonds, an essential move. After drawing trumps in three rounds, you cash the spade suit and return to dummy with a fourth round of trumps. These cards remain:

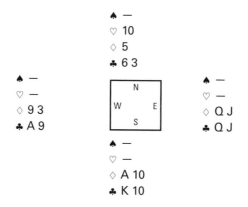

```
                    ♠ —
                    ♡ 10
                    ◇ 5
                    ♣ 6 3
♠ —                           ♠ —
♡ —              N            ♡ —
◇ 9 3        W        E        ◇ Q J
♣ A 9            S            ♣ Q J
                    ♠ —
                    ♡ —
                    ◇ A 10
                    ♣ K 10
```

Dummy's last heart tightens the vice on poor East. Since he knows he has to keep the diamonds intact, he will doubtless throw a club, hoping that West holds the ♣A 10. You discard the ◇ 10 from your hand and set up a club trick to make the slam.

# The stars come out to play:
## the vice squeeze

Our real-life example of the vice squeeze features Geir-Olav Tislevoll, playing in the 1998 Norwegian Premier League.

```
Neither Vul.              ♠ Q 7 3
Dealer East               ♡ J 8 5 2
                          ◇ A 6 5
                          ♣ A Q 2
        ♠ J 10 9 4                        ♠ A 6 5 2
        ♡ 6              ┌─────────┐      ♡ 9 3
        ◇ K 7 3 2        │    N    │      ◇ J 10 9 4
        ♣ 9 7 6 3        │ W     E │      ♣ 10 5 4
                         │    S    │
                         └─────────┘
                          ♠ K 8
                          ♡ A K Q 10 7 4
                          ◇ Q 8
                          ♣ K J 8
```

| West | North | East | South |
|------|-------|------|-------|
|      | Helgemo |    | Tislevoll |
|      |       | pass | 1♡ |
| pass | 2NT   | pass | 3♣ |
| pass | 3NT   | pass | 4♣ |
| pass | 4◇    | pass | 4NT |
| pass | 5♡    | pass | 6♡ |
| all pass |   |      |     |

Helgemo's 2NT was a forcing raise in hearts. South's 3♣ asked if any singleton was held and the 3NT response showed a balanced hand. Two cuebids, followed by Roman Key Card Blackwood, carried the partnership to a somewhat dubious slam. West led the ♠J and Tislevoll won in hand with the king. Looking only at the North-South cards for the moment, what chances can you see of making the contract?

One small possibility is that the ace of spades is doubleton. It can then be ducked out, setting up dummy's queen. Another is to find East with the ◇K as well as the ♠A. When you play off your winners in hearts and clubs East would have to reduce to ♠A ◇K-x and could then be thrown in (a strip-and-endplay).

Tislevoll drew trumps and cashed three rounds of clubs. He then returned to the trump suit. This was the position with one trump still to be played:

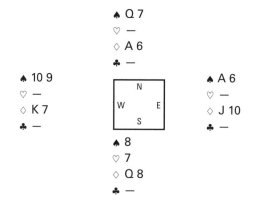

```
                    ♠ Q 7
                    ♡ —
                    ◇ A 6
                    ♣ —
    ♠ 10 9                        ♠ A 6
    ♡ —         ┌─────────┐       ♡ —
    ◇ K 7       │    N    │       ◇ J 10
    ♣ —         │ W     E │       ♣ —
                │    S    │
                └─────────┘
                    ♠ 8
                    ♡ 7
                    ◇ Q 8
                    ♣ —
```

The option of a strip-and-endplay on East was still present, but in fact it was West who paused to consider on the last trump. Hoping that his partner held the ♠8, he eventually released the ♠9. Tislevoll now threw the ◇6 from dummy and led a spade, setting up a twelfth trick in the suit. West had been caught in a vice squeeze.

Suppose West had thrown the ◇7 instead, somehow diagnosing that South held the ♠8. Declarer would throw a spade from dummy and so would East. Declarer would then have to guess which defender held the diamond king. If East held it, he could be thrown in with a spade. If West held it, the card would now be bare and could be dropped.

One final point on this deal. Did it seem to you that declarer would do better to play the queen of spades at Trick 1, forcing East to rectify the count by taking his ace? Such a move might work on some deals but here East could break the simple spade-diamond squeeze on his partner by returning a diamond.

# Quiz ✎

**A.**

♠ K Q 9 6
♡ 7 6 4
◇ K Q 7
♣ J 5 3

```
      N
  W       E
      S
```

♡A led

♠ J 10 8 7 3
♡ Q 9 5
◇ A 4
♣ A K 7

| West | North | East | South |
|------|-------|------|-------|
| pass | pass | pass | 1♠ |
| pass | 3♠ | pass | 4♠ |
| all pass | | | |

West leads the ♡A against your spade game and his partner plays a discouraging ♡2. He switches to ace and another trump, the suit breaking 2-2. Plan the play. Was there a way for West to defend better?

**B.**

♠ Q 9 3
♡ 9 6 4
◇ 7 3 2
♣ K Q J 5

```
      N
  W       E
      S
```

♡8 led

♠ A K J 10 6 2
♡ A 7
◇ K 10 4
♣ A 6

| West | North | East | South |
|------|-------|------|-------|
| | | 3♡ | dbl |
| pass | 4♣ | pass | 4♠ |
| pass | 5♠ | pass | 6♠ |
| all pass | | | |

West leads the ♡8 against your small slam in spades, East playing the ten. Plan the play.

# Answers ✏

**A.** West is a passed hand and has turned up with ♡AK ♠A, so he cannot also hold the ♣Q. You can make the contract on a vice squeeze (surprise, surprise!) if East holds the jack and ten of hearts as well as the club queen. Play three more rounds of trumps, the ♣A, and then the ace and king of diamonds. This type of end position will remain:

```
                    ♠ —
                    ♡ 7
                    ◇ Q
                    ♣ J 5
    ♠ —                             ♠ —
    ♡ K 8          ┌─────────┐      ♡ J 10
    ◇ —            │    N    │      ◇ —
    ♣ 8 6          │ W     E │      ♣ Q 10
                   │    S    │
                   └─────────┘
                    ♠ —
                    ♡ Q 9
                    ◇ —
                    ♣ K 7
```

You now play dummy's last diamond. If the jack or ten of hearts appears from East, you will throw the ♣7 and lead a heart, hoping for a trick in that suit. Otherwise you will play for East's ♣Q to be bare.

West had two ways to break the squeeze. At Trick 2, he could switch to a club, playing another club when he came on lead with the trump ace. This would destroy your two-card threat. Alternatively, he could switch to a diamond at Trick 2, playing another diamond when in with the ace of trumps. You need to play the trumps before the diamonds and this defense would prevent you from doing so.

**B.** Since he opened 3♡, East is unlikely to hold the ◇A in addition to the K-Q-J of hearts. You should play him for the Q-J of diamonds instead. Win the heart lead and play all six rounds of trumps, throwing one heart and two diamonds from dummy. You continue with four rounds of clubs and on the last round East will have to throw one of his diamond honors, to retain a guard against dummy's ♡9. You can then lead a diamond, covering East's remaining honor with the king. West will win with the ace but will have to surrender the last trick to your ◇10.

# The Winkle Squeeze

**P**erhaps you thought that by the time you reached Chapter 17 the squeezes would become rather complicated, and maybe not worthy of your study. Stop right there. Don't chuck the book into the bin! The **winkle squeeze** is not particularly difficult and it's also rather pretty.

In a winkle squeeze, the defender has two losing options when the squeeze card is played. If he retains a high card he will be thrown in with it to concede a trick. If instead he unblocks the card, declarer will be able to set up a trick in the suit of the unblock. Look at this end position, played at notrump:

```
                    ♠ —
                    ♡ A 5
                    ◇ Q 8
                    ♣ —
   ♠ —                              ♠ —
   ♡ K 8          ┌─────────┐       ♡ J 10
   ◇ A 9          │    N    │       ◇ K 10
   ♣ —          W │         │ E     ♣ —
                  │    S    │
                  └─────────┘
                    ♠ —
                    ♡ Q 9
                    ◇ J
                    ♣ J
```

Needing three of the last four tricks, you lead the ♣J. If West discards the ♡8, you will throw a diamond from dummy and score two heart tricks. If instead West discards the ◇9, you can throw him with a diamond to lead away from the ♡K. West's final option gives this squeeze its attractive name. If he throws the ◇A, you can discard the ♡5 from dummy and lead the ◇J to set up dummy's ◇Q. You will have 'winkled' an extra diamond trick.

Let's see a full-deal example of this exotic play:

```
                    ♠ A 9 5
                    ♡ Q J 6 3
                    ◇ Q 10 7 4
                    ♣ 4 3
    ♠ K 10 7 3                      ♠ J 8 6 2
    ♡ 10 8 2          N             ♡ 9 5 4
    ◇ A J 3      W         E        ◇ K 9 6 2
    ♣ 9 8 5          S             ♣ 6 2
                    ♠ Q 4
                    ♡ A K 7
                    ◇ 8 5
                    ♣ A K Q J 10 7
```

When this deal arose at the table, South opened 1♣ and had a tricky rebid problem over partner's 1♡. He invented a reverse to 2◇, raised by his partner, and the bidding eventually came to a halt in 6NT! Seeking a safe lead, West placed the ♣8 on the table. How would you play the contract now?

The only real hope was a squeeze. Declarer needed to find West with the king of spades and to bring him down to a singleton diamond honor. A throw-in might then be possible. The first essential was to cash the hearts. Declarer played four rounds of that suit, throwing a diamond, and then started on the clubs. He soon reached this end position:

```
                    ♠ A 9
                    ♡ —
                    ◇ Q 10
                    ♣ —
    ♠ K 10                           ♠ J 8
    ♡ —               N             ♡ —
    ◇ A J       W          E        ◇ K 9
    ♣ —               S             ♣ —
                    ♠ Q 4
                    ♡ —
                    ◇ 8
                    ♣ 7
```

What could West play on the last club? If he threw a spade, declarer would discard a diamond from dummy and claim two spade tricks. If West threw the ◇J, he would be endplayed on the next trick. The only other chance was to throw the ace of diamonds. Declarer would then discard the ♠9 from dummy and lead a diamond to winkle a trick for himself in that suit. Well bid, partner!

On the next deal East can choose to subject himself to a variety of squeezes.

```
North-South Vul.          ♠ K 9 8 7
Dealer North              ♡ A 4 3
                          ◇ K Q 7 6 4
                          ♣ 7
        ♠ 10 4 3 2                          ♠ 6
        ♡ J 10 8 7 5 2      ┌─────────┐     ♡ —
        ◇ 9                 │    N    │     ◇ J 10 8 5 2
        ♣ 10 9              │ W     E │     ♣ A Q J 6 4 3 2
                            │    S    │
                            └─────────┘
                          ♠ A Q J 5
                          ♡ K Q 9 6
                          ◇ A 3
                          ♣ K 8 5
```

| West | North | East | South |
|------|-------|------|-------|
|      | 1◇    | 4♣   | dbl   |
| pass | 4♠    | pass | 4NT   |
| pass | 5♡    | pass | 6NT   |
| all pass |   |      |       |

West leads the ♣10 against 6NT. How many different squeeze endings can you visualize?

Twelve tricks are easy if East rises with the ♣A at Trick 1. You will have eleven top tricks and, since only East guards the third round of clubs, the run of your major-suit winners will squeeze him in the minors. A simple squeeze.

More interesting are the situations that may arise when East defends more strongly, allowing the ♣10 to run to your king. You play the king of hearts, revealing the situation in that suit, and then follow with four rounds of spades. This position is left:

```
                          ♠ —
                          ♡ A 4
                          ◇ K Q 7 6 4
                          ♣ —
        ♠ —                                ♠ —
        ♡ J 10 8 7 5       ┌─────────┐     ♡ —
        ◇ 9                 │    N    │     ◇ J 10 8 5
        ♣ 9                 │ W     E │     ♣ A Q 6
                            │    S    │
                            └─────────┘
                          ♠ —
                          ♡ Q 9 6
                          ◇ A 3
                          ♣ 8 5
```

East has already discarded one club honor, to retain some flexibility. What can he throw next, though, when you play a heart to the ace?

If he throws the ♣6, a heart to the queen will force him to throw the club queen. You can then exit with the ♣5 to the bare ace, setting up your ♣8. That was a squeeze without the count.

Suppose instead that East throws the club queen, retaining A-6 in the suit. You then cross to the ace of diamonds and lead the ♣5 in this ending:

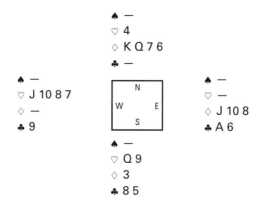

It is a winkle squeeze position. If East overtakes the ♣9 with his ace, your ♣8 will become good. If instead he allows the ♣9 to win, West must exit with a heart and this will squeeze his partner. A suicide squeeze.

If you could follow clearly in your mind what happened on each of the different squeezes there, permit yourself a brief self-congratulation. You have a good understanding of squeeze play.

# The stars come out to play:
## the winkle squeeze

Our first real-life action comes from the 1999 Bermuda Bowl, played (appropriately) in Bermuda. USA I faces USA II.

*North-South Vul.*
*Dealer North*

♠ 10 9 8 7 4
♡ A Q
◇ A J 8 6 5
♣ 2

♠ A 6 5
♡ 8 6 5 2
◇ K Q 3
♣ A 8 5

♠ K J 2
♡ 7
◇ 10 9 7 2
♣ Q 7 6 4 3

♠ Q 3
♡ K J 10 9 4 3
◇ 4
♣ K J 10 9

| West | North | East | South |
|------|-------|------|-------|
| *Meckstroth* | *Stansby* | *Rodwell* | *Martel* |
| | 1♠ | pass | 2♡ |
| pass | 2♠ | pass | 3♡ |
| pass | 4♡ | all pass | |

Chip Martel won the ◇K lead with the ace and played a club to the jack and ace. (It is a measure of how difficult bridge is that Jeff Meckstroth now needed to find an impossible switch to spades to beat the game!) Meckstroth may be superhuman but even he was not clairvoyant enough to switch to spades on the evidence available to him here. When he played a trump instead, Martel won in the dummy, ruffed a diamond and ruffed the ♣9. A further diamond ruff dropped the queen from West.

East showed out on the second round of trumps and declarer continued to draw trumps. This end position was reached:

```
                  ♠ 10 9 8 7
                  ♡ —
                  ◇ J
                  ♣ —
  ♠ A 6 5                           ♠ K J 2
  ♡ 8          ┌─────────────┐      ♡ —
  ◇ —          │      N      │      ◇ —
  ♣ 8          │  W       E  │      ♣ Q 7
               │      S      │
               └─────────────┘
                  ♠ Q 3
                  ♡ 9
                  ◇ —
                  ♣ K 10
```

The last trump squeezed East out of a spade, thereby depriving the defenders of the chance to score three spade tricks. Rodwell chose to throw the spade two and Martel now exited with the spade queen, won with the king. Rodwell returned the ♠J, which West could not afford to overtake. The jack was allowed to win and East then had to surrender two tricks to declarer's club tenace.

As you see, East does no better to throw the ♠J in the diagrammed position. The defender who won the second round of spades would then have to play a club into South's tenace or allow declarer to winkle a spade trick.

On now to the 1990 National Open Teams, in Canberra, Australia. The visiting Indonesians won the main event, aided by this winkle squeeze by Franki Karwur:

Neither Vul.
Dealer North

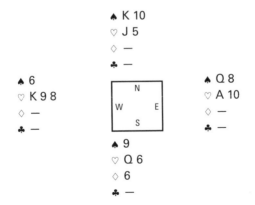

```
                ♠ A K 10 4
                ♡ J 5
                ◇ Q 7 4 2
                ♣ A K J
  ♠ 6 5 2          N          ♠ Q 8 7 3
  ♡ K 9 8 4 3                 ♡ A 10 7
  ◇ A 8      W         E      ◇ 3
  ♣ 6 5 2          S          ♣ 10 9 8 7 4
                ♠ J 9
                ♡ Q 6 2
                ◇ K J 10 9 6 5
                ♣ Q 3
```

| West | North | East | South |
|------|-------|------|-------|
| C.Ackerley | Sacul | D.Ackerley | Karwur |
|  | 1♣ | 1◇ | 2◇ |
| 2♠ | 3◇ | pass | 5◇ |
| all pass |  |  |  |

East's 1◇, over the strong club, showed hearts or both black suits. West's 2♠ requested correction to 3♡, if East held hearts.

So much for the bidding. Franki Karwur arrived in 5◇ with three top losers and Chris Ackerley led the ace of trumps. Should West have diagnosed a heart switch now, do you think? If East's overcall was indeed based on a black two-suiter, dummy's top cards would cover declarer's losers in those suits and then two heart tricks would be the only way to beat the contract. West in fact played a spade next, declarer winning with dummy's ace and unblocking the jack from his hand. East's overcall suggested that the spade queen would be offside. Karwur therefore ran his minor-suit winners, hoping for something good to develop. It did! This was the four-card end position:

```
                ♠ K 10
                ♡ J 5
                ◇ —
                ♣ —
  ♠ 6              N          ♠ Q 8
  ♡ K 9 8                     ♡ A 10
  ◇ —        W         E      ◇ —
  ♣ —              S          ♣ —
                ♠ 9
                ♡ Q 6
                ◇ 6
                ♣ —
```

When the last diamond was led, West and the dummy threw a heart. The spotlight turned to East. What could he throw? A spade would surrender an eleventh trick immediately. If he threw the ♡ 10, a throw-in would surely follow. David Ackerley therefore discarded the ace of hearts.

A smile on his lips, Karwur crossed to the king of spades to extract West's last spade. The jack of hearts went to West's king and he was forced to concede the last trick to South's heart queen. The diamond game had been made.

Even after West's failure to switch to a heart, the defenders had a second chance to defeat the contract. Did you spot it? It would be a remarkable play indeed, but suppose West keeps ♠65 ♡K9 as his last four cards and then throws a heart. The defenders can counter any move by declarer. If he keeps ♠K10 ♡J in the dummy, for example, East can discard the ♡A and wait for a spade trick.

For our final example of a real-life winkle squeeze, we will visit the 1991 Cap Gemini Pandata World Top Pairs. As always, sixteen of the world's top pairs had been invited and we will focus on the table where Canadian aces Mittelman and Kokish faced Brazil's triple world champions Chagas and Branco.

*North-South Vul.*
*Dealer West*

```
                      ♠ A 7 2
                      ♡ Q 6 4
                      ◇ K 9 6 5
                      ♣ 10 8 4
      ♠ K 9                              ♠ J 8 6 5 4 3
      ♡ K 8 5          N                 ♡ 7
      ◇ 7 3        W       E             ◇ Q J 4 2
      ♣ A 7 6 5 3 2      S               ♣ K J
                      ♠ Q 10
                      ♡ A J 10 9 3 2
                      ◇ A 10 8
                      ♣ Q 9
```

| West | North | East | South |
|------|-------|------|-------|
| *Kokish* | *Chagas* | *Mittelman* | *Branco* |
| pass | pass | 2♠ | 3♡ |
| pass | 4♡ | all pass | |

All preemptive openings are somewhat of a gamble. If you open a weak two on a suit such as jack sixth, you take bidding space away from the opponents. You also run the risk that partner will subsequently make a costly opening lead in the suit.

That's what happened here. Marcelo Branco arrived in four hearts and Eric Kokish led the king of spades. Branco won with dummy's ace and ran the queen of trumps to West's king. A second round of spades went to South's queen, a wry look appearing from the Canadians. It was still far from clear how the contract could be made. With two top losers in clubs, declarer had somehow to avoid a diamond loser. Can you see any way that this can be done?

Branco aimed to force the defenders to open the diamond suit. He ran his remaining trumps, arriving at this end position:

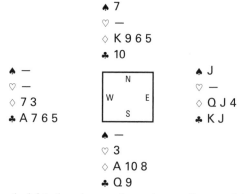

```
              ♠ 7
              ♡ —
              ◇ K 9 6 5
              ♣ 10
♠ —                        ♠ J
♡ —            N           ♡ —
◇ 7 3      W       E       ◇ Q J 4
♣ A 7 6 5         S        ♣ K J
              ♠ —
              ♡ 3
              ◇ A 10 8
              ♣ Q 9
```

Branco now led his last heart, throwing a diamond from dummy. What should East discard? A spade or a diamond discard would raise the white flag immediately, so East had to throw a club. If, hoping to avoid a throw-in, he threw the king of clubs, declarer would winkle himself a club trick. Mittelman eventually chose to throw the jack of clubs.

Branco, who had a fairly sure count on the hand, now exited with the ♣9. West could not afford to put up the ace, or declarer's queen of clubs would be established. He played low and the trick was won by East's bare king. Mittelman cashed the ♠J, South and West throwing clubs, and then had to open the diamond suit. He chose to play the queen and Branco now had to guess whether East was down to Q-J-x in the suit or had played an 'expert' queen from Q-x-x to give declarer a guess. Perhaps reasoning that West might have opened the bidding, with the ◇J in addition to the values already shown, Branco read the suit correctly. He ran the diamond queen to dummy's king and finessed on the return. A fine piece of cardplay!

# Quiz ✐

**A.**

                 ♠ K J 3
                 ♡ 8 6 5
                 ◇ A K J 10 3
                 ♣ A 4

♡K led

|   | N |   |
|---|---|---|
| W |   | E |
|   | S |   |

                 ♠ A Q 9 4
                 ♡ A 9
                 ◇ Q 8 4
                 ♣ Q 7 3 2

You overbid to 6NT and West leads the ♡K. How would you plan the play? Do you see how you might winkle yourself a second heart trick?

**B.**

                 ♠ A Q 3
                 ♡ J 10 6
                 ◇ A K Q 10
                 ♣ J 4 2

◇7 led

|   | N |   |
|---|---|---|
| W |   | E |
|   | S |   |

                 ♠ K 10 5 4
                 ♡ A K Q 9
                 ◇ J 8 4
                 ♣ Q 7

You open a 15-17 1NT and partner raises to 6NT. West gives you a chance by leading the ◇7. Plan the play. (When you play on the red suits, West will show up with two doubletons there.)

# Answers ✎

**A.** Your best chance is to find West with the ♣K. If you can reduce him to K-x of clubs and a heart winner, you will be able to throw him in at Trick 11. Win the first trick and play five rounds of diamonds, throwing two clubs from your hand. You then continue with four rounds of spades. If West has kept ♡QJ ♣ Kx as his last four cards, he will have no escape. Suppose he has foreseen a throw-in and retained a lower heart. The position will be similar to this:

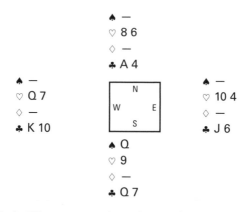

```
              ♠ —
              ♡ 8 6
              ◊ —
              ♣ A 4
  ♠ —                      ♠ —
  ♡ Q 7        N           ♡ 10 4
  ◊ —       W     E        ◊ —
  ♣ K 10        S          ♣ J 6
              ♠ Q
              ♡ 9
              ◊ —
              ♣ Q 7
```

It will do West no good to throw the ♡Q on your last spade. You would then throw the ♣4 from dummy and lead a heart from your hand, winkling a trick for dummy's ♡8. If instead West throws the ♡7, you will discard a heart from dummy and throw West in with a heart.

**B.** You should cash your eight winners in diamonds and hearts, throwing a club from each hand. When West started with four or five spades to the jack (quite likely when he shows up with 2-2 in the reds), he will have to reduce to a singleton club. If he retains the bare ace or king of clubs, you can cash the ace and queen of spades and throw West in with a club. If he attempts to avoid a throw-in by discarding his club honor, you can winkle yourself a club trick. When you lead the bare ♣Q from your hand, East will have to win and concede a trick to dummy's ♣J

# CHAPTER 18

# The Triple Squeeze

The famous Scottish bridge writer, Hugh Kelsey, once wrote a whole book on the **triple squeeze**. It was subtitled 'A must for all pairs players'! We have only a few pages to dedicate to the subject ("Thank goodness!" you are probably saying…), which is probably as it should be. This form of squeeze is relatively rare and a detailed knowledge of the variations possible would bring only a limited reward at the table.

What is a triple squeeze? It is a squeeze on one defender in three different suits. In its most straightforward form, declarer has two one-card threats and one two-card threat (as in the double squeeze). When all these act against the same defender he can be squeezed directly even though the count has not been rectified.

Let's see an example of this straight away.

```
North-South Vul.        ♠ K Q 7
Dealer West             ♡ K Q 8 3
                        ◇ A J 6
                        ♣ 10 6 3
    ♠ A J 4                          ♠ 10 9 8 6 5 2
    ♡ J 9 5 2            N            ♡ 10 7 6
    ◇ K Q 9 8 7      W       E        ◇ 10 3
    ♣ 8                  S            ♣ 9 7
                        ♠ 3
                        ♡ A 4
                        ◇ 5 4 2
                        ♣ A K Q J 5 4 2
```

| West | North | East | South |
|------|-------|------|-------|
| 1◇ | 1NT | pass | 3♣ |
| pass | 3◇ | pass | 3♡ |
| pass | 3♠ | pass | 6NT |
| all pass | | | |

South's leap to 3♣ was a single-suited slam try and the next three bids showed controls. Fearful of a possible diamond ruff, South bid the slam in notrump. A small slam in clubs would have been easy. (If West leads the ◇K, declarer can draw trumps, discard his spade singleton, and eventually lead towards the ◇J). How would you play the more challenging contract of 6NT when West leads the ◇K, won by dummy's ace?

West clearly holds the guards in spades and diamonds but no squeeze can be possible in those suits alone, since neither suit now contains an entry. A squeeze will be possible only if West also holds the heart guard. Note that you are in the state known as 'near rectification' (see Chapter 10). You have eleven winners and have not yet lost a trick.

After winning the diamond lead, you run the club suit. With the ♡A also cashed (for simplicity), you reach this end position:

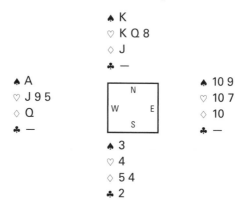

Dummy contains two one-card threats (♠K, ◇J) and a 'threat with an entry' in hearts. All of these act solely against West. When the last club is led, West has to throw one of his guards, giving you an extra trick.

Unusual, isn't it? The count has not been rectified but West's discard gives you an extra trick directly. We saw some squeezes without the count in Chapters 10 and 11 but in every case a trick had to be surrendered, after the squeeze, in order to set up the extra trick. Here, because West guards three suits, his key discard sets up a winner immediately.

With all three threats in the dummy, the squeeze was positional. Switch the West and East hands and dummy would have to discard a threat before East was put to the test. To make the squeeze automatic, one or both of the one-card threats must lie in the South hand. Let's swap the jack and five of diamonds:

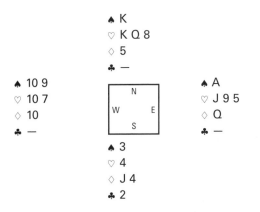

```
              ♠ K
              ♡ K Q 8
              ◇ 5
              ♣ —
  ♠ 10 9                    ♠ A
  ♡ 10 7       ┌─────┐      ♡ J 9 5
  ◇ 10         │  N  │      ◇ Q
  ♣ —          │W   E│      ♣ —
               │  S  │
               └─────┘
              ♠ 3
              ♡ 4
              ◇ J 4
              ♣ 2
```

Now, as you see, the squeeze will work against East too. Dummy has a spare card (the ◇ 5),which can be thrown on the last club. East is left with no good discard. The recessed threat in hearts creates so much extra space opposite that in fact the South hand could have accommodated both one-card threats.

A triple squeeze is possible too when a twin-entry threat (such as A-x opposite K-x-x) has its longer holding alongside the squeeze card. Try your luck here:

```
Both Vul.                ♠ A 6 2
Dealer South             ♡ Q 7
                         ◇ Q 10 8 6 3
                         ♣ J 7 2
      ♠ 8 5 4                            ♠ Q J 9 3
      ♡ 10 9 8 4        ┌─────┐          ♡ A J 6 3
      ◇ 7 5             │  N  │          ◇ J 9 4 2
      ♣ 9 8 5 3         │W   E│          ♣ 6
                        │  S  │
                        └─────┘
                         ♠ K 10 7
                         ♡ K 5 2
                         ◇ A K
                         ♣ A K Q 10 4
```

| West | North | East | South |
|------|-------|------|-------|
|      |       |      | 2♣ |
| pass | 2◇ | pass | 2NT |
| pass | 6NT | all pass | |

West leads the ♡ 10 and you win the trick with the king. You unblock the two top diamonds in your hand, play a club to the jack, and cash the queen of diamonds. No luck is forthcoming — West shows out. How can you recover in this situation?

You have one-card threats against East in hearts and diamonds. To make the contract you will need to find East with the sole guard in spades, too. Not particularly likely but better than nothing. You return to your hand with a club and continue to play on clubs. This will be the end position:

```
              ♠ A 6 2
              ♡ Q
              ◇ 10
              ♣ —
  ♠ 8 5 4        ┌─────────┐      ♠ Q J 9
  ♡ 9 8          │    N    │      ♡ A
  ◇ —            │ W     E │      ◇ J
  ♣ —            │    S    │      ♣ —
                 └─────────┘
              ♠ K 10 7
              ♡ 5
              ◇ —
              ♣ 10
```

On the last club you throw the ♠2 from dummy, leaving yourself with a twin-entry threat in the suit. Although East sits over the two one-card threats the fact that he has to guard three suits is too much for him. He will doubtless throw the ♠9, hoping that his partner holds the ♠10. You will then score three spade tricks to make the slam.

# The repeating triple squeeze

A triple squeeze can sometimes generate two extra tricks. A defender who holds the sole guard in three suits is squeezed out of one of his guards. You then use the established winner as a further squeeze card. The play is called a repeating triple squeeze or a progressive squeeze. Here is an example:

```
Both Vul.              ♠ Q 6
Dealer North           ♡ A Q 10 5
                       ◇ A K J 3 2
                       ♣ A 4
   ♠ 9 5 3          ┌─────────┐      ♠ K 8 7 4
   ♡ 6 4            │    N    │      ♡ K J 9 7 2
   ◇ 9 8 4          │ W     E │      ◇ 7
   ♣ 10 9 5 3 2     │    S    │      ♣ K J 8
                    └─────────┘
                       ♠ A J 10 2
                       ♡ 8 3
                       ◇ Q 10 6 5
                       ♣ Q 7 6
```

| West | North | East | South |
|------|-------|------|-------|
|      | 1◇    | dbl  | 2NT   |
| pass | 3♡    | dbl  | 3♠    |
| pass | 6NT   | all pass |   |

You don't like the bidding, I realize. Twelve tricks would have been easy in diamonds but North — perhaps hoping for a place in this book — decided to bid the slam in notrump. Suppose you were his poor partner. How would you play 6NT on the ♡6 lead?

East's takeout doubles mark him with the missing honors. A successful spade finesse brings you only to ten tricks, however, so you will need two more from a squeeze. The first step is to duck the heart lead. East wins with the nine and exits safely in diamonds. It's not a difficult hand to play. You simply run the diamond suit. This is the position with one diamond to play:

```
                        ♠ Q 6
                        ♡ A Q 10
                        ◇ J
                        ♣ A 4
      ♠ 9 5 3         ┌─────────┐         ♠ K 8 7 4
      ♡ 4             │    N    │         ♡ K J
      ◇ —            │ W     E │         ◇ —
      ♣ 10 9 5 3      │    S    │         ♣ K J
                      └─────────┘
                        ♠ A J 10 2
                        ♡ 8
                        ◇ —
                        ♣ Q 7 6
```

What can East throw on the last diamond? His most likely discard is a spade, in the hope that his partner can help out in the suit. You will then lead the ♠Q, covered by the king and ace. You play a club to the ace (a Vienna Coup) and continue with three more spades. The last of these will squeeze East again. He has no good discard from ♡K J ♣K. The two tricks provided by the squeeze will bring your total to twelve.

Look back at the end diagram. No other discard from East is any better. A heart would surrender two tricks immediately. A club would allow you to use the ♣Q as a further squeeze card, inflicting a major-suit simple squeeze on East for a second extra trick. Who's laughing at that bidding sequence now?

It is worth mentioning an important aspect of defending such positions. Suppose you are East in this end position:

```
                        ♠ A K 8
                        ♡ 7
                        ◇ 5
                        ♣ —
      ♠ 10 4          ┌─────────┐         ♠ Q J 5
      ♡ 10 7          │    N    │         ♡ A
      ◇ 10           │ W     E │         ◇ K
      ♣ —            │    S    │         ♣ —
                      └─────────┘
                        ♠ 9 6
                        ♡ K
                        ◇ Q
                        ♣ 2
```

South plays his last club, throwing a red card from dummy. You are hopelessly squeezed and will have to give declarer a trick. You can, however, avoid giving him *two* tricks! If you throw a spade, he will only make one extra spade trick. If instead you throw one of your red-suit guards, declarer will cash the established winner in the South hand, squeezing you again.

# Triple squeeze with no two-card threat

At the start of this book, we said that nearly every squeeze requires a two-card threat containing an entry. We noted in Chapter 14 that one exception to this rule is the crisscross squeeze. Here is another exception, this time a triple squeeze:

```
Neither Vul.              ♠ A 9
Dealer North              ♡ Q 9
                          ◇ A K 7 5 2
                          ♣ A Q 7 2
        ♠ J 8 7 5 4 2            ┌─────────┐        ♠ K 10
        ♡ 7 4                    │    N    │        ♡ A
        ◇ J 8                    │ W     E │        ◇ Q 10 9 4 3
        ♣ 8 6 4                  │    S    │        ♣ K J 10 9 5
                                 └─────────┘
                          ♠ Q 6 3
                          ♡ K J 10 8 6 5 3 2
                          ◇ 6
                          ♣ 3
```

| West | North | East | South |
|------|-------|------|-------|
|      | 1◇    | 2♣   | 2♡    |
| pass | 3♣    | pass | 4♡    |
| pass | 6♡    | all pass |   |

West leads the ♣6, won with dummy's ace, and your best chance of a twelfth trick is to set up a long diamond. You cash the ◇A and ruff a diamond with the eight. When you play a trump to the queen and ace, East returns a further diamond. You ruff high again, disappointed to see West show out. You cannot now establish a long diamond. Any other ideas?

Although the entry position seems hopelessly adverse, a triple squeeze will be possible if East holds the ♠K. You cross to the ♡9, drawing West's last trump, cash the ◇K and return to hand with a club ruff. When you play the remaining trumps, this amazing end position arises:

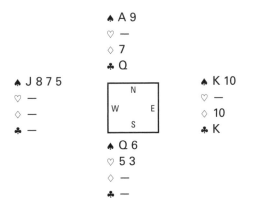

On the penultimate trump you throw the ♠9 from dummy, leaving your-self with no 'two-card threat with an entry'. East holds the sole guard in three different suits. What can he throw? If he unguards one of the one-card threats in the dummy, you will cross to the ace of spades and score the slam-going trick in the unguarded suit. His only alternative is to bare the ♠K. You will then cross to the ace of spades, dropping the king, and return to your hand with a ruff to enjoy the established ♠Q. A strange ending, indeed!

# The stars come out to play:
## the triple squeeze ☆

Our first real-life action comes from the 1991 world championship, from a match between Iceland and Sweden. The annoyingly smooth-looking guy in the South seat is Gudmundur Arnarson.

Both Vul.
Dealer North

```
              ♠ 10 8 5 2
              ♡ A Q 8 2
              ◇ Q 7 6
              ♣ A 4
♠ 7 6 3                        ♠ K Q J 9
♡ J 4          N               ♡ 10 9 7 3
◇ J 10 9 5 4 3  W   E          ◇ A 8 2
♣ 10 9            S            ♣ 8 2
              ♠ A 4
              ♡ K 6 5
              ◇ K
              ♣ K Q J 7 6 5 3
```

| West | North | East | South |
|------|-------|------|-------|
| Morath | Jonsson | Bjerregard | Arnarson |
| | 1◇ | pass | 2♣ |
| pass | 2◇ | pass | 4♣ |
| pass | 4♠ | pass | 6♣ |
| all pass | | | |

North's rebid showed either diamonds or 11-13 balanced. South's 4♣ was Roman Key Card Blackwood for clubs and the response showed two key cards (two aces, from South's perspective). East appears to have an obvious lead-directing double of 4♠ but Bjerregard passed. Not to worry. His partner found a spade lead — the only one to trouble the contract — without any such assistance. Suppose you had been South. How would you have rated your chances?

The hearts might break 3-3 or East might hold a doubleton J-10, J-9 or 10-9, which would allow a third-round finesse of dummy's eight. What will happen if a defender holds both the ace of diamonds and four hearts? The answer is: not much. Since the count cannot safely be rectified, a simple squeeze in the red suits would not materialize.

Arnarson saw that his best chance was to find East with the sole guard in three suits. He played six rounds of trumps to arrive at this position:

```
              ♠ 10 8
              ♡ A Q 8 2
              ◇ —
              ♣ —
  ♠ 7 6                      ♠ Q
  ♡ J 4         N            ♡ 10 9 7 3
  ◇ J 10    W     E          ◇ A
  ♣ —           S            ♣ —
              ♠ 4
              ♡ K 6 5
              ◇ K
              ♣ 5
```

Declarer played his last club, throwing a spade from dummy. Although the count had not been rectified, East was squeezed directly because he had guards in three different suits. He eventually threw the diamond ace, hoping that West held the king of diamonds. It was not to be. Arnarson produced that card and the slam was made. It had been a triple squeeze. The count was near-rectified, rather than rectified, but this is normal for a triple squeeze.

In the other semifinal, Gawrys played 6♣ from the North hand (having opened a Polish 1♣). He reached the same six-card ending, again putting East to a discard on the last club. Brazil's Camacho (East) could see the ◇K in dummy, so he threw the ♠Q instead, hoping that his partner held the spade ten. Declarer now made an overtrick. He crossed to the ace of hearts and played the established ♠10, squeezing yet another trick out of poor East. A discard of either red suit in the diagrammed position would have held declarer to twelve tricks, as happened at the other table.

We will end this section with one of the most spectacular deals from the 1977 World Championship, contested in Manila.

Neither Vul.
Dealer North

|  |  |  |  |
|---|---|---|---|
| | ♠ A K J 2 | | |
| | ♡ K J 8 7 | | |
| | ◇ 7 4 | | |
| | ♣ Q 10 5 | | |

| | | | |
|---|---|---|---|
| ♠ Q 10 6 5 4 | | | ♠ 9 8 7 |
| ♡ A 6 | | | ♡ Q 9 2 |
| ◇ Q 10 3 | N W E S | | ◇ A J 8 6 5 2 |
| ♣ J 7 6 | | | ♣ 2 |

| | |
|---|---|
| | ♠ 3 |
| | ♡ 10 5 4 3 |
| | ◇ K 9 |
| | ♣ A K 9 8 4 3 |

| West | North | East | South |
|---|---|---|---|
| Eisenberg | Passell | Kantar | Hamilton |
| | 1♣ | 2◇ | dbl |
| 4◇ | pass | pass | 4NT |
| pass | 5◇ | pass | 5♡ |
| pass | 5NT | all pass | |

A bizarre auction that would have my wife shaking her head. 'Twenty-four points between them and they get to 5NT?' she would say. 'Did you say they were experts? Norma and I probably wouldn't get to game.'

Hamilton had intended his 4NT as natural. Passell showed one ace, however, and the partnership managed to bail out in 5NT. West led the ◇ 3 to East's ace and a diamond was returned. Declarer won with the king and proceeded to run his club suit. Poor Eisenberg, in the West seat, came under increasing pressure. This was the position when the last club was led:

| | | | |
|---|---|---|---|
| | ♠ A K J 2 | | |
| | ♡ K J | | |
| | ◇ — | | |
| | ♣ — | | |

| | | | |
|---|---|---|---|
| ♠ Q 10 6 5 | | | ♠ 9 8 7 |
| ♡ A | N W E S | | ♡ — |
| ◇ 10 | | | ◇ J 8 2 |
| ♣ — | | | ♣ — |

| | |
|---|---|
| | ♠ 3 |
| | ♡ 10 5 4 3 |
| | ◇ — |
| | ♣ 4 |

Under pressure in three suits, West chose to throw a spade. Hamilton discarded the ♡J from dummy and finessed in spades to score four tricks there for his contract. Suppose West throws the ◇10, the link to his partner's hand, instead. Declarer can then throw a spade from dummy, finesse the ♠J, and duck a heart to the bare ace. At Trick 11 West will have to give the lead to the winners in dummy.

# Chapter 18: The Triple Squeeze • 199

Do you see how the contract might have been defeated? Kantar had to withhold the ◇A at Trick 1! This would prevent declarer from achieving a state of 'near rectification'. In effect, it would allow West to hold one more card in the eventual end position. He could retain the six cards shown in the end position and would not be squeezed. Of course, such a defense was asking a lot of Kantar after the auction he had heard. For all he knew, South might have held Q-x in diamonds. Imagine the uproar then if the defenders failed to take their six tricks in the suit.

The drama on the deal was not finished. At the other table East-West did not enter the auction and North ended in a normal 4♡. After a club lead the game went down. Declarer lost tricks to the ◇A and to the queen and ace of trumps; he also suffered a club ruff. The 5NT bidders therefore gained 10 IMPs for their efforts. Just another bridge hand!

# Quiz

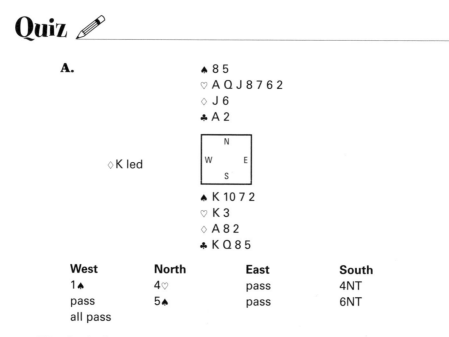

**A.**

♠ 8 5
♡ A Q J 8 7 6 2
◇ J 6
♣ A 2

◇K led

♠ K 10 7 2
♡ K 3
◇ A 8 2
♣ K Q 8 5

| West | North | East | South |
|------|-------|------|-------|
| 1♠ | 4♡ | pass | 4NT |
| pass | 5♠ | pass | 6NT |
| all pass | | | |

West leads the ◇K against your small slam in notrump. Plan the play.

**B.**

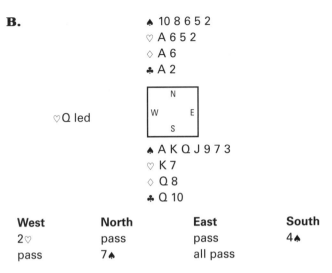

```
              ♠ 10 8 6 5 2
              ♡ A 6 5 2
              ◇ A 6
              ♣ A 2
                    N
♡ Q led        W        E
                    S
              ♠ A K Q J 9 7 3
              ♡ K 7
              ◇ Q 8
              ♣ Q 10
```

| West | North | East | South |
|------|-------|------|-------|
| 2♡ | pass | pass | 4♠ |
| pass | 7♠ | all pass | |

You agree to partner the local madman for a session of pairs and he confirms his reputation on the first board by raising you to a grand slam. How do you plan to survive the experience?

# Answers

**A.** West has the sole guard in diamonds and spades but this is no use to you, on its own, because the opening lead has removed the only entry in those suits. (He was sitting on the wrong side of your threats, anyway.) You will need West to hold at least four clubs too, so that a triple squeeze will be possible. Win the opening lead and run the heart suit. If West did start with at least four clubs, the end position will be similar to this:

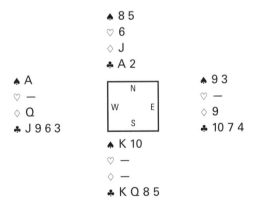

```
              ♠ 8 5
              ♡ 6
              ◇ J
              ♣ A 2
♠ A                    ♠ 9 3
♡ —           N        ♡ —
◇ Q       W        E   ◇ 9
♣ J 9 6 3     S        ♣ 10 7 4
              ♠ K 10
              ♡ —
              ◇ —
              ♣ K Q 8 5
```

You lead dummy's last heart, throwing the ♠ 10. What can West discard? If he throws a spade or a diamond, you will cash the established winner to squeeze him again, scoring an overtrick. If he foresees this and throws a club, you will score four club tricks for the contract.

**B.** You have only eleven top tricks and must aim to score two more tricks via a repeating squeeze, hoping that West holds both the minor-suit kings. Win the heart lead in your hand and draw trumps. You must then cash the two minor-suit aces (a double Vienna Coup). When you run your remaining spades West will have to find one more discard in this position:

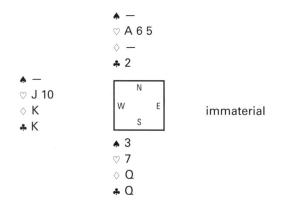

♠ —
♡ A 6 5
◇ —
♣ 2

♠ —
♡ J 10
◇ K
♣ K

N
W    E
S

immaterial

♠ 3
♡ 7
◇ Q
♣ Q

If he throws a heart, you will score two extra heart tricks in dummy. If he throws a minor-suit king instead, you will cash the established queen to squeeze him again. Your partner was not such a lunatic after all. He just knew that you'd been reading a really good book on squeezes...

# The Guard
# Squeeze

$S$uppose you are sitting West, in the endgame, and the club position has been reduced to:

         ♣ 8 6

♣ Q                   ♣ K 10 5

         ♣ A J

Your ♣Q is not a guard on the club suit in the normal sense, since it would fall under South's ace. The card does however protect your partner from a finesse in the suit. If you were to discard the club queen, it would cost a trick.

It is not possible to create a two-suit squeeze where you would be squeezed out of your ♣Q. To force you down to two cards fewer than he himself holds in clubs, declarer needs you to hold a guard in two other suits. A triple squeeze in which one of the defender's guards protects his partner from a finesse is known as a 'guard squeeze'. Here is a straightforward example:

         ♠ J 6 2
         ♡ 10 3
         ◇ Q 9 7 5 4
         ♣ K 7 5

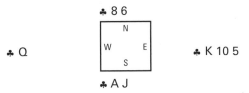

♠ Q 9 8 4                 ♠ 10 7 5 3
♡ 8 6                      ♡ 4 2
◇ K 10 8 2               ◇ J 6 3
♣ Q 8 4                  ♣ J 9 6 2

         ♠ A K
         ♡ A K Q J 9 7 5
         ◇ A
         ♣ A 10 3

Now in the South seat, you reach an ambitious grand slam in hearts and West leads a trump. You win in your hand, cash the ace of diamonds, cross to the ♡ 10, and ruff a diamond high. If it was your birthday you might ruff out the king of diamonds.

No such outrageous luck materializes. You proceed to run the remaining trumps with various squeeze chances in mind. If either defender holds the ♠Q and the sole club guard, there will be a simple squeeze in the black suits. There might instead be a simple squeeze in the minor suits. A third possibilty is that the spade and diamond guards are divided, which will permit a double squeeze with clubs as the pivot suit. The final chance is that both defenders guard the clubs and West has the sole guard in both spades and diamonds. Then — you guessed it — a guard squeeze will arise.

This is the position with one trump still to be played (you have also cashed the ♠A K, to clarify the position in that suit):

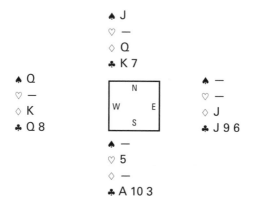

West has no card to spare on the last trump. If he discards a spade or a diamond he will set up an immediate twelfth trick in the dummy. He is forced to discard a club but you will then cross to the ♣K, dropping West's queen, and finesse the ♣10 on the way back.

There is some reading of the cards involved in this ending. If West's last four cards were ♣Q J 8 accompanied by the guard in spades or diamonds, he would again discard ♣8. The winning play would then be to drop the remaining club honor, rather than finesse East for it.

# The double guard squeeze

When a guard squeeze forces a defender to release a guard on one of declarer's one-card threats, the other defender may suffer a simple squeeze as a result. We are reaching deep down into the well of complexity, I realize, but this is in fact the most common form of the guard squeeze. Here is a full-deal example of what is grandly known as the double guard squeeze:

Both Vul.
Dealer South

|  |  |  |
|---|---|---|
|  | ♠ 6 |  |
|  | ♡ Q J 10 6 4 |  |
|  | ◊ A 9 8 6 2 |  |
|  | ♣ 5 2 |  |
| ♠ 10 8 | **N** | ♠ J 3 |
| ♡ A 9 5 | **W   E** | ♡ K 8 7 3 2 |
| ◊ Q 10 7 4 | **S** | ◊ J 5 |
| ♣ Q J 10 8 |  | ♣ K 6 4 3 |
|  | ♠ A K Q 9 7 5 4 2 |  |
|  | ♡ — |  |
|  | ◊ K 3 |  |
|  | ♣ A 9 7 |  |

| West | North | East | South |
|------|-------|------|-------|
|  |  |  | 2♣ |
| pass | 2♡ | pass | 4♠ |
| pass | 5◊ | pass | 6♠ |
| all pass |  |  |  |

West leads the ♣Q against your small slam in spades. How will you tackle the deal?

If you win the first trick you will have nothing very sensible to do next. The best idea is to hold up. If West is half asleep and does not switch to a trump, you can score a club ruff and move swiftly to the next deal.

West is very much awake, unfortunately, and does switch to a trump. What now? With a lone entry to dummy, prospects may seem bleak indeed. Suppose, however, that West has the sole guard on the diamond suit. When you run the trumps he will have to be careful not to discard his heart guard. If he does, 'West will guard the diamonds, East will guard the hearts; neither defender can retain a club guard'. Yes, a double squeeze will develop. So, West has to keep a guard on both red suits. No doubt his club holding was headed by Q-J-10. If he throws both the honors, a finesse of the ♣9 will become possible.

You run the trump suit, then, and this end position results:

|  |  |  |
|---|---|---|
|  | ♠ — |  |
|  | ♡ Q |  |
|  | ◊ A 9 8 |  |
|  | ♣ 5 |  |
| ♠ — | **N** | ♠ — |
| ♡ A | **W   E** | ♡ K |
| ◊ Q 10 7 | **S** | ◊ J 5 |
| ♣ J |  | ♣ K 6 |
|  | ♠ 2 |  |
|  | ♡ — |  |
|  | ◊ K 3 |  |
|  | ♣ A 9 |  |

West has already been squeezed down to a singleton club. (If he kept three diamonds and two clubs instead, a non-simultaneous double squeeze would result, as we foresaw.) He now has no good card to play on the last spade. A diamond will concede immediate defeat. If he throws the ♣J, you can cross to dummy and take a winning finesse in the suit. The only other option is for West to throw the ♡A. The pressure is then on East. He can delay his surrender by throwing a diamond at this stage, but the king and ace of diamonds will then squeeze him in hearts and clubs.

Studying deals of this complexity can cause a headache — for readers and writers alike. The two recommended treatments are aspirin and (my personal recommendation) a well-iced gin and tonic.

# The stars come out to play:
## the guard squeeze

Our real-life example of the guard squeeze comes from the 1989 Far East Pairs final, contested in Jakarta.

```
Neither Vul.              ♠ —
Dealer North              ♡ A 10 9 3
                          ◇ K 10 8 7 2
                          ♣ A 10 9 2

        ♠ Q 10 8 6          N          ♠ J 9 7 5 4 2
        ♡ J 7          W         E      ♡ Q 6 5 4
        ◇ 5 4                           ◇ —
        ♣ Q J 8 7 6         S          ♣ 5 4 3

                          ♠ A K 3
                          ♡ K 8 2
                          ◇ A Q J 9 6 3
                          ♣ K
```

| West | North | East | South |
|------|-------|------|-------|
| Jim | John | Norma | John |
| Borin | Wignall | Borin | Brockwell |
| | 1◇ | pass | 2NT (forcing raise) |
| pass | 3◇ | pass | 4NT |
| pass | 5♡ | pass | 5NT |
| pass | 7◇ | pass | 7NT |
| all pass | | | |

Brockwell bid the grand in notrump, aiming for a pairs top. This must have been a nasty moment for North, who had leapt to 7◇ on the strength of his spade void! West made the risky lead of the ♣Q (why not a safe diamond?) and declarer won with the bare king. Suppose you had been the declarer. How would you have sought a thirteenth trick?

West was known to hold the club guard. If he discarded his spade guard when the diamonds were run, the hand would revert to a double squeeze ('West would guard the clubs, East would guard the spades; no-one could guard declarer's third heart.') If the heart honors were split, West would also need to retain a heart, to prevent declarer finessing against East's honor. The conditions were present for a double guard squeeze!

Brockwell cashed the ace and king of spades, throwing the ten and nine of hearts from dummy — freeing the way for a possible finesse of his heart eight. He then ran the diamond suit. This was the key moment, when West had to give way to the pressure:

```
                    ♠ —
                    ♡ A 3
                    ◇ —
                    ♣ A 10 9
   ♠ Q                               ♠ J 9
   ♡ J 7          ┌──────────┐       ♡ Q 6 5
   ◇ —            │    N     │       ◇ —
   ♣ J 8          │ W      E │       ♣ —
                  │    S     │
                  └──────────┘
                    ♠ 3
                    ♡ K 8 2
                    ◇ 9
                    ♣ —
```

Every card is needed in the South hand, as you see, so it would not have been a good idea to cash dummy's ♣A earlier in the play. When the last diamond was led, West had no good discard. A club was obviously hopeless and a spade would have led to the double squeeze we visualized. Eventually he threw the ♡7. Brockwell then crossed to the ♡A, dropping West's jack, threw his last spade on the ♣A, and took a successful finesse of the ♡8. Grand slam made! The Borins warmly congratulated declarer on his play, even though it probably cost them the title.

# Quiz ✎

**A.**

♠ A 7
♡ A Q 8 4
◇ 7 5 4 2
♣ A 6 4

◇K led

```
      N
  W       E
      S
```

♠ K Q J 10 8 6 2
♡ 5
◇ A J
♣ K 9 3

| West | North | East | South |
|------|-------|------|-------|
| 1♡ | pass | pass | 4♠ |
| pass | 4NT | pass | 5♠ |
| pass | 5NT | pass | 6◇ |
| pass | 7♠ | all pass | |

On the reasonable assumption that West holds all twelve outstanding points, can you see how to make the grand? (West's opening bid shows at least five hearts.)

**B.**

♠ A J 6 4
♡ 9 8 4 2
◇ Q 7 5
♣ A 6

♡J led

```
      N
  W       E
      S
```

♠ 3
♡ A 10 7
◇ A
♣ K Q J 10 7 5 4 3

| West | North | East | South |
|------|-------|------|-------|
| | | 1♡ | 5♣ |
| pass | 6♣ | all pass | |

West leads the ♡J against your small slam in clubs, East playing low. Can you see how to make the slam when West holds one of the missing spade honors? Think carefully whether you should duck the first trick.

# Answers ✎

**A.** Win the diamond lead, draw trumps and finesse the ♡Q. Then ruff a heart in your hand, to isolate the heart guard with West. When you run your remaining trumps an end position similar to this will arise:

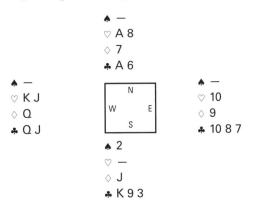

```
              ♠ —
              ♡ A 8
              ◊ 7
              ♣ A 6
   ♠ —      ┌─────────┐      ♠ —
   ♡ K J    │    N    │      ♡ 10
   ◊ Q      │ W     E │      ◊ 9
   ♣ Q J    │    S    │      ♣ 10 8 7
            └─────────┘
              ♠ 2
              ♡ —
              ◊ J
              ♣ K 9 3
```

You lead the last spade and (what a surprise) West is caught in a guard squeeze. If he throws a heart or a diamond, you will score your thirteenth trick directly. If instead he throws a club, you can cross to the ♣A and finesse the ♣9 for the contract.

Try playing the hand again — this time cashing the ♡A and discarding your ◊J. You will still make thirteen tricks, despite the fact that both defenders guard dummy's ◊7. A double guard squeeze will arise:

```
              ♠ —
              ♡ 8
              ◊ 7
              ♣ A 6
   ♠ —      ┌─────────┐      ♠ —
   ♡ K      │    N    │      ♡ —
   ◊ Q      │ W     E │      ◊ 9
   ♣ Q J    │    S    │      ♣ 10 8 7
            └─────────┘
              ♠ 2
              ♡ —
              ◊ —
              ♣ K 9 3
```

If West throws his diamond guard on the last spade, East will be squeezed in the minors.

**B.** If you duck the first round of hearts West will have the chance to scupper any form of squeeze by switching to a spade. You should therefore win the first heart and run all your trumps. When the spade honors are split, the end position will be similar to this:

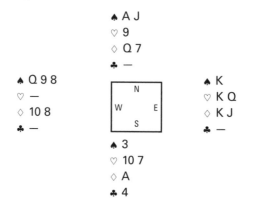

&spades; A J
&hearts; 9
&diams; Q 7
&clubs; —

&spades; Q 9 8
&hearts; —
&diams; 10 8
&clubs; —

&spades; K
&hearts; K Q
&diams; K J
&clubs; —

&spades; 3
&hearts; 10 7
&diams; A
&clubs; 4

You lead the last club, throwing the ♡9 from dummy. East is caught in a guard squeeze without the count. If he throws the ♠K you can finesse in spades. If he throws a diamond, you can cash the ace of diamonds and cross to dummy to score the diamond queen. If he throws a heart, you can concede a heart to set up your ♡ 10, with the diamond ace remaining as an entry to cash it.

# CHAPTER 20

# The Compound Squeeze

The first time I saw a compound squeeze (in print) I remember thinking: Wow! How can that possibly work? The situation is that you have a one-card threat in dummy, sitting over your left-hand opponent and guarded only by him. You have two other suits that are guarded by both opponents. It's too difficult to visualize in abstract, I agree. Let's look straight away at a clean-cut example of the play.

```
                      ♠ K 9 3
                      ♡ A K 7
                      ◇ Q 7 4 2
                      ♣ K Q 2
        ♠ Q 10 8 4 2                    ♠ J 6 5
        ♡ J 9 6 3 2        N            ♡ Q 10 8
        ◇ —            W       E        ◇ J 10 9 8 3
        ♣ 8 6 5            S            ♣ 9 4
                      ♠ A 7
                      ♡ 5 4
                      ◇ A K 6 5
                      ♣ A J 10 7 3
```

You reach 7NT on the South cards and West leads a club, which you win with the king. When you play the ◇Q, West gives you an unpleasant surprise by throwing a heart. How do you assess your chances at this point?

You may be surprised to hear that, provided you read the cards correctly, your contract is 100% whatever the lie of the cards! Why is that? Because when you run your clubs East will have to abandon one of the major suits. You will then have a guaranteed double squeeze, using the other major suit as the pivot.

East has an easy diamond discard on your third club. Let's look first at what will happen if he throws a spade on the fourth club, followed by another spade on the fifth club. You will discard two diamonds from dummy, meanwhile, and these cards will remain:

```
              ♠ K 9 3
              ♡ A K 7
              ◇ 7
              ♣ —
  ♠ Q 10 8                    ♠ J
  ♡ J 9 6 3      N            ♡ Q 10 8
  ◇ —        W       E        ◇ J 10 9
  ♣ —            S            ♣ —
              ♠ A 7
              ♡ 5 4
              ◇ A K 6
              ♣ —
```

The position has evolved into a double squeeze. 'West guards the spades, East guards the diamonds; no-one can hold the hearts.' You play two rounds of spades, forcing East to abandon his heart guard. You then play the ace and king of diamonds, to squeeze West in the majors.

So, when East abandons the spades, you use hearts as the pivot suit. When instead he chooses to abandon the hearts, you will use spades as the pivot suit. This will be the end position:

```
              ♠ K 9 3
              ♡ A K 7
              ◇ 7
              ♣ —
  ♠ Q 10 8                    ♠ J 6 5
  ♡ J 9 6 3      N            ♡ Q
  ◇ —        W       E        ◇ J 10 9
  ♣ —            S            ♣ —
              ♠ A 7
              ♡ 5 4
              ◇ A K 6
              ♣ —
```

'West guards the hearts, East guards the diamonds; no-one can hold the spades.' You cash dummy's two top hearts, forcing East to abandon the spade suit. You then play the two top diamonds, again squeezing West in the majors.

It was unusually easy to read the cards on this example. Since you had two painless diamond discards from dummy on the two long clubs, you could wait to see two discards from East. You could then be almost certain which major he had chosen to abandon.

Too many deals of this type will bring back that headache we both suffered in the previous chapter. Let's see just one more example of this very complicated squeeze.

Both Vul.
Dealer North

```
                ♠ 6 4
                ♡ 5 2
                ◇ A K 10 7 5 2
                ♣ K 9 3
♠ K J 7 5 3          N          ♠ Q 10 8 2
♡ 10 4                          ♡ J 9 6 3
◇ 9 6          W       E        ◇ 8 4
♣ Q 10 4 2          S          ♣ J 8 6
                ♠ A 9
                ♡ A K Q 8 7
                ◇ Q J 3
                ♣ A 7 5
```

| West | North | East | South |
|------|-------|------|-------|
|      | 1◇    | pass | 1♡    |
| pass | 2◇    | pass | 4NT   |
| pass | 5♡    | pass | 5NT   |
| pass | 6◇    | pass | 7NT   |
| all pass |   |      |       |

Your partner opens on a pleasing 10-count. You place him with six diamonds when he rebids 2◇ and, after two rounds of Blackwood, you can count twelve tricks. Since you have accounted for only ten of his points, you hope that a thirteenth trick will be available somewhere and aim for a top score by bidding the grand in notrump. (Playing in diamonds, he could have ruffed the last heart good.)

West leads a diamond and you play four rounds of the suit, throwing a heart from your hand. The first key position has already been reached:

```
                ♠ 6 4
                ♡ 5 2
                ◇ 10 7
                ♣ K 9 3
♠ K J 7              N          ♠ Q 10
♡ 10 4                          ♡ J 9 6 3
◇ —           W        E        ◇ —
♣ Q 10 4 2          S          ♣ J 8 6
                ♠ A 9
                ♡ A K Q 8
                ◇ —
                ♣ A 7 5
```

When you lead dummy's penultimate diamond, East has to surrender his guard in one of the black suits in order to retain four hearts. Let's suppose first that he throws a club. Although you have no clear idea how the cards lie, this is in fact the situation: 'West guards the clubs, East guards the hearts; no-one will be able to hold the spades'. You throw a club from your hand and then play three top hearts, throwing a spade from dummy. Hearts do not break and you continue with the ace and king of clubs. This position has been reached:

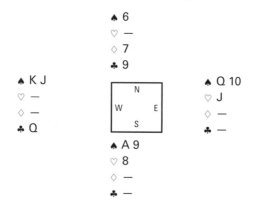

♠ 6
♡ —
◇ 7
♣ 9

♠ K J
♡ —
◇ —
♣ Q

N
W   E
S

♠ Q 10
♡ J
◇ —
♣ —

♠ A 9
♡ 8
◇ —
♣ —

The last diamond effects a double squeeze; neither defender can retain a spade guard and you score your thirteenth trick.

Look back to the nine-card position at the bottom of the previous page and see what happens if East decides to release his spade guard instead. You must then cash dummy's remaining diamond immediately. East throws his last spade, you throw the ♠9, and these cards remain:

♠ 6 4
♡ 5 2
◇ —
♣ K 9 3

♠ K J
♡ 10 4
◇ —
♣ Q 10 4

N
W   E
S

♠ —
♡ J 9 6 3
◇ —
♣ J 8 6

♠ A
♡ A K Q 8
◇ —
♣ A 7

A spade to the ace squeezes East out of his club stop and three rounds of hearts then squeeze West in the black suits. The seven-card ending is a non-simultaneous double squeeze.

# The stars come out to play:
## the compound squeeze

Our real-life compound squeeze comes from the British trials for the ('finger-signal accusation') 1965 world championship to be held in Buenos Aires. Kenneth Konstam sat South, partnered by the mercurial Boris Schapiro.

```
North-South Vul.        ♠ J 10
Dealer East             ♡ A K 10 8 2
                        ◇ 6 4
                        ♣ K J 7 3
     ♠ 3                              ♠ A 4
     ♡ Q 7 5 4          N             ♡ J 9 6
     ◇ Q 9 7 3     W         E        ◇ J 8 5
     ♣ Q 10 8 5        S             ♣ A 9 6 4 2
                        ♠ K Q 9 8 7 6 5 2
                        ♡ 3
                        ◇ A K 10 2
                        ♣ —
```

| West | North | East | South |
|------|-------|------|-------|
| Tarlo | Schapiro | Dr. Lee | Konstam |
| | | pass | 2♠ |
| pass | 3♡ | pass | 3♠ |
| pass | 4♣ | dbl | 4◇ |
| pass | 4♠ | pass | 6♠ |
| all pass | | | |

If West had followed his partner's suggestion, leading a club, declarer would have had a very easy ride indeed. Made suspicious by his own club holding, Louis Tarlo struck upon the fine lead of a trump. His partner won with the ace and returned a second trump, depriving declarer of a diamond ruff.

Konstam won the second round of trumps in the dummy and, recalling East's double of 4♣, called for the club king. Do you see the purpose of this? The club king would be useless as the one-card threat in a compound squeeze because the ace was known to lie over it (after East's lead-directing double). When the king was covered by the ace and ruffed by declarer, there was at least some chance that dummy's jack would now be a threat against West's queen.

So it proved. When Konstam ran his spade suit, a compound squeeze developed. West was left alone to guard the club suit while both defenders guarded each of the red suits. West soon had to abandon one of the red suits. He chose to throw hearts, since if declarer held two hearts a simple club-heart squeeze was certain. East had to retain his ♡J 9 6 and was therefore forced to abandon the diamonds. That left this position:

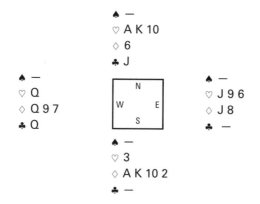

```
              ♠ —
              ♡ A K 10
              ◇ 6
              ♣ J

  ♠ —                        ♠ —
  ♡ Q                        ♡ J 9 6
  ◇ Q 9 7      N             ◇ J 8
  ♣ Q       W     E          ♣ —
                 S
              ♠ —
              ♡ 3
              ◇ A K 10 2
              ♣ —
```

Two rounds of hearts now squeezed West in the minors. Had West chosen to throw diamonds, retaining a heart guard, East would have had to throw his heart guard. Two rounds of diamonds would then have squeezed West in hearts and clubs. There was a pleasing symmetry about the deal.

# Quiz

**A.**

```
              ♠ A J 4
              ♡ A 5 4
              ◇ A 8 3
              ♣ K 4 3 2

                    N
  ♠K led        W       E
                    S

              ♠ 8
              ♡ K 7 2
              ◇ K 9
              ♣ A Q J 9 7 6 5
```

| West | North | East | South |
|------|-------|------|-------|
|      | 1NT   | pass | 3♣    |
| pass | 3◇    | pass | 4NT   |
| pass | 5◇    | pass | 7♣    |
| all pass |   |      |       |

West leads the ♠K against your grand slam in clubs. West guards the spades and both defenders (almost certainly) guard the red suits. You win the spade lead and run the clubs. How will the compound squeeze develop if West first abandons (a) the hearts, (b) the diamonds?

# Answer ✎

**A.** You run the trump suit, throwing a spade and a heart from dummy. If you judge that West has abandoned hearts, the end position will be similar to this:

```
              ♠ J
              ♡ A 5
              ◇ A 8 3
              ♣ —
♠ Q 5                          ♠ —
♡ J          ┌─────────┐       ♡ Q 9 6
◇ J 7 6      │    N    │       ◇ Q 10 5
♣ —          │ W     E │       ♣ —
             │    S    │
             └─────────┘
              ♠ —
              ♡ K 7 2
              ◇ K 9
              ♣ 6
```

You play the ace and king of hearts, confirming the position in that suit, and then lead the last club. A simultaneous double squeeze occurs with diamonds as the pivot suit. West has to throw a diamond to retain the spade queen. You release the ♠J from dummy and East must abandon his guard in one of the red suits.

Suppose instead you judge that West has abandoned the diamonds. Since you are now planning a double squeeze with hearts as the pivot suit, you should cash the ace and king of diamonds. These cards will remain:

```
              ♠ J
              ♡ A 5
              ◇ 8
              ♣ —
♠ Q                            ♠ —
♡ J 10 8     ┌─────────┐       ♡ Q 9 6
◇ —          │    N    │       ◇ Q
♣ —          │ W     E │       ♣ —
             │    S    │
             └─────────┘
              ♠ —
              ♡ K 7 2
              ◇ —
              ♣ 6
```

When you play the last club West releases a heart and you can spare the ♠J from dummy. East has to throw a heart too and you score three heart tricks to make the grand slam.

Was that compound squeeze such a difficult hand to play, do you think? In a word... yes! It's just as well for all of us that these deals are relatively rare. The lumbering mammoths of the squeeze world are greatly outnumbered by the more straightforward plays — those that we saw in the early part of the book. They're the ones to look out for, next time you sit down at the bridge table.

You will find that around one deal in five offers some opportunity for squeeze play. Happy hunting!

# Squeeze Glossary

**Automatic squeeze.** A squeeze that will work against either defender. It succeeds because a solitary defender cannot guard against threats that declarer holds in two separate hands.

**Blocked threat.** A threat that faces one or more bare winners in the opposite hand (for example Q-x opposite a bare ace).

**Compound squeeze.** A triple squeeze on one defender, which resolves to a double squeeze when the defender releases one of his guards.

**Criss-cross squeeze.** A rare form of the simple squeeze where both threats are blocked.

**Double guard squeeze.** A guard squeeze on one defender, followed by a simple squeeze on the other defender.

**Double squeeze.** An end position in which both defenders are subjected to a simple squeeze.

**Double trump squeeze.** A two-suit double squeeze where declarer threatens to ruff a trick good, either by dropping an honor from one defender or by pinning an honor from the other defender.

**Entry-shifting squeeze.** Alternative name for the 'see-saw squeeze'.

**Guard squeeze.** A rare form of the triple squeeze where a defender has to retain a bare honor to guard against his partner being finessed in the suit.

**Isolating the guard.** A technique whereby one defender's guard of a suit is removed, leaving the other defender with the sole guard. (The play is sometimes called 'isolating the menace'.)

**Losing-card squeeze.** A squeeze where the squeeze card is a loser and performs the secondary role of rectifying the count.

**Menace.** A card that is not a master but will become so if a defender releases his guard on it. Identical in meaning to 'threat'.

**Near-rectification of the count.** The state where declarer has lost all but one of the tricks that he can afford to lose.

**Non-material squeeze.** A squeeze that does not generate a trick directly but forces a defender to throw a card that will reduce his communications or improve those of the declarer.

**One-card threat.** A single card that threatens to become good if one or both defenders release their guard on it.

**Pivot suit.** The suit in a double squeeze that both defenders guard. Each defender in turn has to retain a guard on some different suit and must therefore abandon the guard on the pivot suit.

**Positional squeeze.** A squeeze that will work against only one of the defenders. It succeeds because that defender has to discard before the hand that contains the threats.

**Progressive squeeze.** A triple squeeze that gains two tricks. When the defender abandons the first of his three guards, declarer uses the established winner as a new squeeze-card.

**Recessed threat.** A threat accompanied by more winners than there are non-winners in the opposite hand (for example, the two nine-spots in: $\diamond$ A K 9 opposite $\diamond$ 2, or $\clubsuit$ A Q 9 6 opposite $\clubsuit$ K 5).

**Rectifying the count.** The deliberate losing of those tricks that declarer can afford to lose, with the aim of removing spare cards from the defenders' hands and thereby tightening the end position. For example, in a small slam the loss of one trick would rectify the count.

**Repeating squeeze.** Another name for the progressive squeeze.

**Ruffing squeeze.** Alternative name for 'trump squeeze'.

**See-saw squeeze.** A squeeze where you overtake the squeeze card or not, depending on which suit the key defender discards.

**Show-up squeeze.** A simple squeeze against one defender which permits declarer to knowingly drop an unguarded honor from the other defender.

**Simple squeeze.** A squeeze of one defender in two suits.

**Split two-card threat.** A two-card threat where the threat itself lies opposite the winner in the suit, for example, A-x opposite Q-x.

**Squeeze.** A play which forces one or both defenders to release their guard(s) on a threat card, thereby establishing it.

**Squeeze without the count.** A squeeze which takes place without the count being rectified. Declarer surrenders one or more tricks after the squeeze has taken place.

**Squeeze card.** The card that is played to extract a discard from the player being squeezed.

**Stepping stone squeeze.** A rare form of the simple squeeze where one threat suit is blocked but declarer has the option of overtaking (for example, he holds K-Q opposite A-10-x). A defender who retains J-x-x to prevent an overtake renders himself vulnerable to a throw-in.

**Strip squeeze.** See 'strip and endplay'.

**Strip and endplay.** A play that squeezes a defender out of one or more winners, and/or safe exit cards, after which he is thrown in to lead into a tenace. (This play is alternatively known as a 'strip squeeze'.)

**Suicide squeeze.** A squeeze where the squeeze card is led by the partner of the player being squeezed.

**Threat.** A card that is not a master but will become so if a defender releases his guard on it.

**Transferring the guard.** A technique whereby the guard of a suit is switched from one defender to the other.

**Triple squeeze.** A squeeze against one defender in three different suits.

**Trump squeeze.** A squeeze where a winner is ruffed good after the defender who was guarding the suit has been squeezed.

**Twin-entry threat.** A third-round threat that is accompanied by entries to both hands. For example, K-10-x opposite A-x, where the ten is the actual threat.

**Twin-entry recessed threat.** A fourth-round recessed threat that is accompanied by entries to both hands. For example, K-Q-9-x opposite A-x, where the nine is the actual threat.

**Two-card threat.** A threat that is accompanied by a winner.

**Vice squeeze.** A rare form of the 'squeeze without the count' where a defender holds middle cards in a suit (for example, Q-J under K-10 with the other defender holding the ace). He cannot throw one of these without allowing declarer to set up a winner.

**Vienna Coup.** The playing of a winner to free a card in the opposite hand to act as a threat against either defender.

**Winkle squeeze.** A rare form of the 'squeeze without the count' where a defender has to choose between retaining a high card (allowing himself to be thrown in) or discarding the high card (after which declarer will be able to set up a trick in that suit).

# More Bridge Titles from Master Point Press

## ABTA Book of the Year Award winners

**25 Bridge Conventions You Should Know**
by Barbara Seagram and Marc Smith (foreword by Eddie Kantar)
192pp., PB             Can $19.95        US$ 15.95

**Eddie Kantar teaches Modern Bridge Defense**
**Eddie Kantar teaches Advanced Bridge Defense**
by Eddie Kantar
each 240pp., PB    Can $27.95         US$ 19.95

*Interactive CD-ROM Editions*

**Modern Bridge Defense**          Can $69.95, US$ 49.95
**Advanced Bridge Defense**        Can $69.95, US$ 49.95

---

## The Bridge Technique Series
### by David Bird & Marc Smith
each 64pp. PB, Can $7.95 US $5.95

| | |
|---|---|
| Entry Management | Reading the Cards |
| Safety Plays | Tricks with Finesses |
| Tricks with Trumps | Planning in Defense |
| Eliminations and Throw Ins | Planning in Notrump Contracts |
| Deceptive Card Play | Defensive Signaling |
| Planning in Suit Contracts | Squeezes for Everyone |

---

**Around the World in 80 Hands** by Zia Mahmood with David Burn
256pp., PB                        Can $22.95          US $16.95

**A Study in Silver** *A second collection of bridge stories*
by David Silver
128pp., PB                        Can $12.95          US$ 9.95

**Becoming a Bridge Expert** by Frank Stewart
300pp., PB                        Can $27.95          US $19.95

**The Best of Bridge Today Digest** by Matthew and Pamela Granovetter
300pp., PB                        Can $27.95          US $19.95

**Bridge Problems for a New Millennium** by Julian Pottage
212pp., PB                        Can $19.95          US $14.95

**Bridge the Silver Way** by David Silver and Tim Bourke
192pp., PB                                          Can $19.95              US $14.95

**Bridge: 25 Ways to Compete in the Bidding**.
by Barbara Seagram and Marc Smith
220pp., PB                                          Can.$19.95             US $15.95

**Bridge, Zia... and me** by Michael Rosenberg
(foreword by Zia Mahmood)
192pp., PB                                          Can $19.95              US $15.95

**Challenge Your Declarer Play** by Danny Roth
128pp., PB                                          Can. $12.95            US $ 9.95

**Classic Kantar** a *collection of bridge humor* by Eddie Kantar
192pp., PB                                          Can $19.95              US $14.95

**Competitive Bidding in the 21st Century** by Marshall Miles
254pp.,PB                                           Can. $22.95            US. $16.95

**Countdown to Winning Bridge** by Tim Bourke and Marc Smith
92pp., PB                                           Can $19.95              US $14.95

**Easier Done Than Said** *Brilliancy at the Bridge Table*
by Prakash K. Paranjape
128pp., PB                                          Can $15.95              US $12.95

**For Love or Money** *The Life of a Bridge Journalist*
by Mark Horton and Brian Senior
189pp., PB                                          Can $22.95              US $16.95

**Focus On Declarer Play** by Danny Roth
128pp., PB                                          Can $12.95              US $9.95

**Focus On Defence** by Danny Roth
128pp., PB                                          Can $12.95              US $9.95

**Focus On Bidding** by Danny Roth
160pp., PB                                          Can $14.95              US $11.95

**I Shot my Bridge Partner** by Matthew Granovetter
384pp., PB                                          Can $19.95              US $14.95

**Murder at the Bridge Table** by Matthew Granovetter
320pp., PB                                          Can $19.95              US $14.95

**Partnership Bidding** a *workbook* by Mary Paul
96pp., PB                                           Can $9.95               US $7.95

**Playing with the Bridge Legends** by Barnet Shenkin
(forewords by Zia and Michael Rosenberg)
240pp., PB                     Can $24.95        US $17.95

**Saints and Sinners** *The St. Titus Bridge Challenge*
by David Bird & Tim Bourke
192pp., PB                     Can $19.95        US $14.95

**Samurai Bridge** *A tale of old Japan* by Robert F. MacKinnon
256pp., PB                     Can $ 22.95       US $16.95

**Tales out of School** *'Bridge 101' and other stories* by David Silver
(foreword by Dorothy Hayden Truscott)
128pp., PB                     Can $ 12.95       US $9.95

**The Bridge Magicians** by Mark Horton and Radoslaw Kielbasinski
248pp., PB                     Can $24.95        US $17.95

**The Bridge Player's Bedside Book** edited by Tony Forrester
256pp., HC                     Can $27.95        US $19.95

**The Bridge World's 'Test Your Play'**
by Jeff Rubens
164pp., PB                     Can $14.95        US $11.95

**The Complete Book of BOLS Bridge Tips** edited by Sally Brock
176pp., PB (photographs)       Can $24.95        US $17.95

**The Pocket Guide to Bridge** by Barbara Seagram and Ray Lee
64pp., PB                      Can $9.95         US$7.95

**There Must Be A Way**... *52 challenging bridge hands*
by Andrew Diosy (foreword by Eddie Kantar)
96pp., PB                      $9.95 US & Can.

**Thinking on Defense**
by Jim Priebe
216pp., PB                     Can $19.95        US$15.95

**You Have to See This**... *52 more challenging bridge problems*
by Andrew Diosy and Linda Lee
96pp., PB                      Can $12.95        US $9.95

**Win the Bermuda Bowl with Me** by Jeff Meckstroth and Marc Smith
288pp., PB (photographs)       Can $24.95        US $17.95

**World Class** — *conversations with the bridge masters* by Marc Smith
288pp., PB (photographs)       Can $24.95        US $17.95